Farewell to Arms

The Other One Percent
Sanjoy Chakravorty, Devesh Kapur, and Nirvikar Singh

Social Justice through Inclusion
Francesca R. Jensenius

Dispossession without Development
Michael Levien

The Man Who Remade India
Vinay Sitapati

Business and Politics in India
Edited by Christophe Jaffrelot, Atul Kohli, and Kanta Murali

Clients and Constituents
Jennifer Bussell

Gambling with Violence
Yelena Biberman

Mobilizing the Marginalized
Amit Ahuja

The Absent Dialogue
Anit Mukherjee

When Nehru Looked East
Francine Frankel

Capable Women, Incapable States
Poulami Roychowdhury

Farewell to Arms

How Rebels Retire without Getting Killed

RUMELA SEN

OXFORD
UNIVERSITY PRESS

Oxford University Press is a department of the University of Oxford. It furthers
the University's objective of excellence in research, scholarship, and education
by publishing worldwide. Oxford is a registered trade mark of Oxford University
Press in the UK and certain other countries.

Published in the United States of America by Oxford University Press
198 Madison Avenue, New York, NY 10016, United States of America.

Library of Congress Cataloging-in-Publication Data
Names: Sen, Rumela, author.
Title: Farewell to arms : how rebels retire without getting killed / Rumela Sen.
Description: New York, NY : Oxford University Press, 2021. |
Series: Modern South Asia series | Includes bibliographical references and index.
Identifiers: LCCN 2020032559 (print) | LCCN 2020032560 (ebook) |
ISBN 9780197529867 (hardback) | ISBN 9780197529874 (paperback) |
ISBN 9780197529898 (epub)
Subjects: LCSH: Peace-building—India. | Insurgency—India. |
Naxalite movement—India. | Communist Party of India-Maoist.
Classification: LCC JZ5584.I4 S36 2021 (print) | LCC JZ5584.I4 (ebook) |
DDC 303.6/40954—dc23
LC record available at https://lccn.loc.gov/2020032559
LC ebook record available at https://lccn.loc.gov/2020032560

DOI: 10.1093/oso/9780197529867.001.0001

1 3 5 7 9 8 6 4 2

Paperback printed by LSC Communications, United States of America
Hardback printed by Bridgeport National Bindery, Inc., United States of America

To my family

Contents

Acknowledgments

This book began as a PhD dissertation that I defended at Cornell University in 2017. The project benefited enormously from the advice I received from members of my PhD committee: Ron Herring, Andy Mertha, and Tom Pepinsky. My first debt of gratitude is to them. Ron has been unfailingly supportive in this scholarly journey, offering his good-natured encouragement without ever compromising on scholarly rigor. I fondly remember our meetings in Ithaca, sprinkled with the most interesting discussions about leftist politics and Kerala-style fish curry. Andy has been a wonderful mentor to me. A supportive committee member, he intuitively knows the perfect combination of carrot and stick to motivate students. I'm grateful to him for taking interest in my work and for offering a mix of mentorship, support, and friendship that is rare to come by. Tom is a valued committee member for anyone because he brings an inspiring combination of academic acumen, work ethic, and commitment to students that I can only aspire to. He made time to read my drafts and offer detailed criticisms. Every conversation with him has been immensely productive. I'm also deeply indebted to Emmanuel Teitelbaum for reading my work. I met Manny at conference in Chicago during my first year of graduate school. With him, I co-authored my first paper on the Maoist insurgency in India. In many ways, this book began with that paper, and for that I am forever grateful to Manny.

This research would not have been possible without the financial support provided by American Institute of India Studies, John D. Montgomery fellowship at Pacific Basic Research Center, and my postdoctoral fellowship in the department of political science at Columbia University. At various stages of converting the dissertation into book manuscript, I received valuable feedback from Bill Ascher, Bilal Baloch, Richard Bownas, Kaustav Chakrabarti, Kanchan Chandra, Shibashis Chatterjee, Nandini Dhar, Mark Frazier, Tim Frye, Ajay Gudavarthy, John Harriss, Macartan Humphreys, Devesh Kapur, David Ludden, Rahul Mukherji, Shivaji Mukherjee, Phil Oldenburg, David Patel, Alpa Shah, Jake Shapiro, Jack Snyder, Tariq Thachil, and Ashutosh Varshney. I am especially thankful to Ashu for including this book in the Modern South Asia series.

My great appreciation goes to the three anonymous reviewers of this manuscript for providing incredibly useful, detailed feedback and critical guidance that turned my manuscript into a published book. There were times when I spurned their wisdom. But as I made painful cuts, dropped arguments, added material, I realized how much they helped strengthen my arguments. The shortcomings that still remain are all mine. I share my appreciation for the production team at Oxford University Press, David McBride, Holly Mitchell, and Suganya Elango. Special thanks to the very talented Prasun Basu (Offish Studio) who took time out of his busy schedule to design the cover of my book.

This book would not have been possible without the generosity of many former rebels and ordinary people I met in the conflict zones in India. Over the course of several months of fieldwork in India, they opened their homes to me, shared painful memories, and took interest in my work. They go unnamed in this book, but not unacknowledged. I also wish to thank several individuals who proved critical to my experience in the field in India. My fieldwork in Telangana would not have been possible without the generous assistance and friendship of N. Chandrasekhar Rao, who is currently a professor at the Institute of Economic Growth. For sharing their perspectives and rich experience, I'm deeply grateful to Amit Bhattacharya, late Purusottam Bhattacharya, G. Haragopal, Vasantha Lakshmi, Dappu Ramesh, Jairam Ramesh, late Santosh Rana, Varavara Rao, G.N. Saibaba, Stan Swamy, late Bojja Tharakam, some of whom are now unfortunately in jail in India. I must acknowledge the institutional affiliation and research assistance I received at the Center for Economic and Social Studies, Hyderabad, and Jadavpur University, Kolkata. I'm also grateful to many friends, acquaintances, and their families who provided me with contacts for potential interviews, as well as logistical support during my fieldwork in India and Nepal: special thanks to Amitava Bhattacharya, Arpita Sutradhar, Anand Swaroop Verma, and Naresh Gyawali.

I received useful feedback at seminars and workshops at Columbia University, Princeton University, University of Pennsylvania, Brown University, George Washington University, East West Center, Soka University of America, Jawaharlal Nehru University, Claremont Mckenna College, New York University, and the New School. I also benefited from helpful comments at the Annual South Asia Conference at Madison, AIIS Book Workshop convened by Susan Wadley and Geraldine Forbes, GW CIBER Summer Doctoral Institute, Empirical Studies of Conflict Program,

Center for Advanced Study of India, and Brown Harvard MIT Joint Seminar on South Asia.

Finally, my family deserves to be thanked for their invaluable support during several years of research and writing. A PhD from the United States can be a long arduous process not simply for the students but also their families. My late grandfather wished that I would write this book one day, and here I am. My husband Niloy kept the wind to my back throughout the process. Much like other immigrant families, struggling to gain a foothold in a new country, there hasn't ever been enough time left to be together. But without him, and our children, Rajanya and Nevan, this book would not have been possible. My parents have always been my biggest, unwavering pillars of support. They believed I could, so I did. Their love and patience have sustained me through moments of exhaustion, of which there have been many. This book is dedicated to them.

Farewell to Arms

1

Introduction

How do rebels give up arms and return to the same political processes that they had once sought to overthrow? The question of weaning rebels from extremist groups is highly significant in the context of counterinsurgency policy and in the broader context of pacification of insurgencies. Existing explanations for conflict mitigation focus mostly on state capacity, the efficacy of counterinsurgency operations, or on socioeconomic development. This book builds on the existing scholarship and highlights what is almost always missing in it: the rebel's perspective. Moving away from the dominant trend of portraying rebellions and their alleviation from the perspective of policymakers, it breaks down the protracted process of rebel retirement into a multi-staged process as the rebels see it. From the rebel's perspective, what is of paramount importance is in whether or not they quit extremism is the ease with which they can exit and lay down their arms without getting killed in the process.

The central empirical puzzle of this book manifests itself in the Maoist conflict in North and South India, which claimed 6,760 lives between 2005 and 2015.[1] By 2008 a total of 223 districts across 20 (out of 29) states in India came under Maoist influence (SATP 2017). This book draws on several rounds of interviews with current and former Maoist rebels, as well as security personnel, administrators, activists, politicians, and ordinary people outside of the Maoist movement. This book also highlights how the various steps in the process of disengagement from extremism are linked more fundamentally to the nature of societal linkages between insurgencies and society, thereby bringing civil society into the study of insurgency in a theoretically coherent way.

The Maoists in India are distinct from the mainstream communists, primarily on the question of whether to pursue armed struggle or seek change through participation in elections.[2] The first invocation of Mao's idea of a peoples' war in India dates to the Telangana rebellion in the South of India between 1946 and 1951. However, it was only after the violent uprising of landless peasants and sharecroppers in Naxalbari in the Darjeeling district of North Bengal

Farewell to Arms. Rumela Sen, Oxford University Press (2021). © Oxford University Press.
DOI: 10.1093/oso/9780197529867.003.0001

in May 1967 that the idea of a Maoist revolution spread like wildfire, creating a contagion of planned seizure of land and confiscation of food grains by the poor in various parts of India (Banerjee 1980, 1984; Basu 2000; Ghosh 2009; Donner 2004). These were tumultuous times in Indian politics. Economic problems, like chronic food shortages, sharp inflationary price spirals, unemployment, low industrial output, and stagnant rates of public investment, created mounting popular frustration. The Congress Party, known to bear the formidable legacy of Gandhi and India's freedom struggle, was, for the first time since independence, defeated in eight states in the 1967 elections.

The early Maoists, known as Naxalites based on their resurgence in Naxalbari in 1967, attacked not only the localized systems of exploitation but also called for the violent takeover of the foundational institutions of the democratic state of India that they considered irrevocably complicit in the exploitation of the poor. However, the Naxalite leadership in the 1960s was largely college-educated and urban middle class, who the Indian state swiftly identified, arrested, or executed, fully disbanding the movement by 1972. Surviving cadres disintegrated into many bickering factions and retreated into virtual oblivion until 2004, when they sprung back into national headlines as various Maoist factions in different parts of the country unified to form the CPI(Maoist) (Mohan 1971; Mohanty 1977; Balagopal 2006).[3] During their nearly three-decades (early seventies to late nineties) long strategic retreat from the public eye, Maoists incrementally built localized support bases in various parts of India and raised a guerrilla army of the rural poor trained to confront the might of the Indian state. By 2006, the former prime minister of India identified CPI(Maoist) as "the biggest internal security threat the country has ever faced."[4]

Yet as the conflict raged on, a number of Maoist rebels also quit the ongoing insurgency, more so in their strongest pockets of influence in the South of India than in the North. According to South Asia Terrorism Portal (SATP) data, between 2006 and 2012, 781 Maoist rebels disarmed in the conflict zones in the South of India (primarily the states of Telangana and Andhra Pradesh), while only 54 rebels quit in the North (comprising primarily the state of Jharkhand) during the same period.[5] Although this data is in absolute numbers rather than a proportion of the total number of rebels in each state (that data is not available), the huge North-South variation in the number of surrender event holds up when the percentage SC/ST (scheduled caste/scheduled tribe) population (the recruitment pool of Maoists) and conflict intensity in Andhra Pradesh are taken into account.[6]

It is common knowledge in India that there is a regional variation in surrender of Maoists across various states, and the SATP data illustrates it well.[7] In course of my study, I found that all the politicians, bureaucrats, media persons, and scholars in India that I interviewed already knew and further substantiated this pattern of subnational variation and the success of former Andhra Pradesh (including Telangana) compared to all other Maoist-affected states.[8] This huge regional variation in retirement from the same insurgent movement is an interesting puzzle particularly because the Maoist Party is a highly centralized organization and the counterinsurgency policy of the Indian government against the Maoists, although locally executed, is funded and managed centrally through the Integrated Action Plan (Lalwani 2014).[9] In other words, the popular explanations of surrender of armed rebels in terms of variation in strength of insurgent organization, counterinsurgency operations, and intensity of conflict fall short in explaining why so many Maoist rebels retire in the South while so few do the same in the North. What can this regional variation of Maoist surrender in India tell us about the process of retirement from extremist organizations in general?

This question about factors contributing to rebel retirement resonates around the world, from Afghanistan to Sierra Leone, from Syria to Colombia. The use of the term "retirement" to describe the protracted process of disengagement of Maoists from the insurgent organization, as discussed later in this chapter, was born in the field.[10] By retired rebels, this book refers to former Maoist combatants who were active in the militant or political wings of the Maoist Party and eventually quit the insurgency to return to the mainstream. I have included only those retired rebels who have been "underground" in the organization for at least five years. I interviewed many activists, poets, academics, and journalists who were involved in various frontal organizations of the Maoist movement in different capacities. But they do not count as retired rebels in this study.[11] From the perspective of these retired rebels, the process of retirement begins as soon as armed actors decide to leave their organization and lay down arms, and it continues through the actual surrender of arms to the early stages of reintegration. Policymakers, in sharp contrast, focus mostly on surrender of arms by rebels, which, in reality, is only an intermediate step in the process of retirement. It is often assumed that material incentives are effective to lure rebels away from extremism because "ex-combatants must be able to earn a livelihood through legitimate means" (International Peace Academy 2002) to stay away from extremism. Given that a higher risk of conflict is associated with an absence of income-earning opportunities for young men, the trajectory of disengagement is expected to be a mirror image of the process of radicalization. For example, the U.S. military in Afghanistan calls its approach to the reintegration of insurgents "golden surrender," which promises rebel reintegration into their communities with "dignity and honor," "protection and security," education, vocational training, and cash awards (Waldman 2010; Horgan and Braddock 2010; Kurtenbach and Wulf 2012).

The government of India, in its policy statement on the Surrender and Rehabilitation of Maoists, also places a premium on economic incentives to "wean away the misguided youth . . . who have strayed into the fold of Naxal movement." The Surrender and Rehabilitation program, drawn primarily from the literature on disarmament-demobilization-reintegration (DDR) and security sector reform (SSR), argues: "As the (Maoist) problem has arisen on account of real and perceived neglect, deprivation, and disaffection, mainly towards the downtrodden, the solution should aim at providing gainful employment and entrepreneurial opportunities to the surrendered Maoists so that they are encouraged to join the mainstream and do not return to the fold of the movement."[12] Surely, financial assistance, when it really reaches former combatants, is not detrimental to their well-being, and perhaps certain kinds of insurgencies are more amenable to such enticements than others (Weinstein 2006). However, these incentives only become relevant during reintegration, after the rebels have already disarmed. By focusing on them, the literature sidesteps the arduous process of rebels' disengagement that precedes the formal surrender of arms and subsequent process of reintegration.

This book breaks down the protracted process of rebel retirement into multiple stages according to the rebels' point of view. I highlight the crucial role of informal exit networks in encouraging and facilitating rebel return and reintegration. These networks grow out of grassroots civic associations in the gray areas of the state-insurgency interface. High retirement in the South is due to the emergence of "harmonic" exit networks that weave together multiple stakeholders in an amalgam of roles and alliances to build momentum for exit and manage myriad uncertainties of reintegration. In contrast, retirement from the same insurgent group is very low in the North of India due to the development of "discordant" exit networks that exacerbate mistrust and fear among key players, deterring retirement significantly.

The State of the Art

A lot has been written on why men and women rebel (Gurr 1970; Scott 1977; Lichbach 1994; Wood 2003; Collier and Hoeffler 2004; Kalyvas 2006). A rich, methodologically diverse literature has also developed on the Maoist insurgency in India, particularly since 2010. It is focused mostly on explaining the origins, spread, and patterns of Maoist violence (Kapur, Gawande, and Satyanath 2012; Shah 2006; Shah 2009; Hoelscher, Miklian, and Vadlamannati 2012; Miklian and Carney 2010; Khanna and Zimmermann 2014; Dasgupta, Gawande, and Kapur 2014; Balagopal 2011; Sen and Teitelbaum 2010). But we know very little about how rebels, particularly Maoist rebels, retire.[13]

There is a large literature on insurgent democratic transition, including policy research on ex-combatants, transitional justice, and reintegration in the context of various conflicts in Africa, Central America, and Latin America. Looking at this broader literature for clues, one explanation of insurgent democratic transition is *institutional cooptation* in which movement leaders "demobilize mass defiance" by scaling down organizational goals to avoid conflict and accommodate societal norms (Jenkins 1983). In various quid pro quo arrangements with the state, the leaders defang the movement's ideological content, dilute their demands, and gradually surrender, forcing the cadres to retire, too. Collective disengagements are typically executed as a result of calculated strategy on the part of the group's leadership (Ribetti 2010). Along similar lines, other explanations centered on *elite strategy* argue that movement leaders shun bullets and choose ballots if the probability they attach to being victorious in democratic competition is greater than some minimum (Przeworski 1991; Weingast 1997; Colomer 2000). Specific to India, where militant movements are frequent, they are expected to follow an inverted U-curve of rapid escalation and eventual dissipation, if the democratic institutions are strong enough and their capacity to compromise and accommodate is high (Kohli 1997). These explanations reduce the ordinary people in conflict zones to mere bystanders, although they often have family members in the movement and share a very high stake in the prospect of their return.

A rich literature on the *exposure to violence on the part of noncombatants* (Dyregrov, Gjestad, and Raundalen 2002; Husain et al. 1998), on the other hand, concedes that ordinary people do have an impact on rebel transition insofar as high civilian casualties breeds hostility toward returning rebels, who are resented locally for their role in the mayhem. Some single-country studies, in Sierra Leone, for example, have highlighted distinctive dynamics in the reintegration process of particular subgroups of combatants, notably youth (Richards et al. 2003) and women and girls (Mazurana et al. 2002). Other studies found that individuals do leave terrorist movements and paramilitaries in Colombia for largely *idiosyncratic reasons*: fear of excessive punishment, disillusionment with the group's leadership, or recognition of the impossibility of achieving the group's goals (Kaplan and Nussio 2018; Nussio 2011). This literature, however, focuses more on the various conditions under which rebels choose to quit or rearm and sheds little light on the long, tortuous trajectory of disengagement.

The literature on disarmament-demobilization-reintegration (DDR) and security sector reform (SSR) focuses directly on weaning rebels from extremism but reduces the challenge of rebel exit to one of economic anxiety and poor institutions. As a result, this literature is limited to proposing the most lucrative incentives (land, cash, or vocational training) policymakers can design to entice rebels away from extremism, while simultaneously increasing the accountability and effectiveness of security institutions (via human rights and rule of law). It also recommends removing armed actors from politics as a condition for durable peace (Humphreys and Weinstein 2005; Gilligan, Mvukiyehe, and Samii 2013; Baaré 2005; Paes 2005; Alden 2002). The vast policy literature on democracy promotion, and associated academic research on peacebuilding and international election monitoring, on the other hand, generally concur in advocating rebel electoral participation under international oversight as a path to durable peace (Soderberg Kovacs 2007; Girod 2008; Kelley 2008; Carothers 1997; Bjornlund 2004; Brancati and Snyder 2009; Manning 2008; Fortna 2008). Recent research on rebel governance and postwar trajectories of rebel factions investigate the transition from civil conflict to peace, but the process of retirement is at best peripheral to these accounts (Arjona 2016; Daly 2016; Balcells 2017; Matanock 2017).

Both the DDR-SSR and democracy promotion literature largely build on the untested assumptions that rebels are beset either by economic insecurities or political ambitions, which lucrative surrender packages and electoral participation provisions can address, tempting them to retire. Regardless of whether economic rehabilitation is more enticing to certain kinds of insurgencies than others (Weinstein 2007), as mentioned, these incentives only become relevant during reintegration, after the rebels have already disarmed. Scholars have begun to emphasize that ex-combatants who gain acceptance from family members, friends, and neighbors through formal or informal processes of reconciliation are more likely to integrate into civilian life (Hwang 2018). However, stories of parental persuasion in bringing their children back from extremism do not explain why these networks are available to some rebels and in some places and not others, which is one of the central contributions of this book.

The widespread use of the term "surrender" to indicate the process of return of rebels to the mainstream is problematic primarily because it implies that rebels disarm under duress, and it ignores that rebels, as in the case of many former Maoists I interviewed, also quit voluntarily for myriad reasons. This book shows that the process of Maoist rebels quitting the insurgent organization cannot be called desertion because many former rebels secured permission of the Maoist Party to quit the organization (McLauchlin 2011; Oppenheim et al. 2015). In addition, "defection," defined as a faction leaving one side of a conflict to collaborate with the opposing side, also does not adequately capture the Maoist exit depicted here (Christia 2012; Kalyvas 2008; Staniland 2012; Bakke, Cunningham, and Seymour 2012; Findley and Rudloff 2012; Fjelde and Nilsson 2012; Tanner, Tubiana, and Griffin 2007). Former Maoist combatants, more in the southern conflict zone than in the North, revealed during conversations with this author, that in rejecting violence and ceasing combat they did not agree to fight against their former comrades. Thus side switching is not an appropriate description of this phenomenon. Side switching takes factions as units of analysis, and focuses more on the group dynamic rather than individual incentives, and it does not adequately capture the dynamics of individual rebels leaving the insurgent organization (Seymour 2014; Otto 2018). Former rebels referred to themselves as "retired." Many, more so in the South than in the North, asserted their abiding belief in the Maoist ideology of armed revolution and expressed no remorse for taking up arms against the state that they still considered essentially unjust. The reasons for quitting the insurgency were idiosyncratic, and those reasons are not the focus of this book. Regardless of their respective reasons, the rebels perceived the process of quitting insurgency as ending their life long career, much like retirement. After voluntarily retiring from the insurgency, the rebels do not necessarily deradicalize or join the state forces, which makes this process distinct from surrender, defection, or side switching used customarily in the literature.

The Empirical Puzzle

Around the same time (2004–2012) the Maoist insurgency spread to various Indian states, recruiting and carrying out a series of brazen assaults—including beheading an inspector, hijacking a crowded passenger train, kidnapping bureaucrats, attacking elected politicians, killing almost the entire Chhattisgarh state committee of the Congress Party, and slaughtering 76 officers of the Central Reserve Police Force (CRPF)—Maoist rebels also began to quit the party, more so in the South than in the North. Between 2006 and 2012, for example, compared to 781 surrender events in the state of Andhra Pradesh in South India, only 54 surrendered in the state of Jharkhand in North India.[14] Figure 1.1 illustrates the variation in the number of Maoist surrender cases across affected states.

By the time of my fieldwork in the South in 2013–2014, ordinary people in my fieldwork areas in the South (Telangana region, formerly part of Andhra Pradesh), in the historically worst affected districts of Nalgonda, Warrangal, Karimnagar, Adilabad, and Khammam, reported that they had not seen as many armed guerrillas scouting their villages for recruitment in the last four years (2009–2013) as previously.[15] They shared vivid memories of rebels visiting their villages almost regularly before that for propaganda, recruitment, or recreation purposes. The most tangible reminders of the violent uprisings in these areas that date to the 1970s and 1980s are the numerous tombs that the rebels erected across rural Telangana to honor their dead comrades. These modest structures are now shrouded in thorny shrubs and animal excrement, lying dilapidated by the pitch-black roads built recently by state governments to connect villages that were once remote.[16] However, during

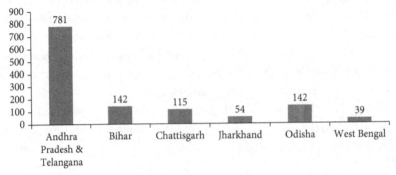

Figure 1.1 State-level Variation in Rebel Retirement, 2006–2012

my visits, I was witness to body bags still coming to villages, mostly from the neighboring state of Chhattisgarh.

The retired rebels are known as "*majhis*" in the South. This is a unique, local honorific used to refer to former Maoists, with no comparable equivalent in Maoist-affected states in the North.[17] The dominant popular sentiment in the South, as I have experienced it over the years, is respectful and sympathetic toward majhis. During interviews, ministers, activists, lawyers, poets, journalists, academics, bureaucrats, and policemen eagerly proclaimed their past association with Maoist politics that reportedly left an indelible mark on their personal lives, political views, and public careers. In the villages, despite initial hesitation, there were hushed admissions of how the revolutionaries gave them hope and self-confidence.

In contrast, I found that ordinary people were either critical or fearful of the Maoists in the North. Government officials, media persons, civil society activists, and ordinary villagers were quick to denounce Maoists as violent thugs terrorizing people and extracting rent from local miners and small businesses. At the most sympathetic end, my informants in the North condemned the Maoists for their military excesses and corrupt rent-seeking practices that included kidnapping for ransom, which negated their past progressive politics and revolutionary zeal.

Retired rebels in the North live secluded lives around the capital city, away from their villages and families and protected by their own private militia or bodyguards. They work either as informants for the police, as part of political/mining mafia, or as aspiring politicians. I met them in various locations, including shady roadside dance bars, inside the premises of state legislative assemblies, in street corner tea shops, or in empty apartments, with them always heavily guarded by privately hired armed men. I found them bitter and beaten, rejected by the people, and hunted by their former comrades for betrayal of the revolutionary cause.

This is in sharp contrast to the retired rebels in the South who have gone back into virtual anonymity of quiet, "normal" life with their families, which indicates their successful reintegration. They are well assimilated into diverse professions, from farmer and homemaker to doctor, professor, and village headman (or headwoman). Figure 1.2 shows the current professions of the 67 retired rebels I met in the South and 50 former rebels I met in the North.

There are two other aspects of the retirement data that are significant in explaining the process of rebel retirement. First, although most studies on Maoist insurgency in India focus on post-2005 data (Gwande, Kapur, and

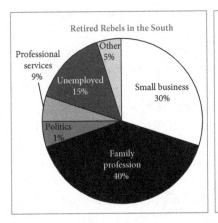
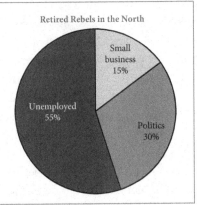

Figure 1.2 North-South Comparison of Post-Retirement Occupations of Retired Rebels

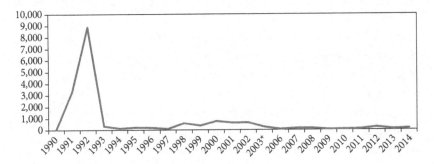

Figure 1.3 Rebel Retirement in the South, 1990–2014

Satyanath 2012; Hoelscher, Miklian, and Vadlamannati 2012; Khanna and Zimmermann 2014), Maoist surrender in the South was actually notably higher in the 1980s and 1990s (Figure 1.3). Thus rebel retirement in the South was high even when the insurgency was still popular and strong. The special commando police (Greyhounds) credited with driving rebels to surrender was barely constituted back then, and the lucrative surrender package of the southern state had not yet been introduced.[18] This sequence of events pokes holes in the dominant narrative that credits efficient policing, arrests and assassinations of Maoists, and lucrative financial incentives for high rebel retirement in the South (Ramana 2009, 2006; Singhal and Nilakantan 2012).

Second, district-level data reveals that rebel retirement, both in the North and South, were concentrated in certain districts and not others

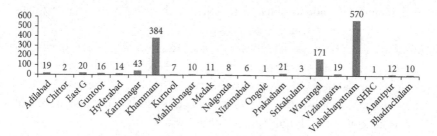

Figure 1.4 District-level Rebel Retirement in the South (Andhra Pradesh), 2006–2013

(Figure 1.4). For example, in the South, rebel retirement was concentrated in two districts (Warrangal and Khammam) in Telangana and one district (Vishakhaptnam) in coastal Andhra Pradesh, although other districts (particularly Karimnagar, Nalgona, and Adilabad) were equally affected by the insurgency. In Jharkhand in the North, retirement was also concentrated in two districts (Khunti and Ranchi).[19] This pattern holds up in other Maoist-affected states as well. Police capability, welfare policies, and financial inducements, the three most popular explanations of rebel retirement among policymakers, varies little across districts.

Throughout the rest of the book, I show that this specific spatial pattern of rebel retirement—higher in the South and concentrated in some districts and not others—is a function of informal exit networks that grow, drawing sustenance from local associational life, in some places and not others.

Theoretical Strategy

The theoretical premise of this book is derived from what former rebels shared with me during more than 100 conversations in both the North and South of India.[20] The primary dilemma that holds rebels back even when they want to quit is this: While they might be killed and their families massacred as after they disarm, the state would not lose much if they failed to keep their side of the bargain. The threat to rebels' lives comes from families they attacked during their rebel career or, in some cases, from the police and their former comrades. Theorizing the rebel's dilemma as a problem of credible commitment, I argue that informal exit networks resolve this problem locally by offering alternative enforcement mechanisms that facilitate retirement in the South, but not so much in the North. These informal exit networks flourish in the South where grassroots associational life is vibrant, but not in the North where civic associations are weak and sparse. Therefore, the theory has two parts: First, an explanation of the credible commitment problem that makes informal networks necessary. Second, a framing of the role of grassroots civic associations that enable the growth of robust and beneficial exit networks in the South but not in the North.

The Problem of Credible Commitment

Rebels are well aware that their lives (and those of their families and friends) would be at stake if they disarmed and returned to the mainstream. In the South, most rebels reported that they feared retaliation from their former enemies (rich, upper caste landlords, money lenders) who they had attacked during their insurgent careers. In the North, former Maoists also listed their former comrades as potential sources of violent retaliation post disarmament. The Indian state loses nothing should it renege on its commitment to protect retired rebels, especially once the initial fanfare around surrender events dies down and the media glare shifts to the latest breaking news.[21] This is the problem of credible commitment. Yet there is no institutional mechanism in place to address this anxiety among rebels, which hinders their ability to give up arms. State-surrender policies that focus primarily on cash rewards and employment opportunities fail to address this fear. Rebels made it clear that the looming threat to their lives from former enemies or former comrades presented a predicament far more pressing and proximate than the predicament of finding a post-retirement livelihood.

Security personnel pointed out to me that it would hurt their reputation if they could not protect retiring rebels, which would, in turn, discourage retirement. Rebels also admitted that they knew that the security personnel have career rewards tied to securing high retirement, but the institutional mechanisms of surrender and rehabilitation, in absence of informal exit networks, were not enough to convince the rebels that the security officials would not collude with the known local enemies of retiring rebels with an aim to attack retired Maoists and their families. A former rebel in the South explained that after he decided to quit he took two more years to finally surrender arms because the specific superintendent of police whom he wanted to oversee the process was transferred out of his area and he did not feel comfortable reaching out to someone he did not trust. This level of trust vis-à-vis a specific law enforcement officer came from (a) his reputation that he went to the same high school as one of the popular local rebel leaders and was known to be sympathetic to the rebel cause, and (b) his successful supervision of other rebel disarmament processes and facilitation of the rebels' return to their families.

Theoretically, the problem of credible commitment is straightforward: how to bind players to an agreement over time. Game theory provides an intuitive answer to this question: The players can be bound when the gains from living up to the agreement exceeds the gains from defecting. Others will merely reason backward to predict whether players have incentives to follow through and keep a promise. In the context of rebel retirement, this problem could be resolved if the rebels knew that the state would also pay a price if it failed to keep its side of the bargain. A straightforward way to establish credibility and convince others of a player's commitment to certain terms of a bargain is to put in place formal rules that declare the punishment for reneging and thereby reduce transaction costs (North 1990, 1993; Wendt 2001). But when formal rules are inadequate to bind players to an agreement, as in the case of rebel retirement, there are historical precedents where formal rules have been supplemented effectively by informal institutions that also reduce enforcement costs. Such arrangements have been identified as key institutional features that bolstered the rapid economic development in many East Asian countries and post-Soviet Russia, managed emerging technologies in Africa, and even asylum governance in Europe (Furlong 2012; Puetter 2004; Harsh 2005; Ledeneva 2006).

One of the loose generalizations in the field is that the effect of participation in the informal, unauthorized networks of social relationships and webs of influence are different in different parts of the world. In well-functioning liberal democracies of the West, the unwritten rules of informal governance are expected to create greater flexibility in the formal institutions that work alongside them. But in "defective democracies" of the non-Western world, informal networks inevitably erode transparency and accountability in ways that destabilize and undermine legitimate public institutions (Merkel and Croissant 2000, 2004). However, this book problematizes this old West/non-West binary by showing how the impact of informal networks varies within the same country: In the South of India, on the one hand, informal exit networks are complementary to formal institutions and "fill in the gaps" that formal institutions are unable to address. In the North of India, on the other hand, they undermine the formal process of rebel retirement and restrict their reintegration. For example, contrary to my expectations, former combatants in the South acknowledged that informal exit networks convinced them to work with certain security and law enforcement officers despite that the rebels were ideologically primed to distrust the state security forces they had exchanged gunfire with during their long insurgent careers.

Indeed, informal exit networks sometimes allow and encourage some bending of the formal rules with an aim to achieve the same goal as formal institutions, namely maximum retirement of rebels (Helmke and Levitsky 2004; Lauth 2000; Stiglitz 2000; Tsai 2006; Williamson 2009). Further, actors operating even within the formal institutional context, such as bureaucracy, law enforcement, and the legislature, develop norms, procedures, and dense networks with private sector actors in ways that expedite their work or address problems unanticipated by the formal rules.

Another important characteristic of these informal exit networks in my fieldwork areas is that, although they are not entirely immune to local cultural norms and social hierarchies, they are rooted more in shared expectations than in shared cultural values. This means that unlike the "primordial" institutions (e.g., caste) that tend to be too deep-rooted to accept incremental changes, these bottom-up exit networks, by co-evolving with democratic and insurgent politics in the conflict zones of North and South India, are more adaptive. Often, Dalits, still socially marginalized in the villages, played key leadership roles in the functioning of harmonic exit networks at the village level, even when the retiring rebel did not belong to the Dalit castes. With repetition and diffusion, these informal networks built by everyday people compensating for perceived institutional drawbacks may take on an institutional reality of their own, or these less costly alternative enforcement mechanisms may hinder costly institutional development. Although that inquiry is outside the scope of this book, suffice it to say here that the non-ascriptive and voluntary nature of these informal networks make them more valuable to a vibrant civil society, thus deepening democracy (Habermas 1991; Heller 2009; Krishna 2002; Varshney 2003).

Grassroots Civic Associations

A flourishing civil society, most evident in the availability of grassroots civic associations as well as dense quotidian ties among citizens, has long been held as the key factor that can make or break democratic governments, driving key political, social, and economic outcomes (Berman 1997; Putnam 1995; Berman 2009). In demonstrating the role of grassroots associational life in the process of rebel retirement, this book also shows how conflict zones are not merely landscapes of lawlessness (Arjona 2016). Societies do not exist in a binary of conflict or peace. What I witnessed instead in the conflict zones of India is the gray zone of overlap between the state and insurgency where, underneath the façade of disorder and chaos, ordinary people experience insurgent activities constantly evolving with a well-functioning state. Grassroots politics, both the legitimate variety via membership in civic organizations and the illegal variety via participation in insurgent mass mobilization, also transpire in these gray zones. Membership in one does not preclude participation in the other.

Prior research suggests that cooperative behavior is a stable characteristic of a political system: For example, social capital that enables local governments in Northern Italy to function better than those in the South derives from the fourteenth century, and inter-ethnic associations that deter Hindu-Muslim violence in modern India have their roots in the colonial era (Varshney 2001; Putnam Leonardi, and Nanetti 1994). Similarly, the emergence of retirement-boosting, harmonic exit networks in the South and retirement-stifling, discordant exit networks in the North are path-dependent processes contingent on the strength of grassroots civic associations, which, in turn, is a historically determined outcome. However, the informal exit networks that emerge in the North and South are distinct, which, I show, is an outcome contingent on regionally distinctive (a) prewar social bases of the rebels going back to the 1950s and (b) the insurgent organizational ties, which jointly affect the nature of the insurgency-democracy interface where retirement transpires.

Research Strategy

Importantly, this book contributes to the methodology of the study of civil conflict and postconflict outcomes. To show how rebel retirement from the same insurgent group varies in two conflict zones, I draw on empirical materials from the extraordinary comparative laboratory of contemporary India.

The primary evidence for the role of informal exit networks in rebel retirement is drawn from intimate conversations with over 100 retired rebels and other stakeholders in two conflict zones of India, including squad members, area commanders, and district and central committee members of the Maoist Party. Of these 102 interviews, 35 were long, open-ended conversations in life history format where respondents decided what they were comfortable sharing, which not only complied with standards of ethically responsible research in postwar settings, but also seemed intuitively respectful (do no harm) particularly given my higher status in the research sites (Büthe et al. 2015; Dauphinée 2016; Pachirat 2011; Wood 2006). This also prevented me from asking leading questions, which create social desirability bias, particularly in a postconflict context where its likelihood is very high. Earlier on during this study, when I asked former rebels when and how they quit, they did not delve into their personal experiences or the role of the informal network. Instead they shared clips of news stories of their surrender that they saved in file folders, which also emphasized the legal, formal process involving police and administration (Tourangeau and Yan 2007; DeMaio 1984; Bradburn et al. 1978; Nadeau, Niemi, and Amato 1995). Many admitted later that they did not think anyone would be interested in the myriad maneuverings they had to engage in to ensure their personal safety. In addition, they were afraid that an outsider could stigmatize their interlocutors as crooked, fraudulent, or even criminal.

This book, in full acknowledgment of the needs for research transparency, pays attention not only to providing a clear and reliable account of the sources but also to laying out how inferences are made from analysis of available qualitative and quantitative data. However, de-identification of my interlocutors in this particular project goes beyond merely removing the name, title, location, or institutional affiliation of my research participants (Parkinson and Wood 2015). It requires keeping names and attributes of informants and their location (district and villages) confidential, as these details provided as evidence can be enough for a local person to identify the identity of key players and/or informants. For example, in my conversations with former rebels and activists, I would begin with one question: How did you become a Maoist rebel or grassroots rights activist? Their answers inevitably consisted of detailed accounts of the violence that they and their families observed or experienced in very specific ways that would be identifiable even if I removed the research participant's name and shared their location.[22]

For the purpose of documentation and balancing the needs for respondent anonymity and research transparency, I divided my various field interactions into 8 categories. I met Maoist leaders of varying stature within the organization (Category 1), as well as leaders of various political parties of various national and regional parties, including members of parliament (MP) and members of legislative assembly (MLA), who had experience contesting elections in Maoist-affected constituencies in Jharkhand and Telangana (Category 2).[23] I also met 102 retired rebels (Category 5), and the respondents are coded with their regional identifier, North (N) or South (S), and serial number (RN 1–37, RS 1–65). In addition, I conducted semi-structured interviews with police (Category 3), bureaucrats (Category 4), academic and journalist experts (Category 6), and activists (Category 7).[24] Many activists (Category 7) working in my fieldwork areas had overlapping affiliations with professional associations and various Maoist frontal organizations including Jana Natya Mandali (Maoist Cultural Wing), Virasam (Revolutionary Writer's Association), Kulanirmulana Porata Samiti (Committee for Annihilation of Caste).[25] This simultaneous involvement in both legal and insurgent organizations was true of some human rights activists affiliated with Human Rights Forum (HRF), Committee for Release of Political Prisoners (CRPP), and Association for Protection of Democratic Rights (APDR), among others.[26] I also interviewed civilians in both conflict zones (Category 8) through two 100-respondent pilot surveys in North and South India. I also held focus groups in the villages and had one-on-one conversations with civilians.[27] I eventually abandoned my plan for larger surveys because I came to question their usefulness in my research. In the field it became clear to me that conflict zones are steeped in ambiguities bred by the simultaneous acceptance and rejection of both the state and the insurgents. Civilians I spoke to had to navigate dangers from both state and rebels, often working as informers (by choice or by lack of it) for insurgents or police. Many of my respondents shared how they offered food and shelter to rebels to help them hide while they recuperated from battle wounds. Others cheered for the Maoist students, youth, and women's organizations, while keeping their day jobs intact in government or private organizations, paying taxes and participating in local elections and peaceful political protests, rallies, voted, and paid taxes.

On the one hand, 60% of civilian respondents in the pilot surveys reported that they were afraid and mistrustful of state law enforcement, and that they also disapproved of rebel excesses, particularly local incidents of indiscriminate violence that killed civilians. On the other hand, the same people applauded the rebels for their heroism, personal sacrifices, and principled, unselfish politics of the rebels and praised their contribution to reducing incidents of landlord harassments against the poor, lower caste, and women. Over 80% of these same respondents when asked also admitted that there is a good side of the state, particularly visible in state-welfare schemes like rural employment guarantee scheme or boarding schools for the poor Dalits in Telangana. It is in this ambiguity of allegiance in the state-insurgency interface that clandestine crosscutting connections are forged among various actors in conflict zones in ways that eventually facilitate rebel retirement in some places and not others. Although some respondents in Categories 2 (politicians), 3 (police), 4 (bureaucrats), 6 (academics and journalists), and 7 (activists) did not request anonymity, and some did, numbers have been assigned to all respondents to ensure a uniform standard of reporting interview data. Citations with names of respondents are included where respondent identity and the shared information are already in the public domain.

In this book I have avoided using direct quotes from rebels even if it would serve my interests to add more credibility to my case studies.[28] Researchers are particularly open to the charge of cherry-picking the most eye-catching statements, without regard to context and representativeness. It is important to represent that the quotation is representative of the average intensity and direction of response. To convey more concretely that respondents mostly agree on a particular point, I summarize the number of respondents expressing the position as percentage of total number of respondents, as percentage of respondents specifically asked about it, and as percentage of respondents who spontaneously volunteered this opinion (Bleich and Pekkanen 2013; Büthe et al. 2015). The Appendix 1, 'Research Methods' discusses sample frame construction, interview methods, and concerns about quality of information and accuracy of reporting in further details.

I learned about rebels who were leaving the Maoist movement during my preliminary visits to Maoist-affected areas around Jhargram in West Bengal in 2010–2011, when the insurgency was at its peak. During this time there was an explosion of interest in exploring the success of the Maoists through statistical analysis of various underlying structural factors. The national and international media were obsessively talking about the rise of the Maoists from the ashes, harping on some spectacular episodes of their attacks on public properties and police stations.[29] At the same time, local journalists, activists, and administrators confirmed that there were many Maoist rebels who were surrendering their arms and trying to return to their pre-insurgent lives. Interested in reading about the pathways rebels take out of an insurgency into normal lives, it became quickly apparent that voices and points of view of retired rebels were largely missing both in the academic literature and policy pieces. Where available, they were mostly stigmatized and sidelined in both in insurgent and state discourse, seen as embittered by failure, betrayal, desertion, and disillusionment. There were some scattered stories in the media of former Maoists running for office, becoming dreaded real estate agents, or earning an honest living running tea stalls. Regional newspapers published stray accounts of women rebels who fondly remembered how their military uniform in the Maoist army liberated them from the clutches of gender and caste discriminations rampant in their pre- and post-insurgent lives. In choosing the topic for my research, I was guided by something that sparked my curiosity, and in conducting the research I have allowed myself to be guided by what I found in the field rather than by the dominant narratives in rebel politics, methodological direction in the field of conflict research, or gaps in the literature.

My earliest intuitions about rebel retirement, from the perspective of rebels, were drawn from my long conversations with former rebels from the first phase of the Naxalite uprising in West Bengal in the 1960s. It was also useful to hear firsthand accounts of top and mid-level Maoist organizers from the 1960s, who shared their experience of how, as young insurgents, they first moved into a rural area, prepared detailed field reports highlighting the potential axes of polarization of antagonistic classes with the least military cost, built local alliances and attracted a broader support base of urban intellectuals and activists, and responded to directions from the central leadership of the party when their own instincts, based on their local experience, went against them. These insights helped me cross-check the various published and unpublished documents that I amassed over the last decade on the Maoist organization. Comparing these accounts with more recent accounts of intra-organizational dynamics and organizational ties to civilians among rebels who retired post-2004 further reinforced my understanding that retirement processes and outcomes were historically contingent and locally embedded. Thus path dependence and its local embeddedness are the abiding themes in this book.

Through interview after interview with police, administrators, politicians, and former rebels, I cross-checked accounts of militant mass-mobilization strategy, recruitment methods, day-to-day interactions with civilians and political parties, military training, and exchange of fire with between the rebels and security forces.[30] It was over many rounds of discussions with diverse stakeholders in conflict zones that I realized that the unbridgeable divide between the state and the insurgents fighting for monopoly over violence is more a theoretical construct than a reality in the experience of ordinary people in conflict zones. Over 60% of respondents spontaneously admitted they were afraid and mistrustful of state law enforcement, but on the question of their retirement and reintegration, those sentiments were insignificant compared to the overriding need for approval of and encouragement from their families and neighbors.

The dominant trend in political science is to employ a complementary mix of qualitative and quantitative approaches. With that in mind, I set out to do large N statistical tests complemented by analysis of my extensive primary qualitative data collected over a period of more than five years (2009–2014). I created a district-level data set on Maoist surrenders over a period of 10 years (2005–2014) in 318 districts of 10 Maoist-affected states of India known as the "Red Corridor." Data were drawn from media reports collected by the South Asia Terrorism Portal and cross-checked with government data shared on the website of the Ministry of Home Affairs. The most significant contribution of this exercise to my project was bringing into focus the sharp regional variation in rebel retirement between the North and the South, with concentration in certain districts. This big picture of spatial distribution eventually shed light on the process of rebel retirement and raised questions on the efficacy of counterinsurgency or development explanations of retirement that do not vary across districts.

I conducted negative binomial regression to assess various alternative explanations of retirement. My primary hypothesis was that local grassroots civic associations are likely to play a positive role in retirement, which I operationalized using household-level survey data on membership in various civic organizations (India Human Development Survey) collapsed to district-level indictors of organizational density. My intuitions about the role of civic associations in rebel retirement were borne out by statistically significant positive correlations between rebel retirement and organizational density. Between 2013 and 2014 I conducted in-depth fieldwork, specifically in the Telangana region of the state of Andhra Pradesh in the South and in Jharkhand in the North, for a continuous stretch of 18 months to uncover the causal mechanisms that connected civic associations with rebel retirement.

In addition, I returned to the field in Nepal in 2018, where I interviewed former Maoist commanders and political organizers, including former Prime Minister Dr. Baburam Bhattarai and other top leaders who were involved in the process of democratic transition. The case of Nepal helps test some of the implications of the theory of rebel retirement through informal networks in an out-of-sample case.

In the Telangana region, I conducted my fieldwork in five out of its 10 districts (Adilabad, Karimnagar, Warangal, Khammam, and Nalgonda), of which Warangal and Khammam had the highest incidence of Maoist rebel retirement events in Andhra Pradesh between 2005 and 2015, Karimnagar had a moderate incidence, and Adilabad and Nalgonda had the lowest incidence of retirement events. In order to investigate the curious spatial pattern of Maoist surrenders with a high concentration in certain districts and not others (as shown in Figure 1.5), examining districts with the highest and lowest values on rebel retirement was a conscious attempt to maximize variance on the dimension of interest.

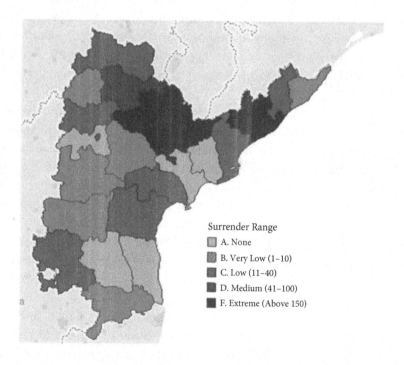

Surrender Range
- A. None
- B. Very Low (1–10)
- C. Low (11–40)
- D. Medium (41–100)
- F. Extreme (Above 150)

Figure 1.5 District-Level Rebel Surrender in the South, 2006–2013

This approach reduced the number of study cases, but the combination of careful comparisons within a shared political setting and militant group, attention to path dependence, and rich empirical details of the causal processes make my inferences more credible than those that I might have drawn from a more heterogeneous and less detailed set of cases. In addition, each of these three districts is large and varied and should not be thought of as a single case but rather as the locations where I engaged in in-depth research of several case studies. I selected these places because they provided important variation in retirement events and the availability of networks.

For each of the five selected districts, I randomly chose one highly affected mandal, one moderately affected mandal, and one non-affected mandal, which added up to 15 mandals (sub district unit equalivalent to subdivision in Jharkhand and West Bengal). In each of the five heavily affected mandals in Telangana, I randomly selected two villages (a total of 10 highly affected villages per district). In the five moderately affected mandals, I randomly selected one village (a total of five moderately affected villages per district). Finally, in each of the five non-affected mandals, I randomly selected one village (five non-affected villages per district). Table 1.1 contains the list of mandals and villages selected for fieldwork in the Telangana region of former Andhra Pradesh. Given my interest in understanding the role of ordinary people in rebel retirement, I also designed focus groups with civilians in conflict zones in Telangana, in all chosen villages with both high and low rebel retirement.

In an ideal world, in order for me to argue why some rebels quit and others do not, I would need the perspective of those Maoist guerrillas who wanted to quit but did not and continue to be deployed. But security and accessibility were important considerations. Since I was more interested in the process of retirement than why some rebels retire and others do not, it was not equally important for me to contact both active and retired rebels. Ideally, I also wanted to conduct focus groups in West Midnapore district in West Bengal (Jangalmahal area). But the 2013 village local elections (*panchayat*) in the state made field research on questions related to the Maoist movement, which was a central issue in the elections, too politically sensitive to extract any useful insight.

In the North, despite Maoist concentration in North, South, and East Jharkhand, Maoist retirement has been concentrated mostly in the capital city, Ranchi, and the neighboring Khunti district (dark areas on the map in Figure 1.6). Even though many Maoist rebels were born in Palamu or Latehar

Table 1.1 Fieldwork Areas in the South

	Nalgonda *Low Exit*	Adilabad *Low Exit*	Karimnagar *Moderate Exit*	Warangal *High Exit*	Khammam *High Exit*
Highly Affected	Munugode Mandal *Villages* 1. Munugode 2. Cholledu	Indervelly Mandal (Vaipet forest) *Villages* 1. Rajampet 2. Tejapur	Husnabad Mandal *Villages* 1. Gouravelli 2. Ramavaram	Geesugonda Mandal *Villages* 1. Mogilicherla 2. Manugoda	Charla Mandal (Chennapuram forest area) *Villages* 1. Pusuguppa 2. Unjapalli
Moderately Affected	Narayanpur Mandal *Village* 1.Rochakonda (Lambada tribal)	Laxetipet Mandal *Village* 1. Pothepalle	Bheemdevarapalli Mandal *Village* 1. Manikyapoor	Station Ghanpur Mandal *Village* 1. Sitarampur-Kondapur	Venkatapuram (tribal area) *Village* Laxmipuram
Not Affected	Nalgonda Mandal *Village* 1. Samastha Narayanpuram	Neredigonda Mandal *Village* 1.Kuntala	Manthani Mandal *Village* 1. Pandullapalle	Venkatapur Mandal *Village* 1. Vetturalapalli	Khammam (Urban) *Village* 1. Manchugonda

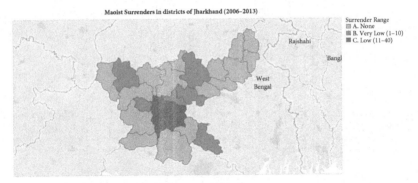

Figure 1.6　District-Level Rebel Surrender in the North, 2006–2013

in northern Jharkhand, they mostly surrendered at the police headquarters in Ranchi.

Unlike Telangana, the two districts with highest surrender events in Jharkhand were not among the 12 Maoist-affected districts in the state. In addition to the capital Ranchi, adjacent rural areas and Khunti districts where Maoist surrender is highest and where Maoists who have surrendered live, I distributed my fieldwork (Table 1.2) in the three Maoist pockets in North, East, and South Jharkhand.[31] In Giridih district (in the east, contiguous with West Bengal), Palamu district (in the north, contiguous with Bihar) and West Singhbhum district (in the southeast, contiguous with Orissa), shown in medium dark shade in Figure 1.6, movement intensity is high and surrender is moderately high.[32]. In the Dhanbad district, movement intensity is high, but surrender is very low Contiguous with East Singhbhum district is West Midnapore district (Jangalmahal) of West Bengal, where I met surrendered Maoists in Binpur I & II and in Gopiballabhpur I & II subdivisions.[33]

In course of the study I was constantly aware that high-quality micro-level data on conflict experiences beyond violence are extremely rare. In methodological terms, I understood firsthand that the utility of questionnaires and surveys is limited when studying sensitive topics and subjective processes in conflict zones, particularly in a climate of great distrust and fear (as in the North).[34] Further, it also became increasingly clear during the fieldwork that the explanation for high retirement in the South lies not only in the availability of grassroots civic associations but also in informal networks that grow out of those associations. My growing interest in the mechanisms of formation and inner workings of informal networks required evidence of clandestine and semi-clandestine connections among people, which was

Table 1.2 Fieldwork Areas in the North

Districts	Region/States	Movement Intensity	Surrender Events	Village/Block
Ranchi	Around capital city, Ranchi/Jharkhand	Low	Highest	Ranchi Town, State Secretariat, Police Headquarters
Kundhi	Adjacent to Ranchi	Low	Highest	Lebed and Korba/Arki block
Palamu	North Jharkhand	High	Low	Bishrampur, chhatarpur, Chainpur, Lesliganj blocks
Giridih	East Jharkhand	High	Low	Dumri and Jamoa blocks
West Singhbum	South Jharkhand	High	Low	Manoharpur block
Dhanbad	East Jharkhand	Low	Low	Topchachi and Dhanbad
West Mindapore	Adjacent to East Singhbum	High	High	Binpur I & II, Gopiballabhpur I & II Subdivisions

neither amenable to structured interviews nor pinned down in any black and white statistics. The emerging evidence of informal networks driving the process of rebel retirement made conversing and observing rather than just interviewing necessary. Thus this book also relies largely on semi-structured interviews complemented with informal conversations and participant observations during a sustained presence in the fieldwork areas, which generated rich ethnographic evidence of how ordinary people in conflict zones live their entire lives in gray zones of state-insurgency interface, straddling across the divide between the two domains (state and insurgency) taken as sacrosanct in policy writings, insurgent documents, and in academic research.

The case studies offer detailed and firsthand accounts of the trajectory, incentives, and intervening variables in the process of rebel retirement from the perspective of the rebels rather than policymakers. Using these qualitative methods, however, required intimate and nuanced understanding of the insurgent organization. Wherever possible, I tried to cross-check the information given to me and to develop a sense of history from many different perspectives. Maoist leaders, former rebels, politicians, and activists, perhaps as an assertion of their control over the process of sharing information, also continuously vetted the project during initial interviews. They quizzed me on the various details of the Maoist ideology and history, asked direct questions about my family's voting preferences (left or right), and demanded assurances about what I would and would not write. As a result, multiple meetings became necessary to win their trust and to broach the sensitive topics I wanted to talk about. As a rule, I was extra careful to be polite but firm, and completely transparent about the nature and purpose of my research. Whenever requested, I promised to never reveal the identities of those I met and spoke with (except the elites), a pledge I have honored. The interviews and associated fieldwork "required certain precautions and incredible delicacy" and raised significant challenges of personal safety, both for those interviewed and for myself. The field conditions made research procedures of informed consent and confidentiality of informants absolutely crucial.[35] However, in general, my probes and inquisitions into intimate details of incentives, motivations, and trust was met with enthusiastic collaboration from many respondents, who opened their homes and hearts to me and were surprisingly generous in sharing painful memories of betrayal and traumatic experiences of losing friends and family members in the recent past. There was almost a need to share and a sense of pride that someone came all the way from a far away university to learn about their lives, their struggle, their losses, and their victories. Other researchers have found similar enthusiasm to share experience with outsiders among survivors and participants of violence in Gujarat (India), El Salvador, Mozambique, Rwanda, and elsewhere (Chakravarty 2015; Chatterjee 2017; Nordstrom and Robben 1995; Wood 2003).

Policy Implications

An understanding how rebels approach the questions of their retirement and reintegration offers very clear policy implications. Policymakers worldwide devote extraordinary resources to weaning people away from extremism. Yet, they continue to limit attention and resources to creating opportunities of economic rehabilitation and political participation for retired rebels, without addressing the main constraint that really discourages rebel retirement. The theory presented in this book reveals the key factor that deters rebel retirement, namely concerns for personal safety and the well-being of their (estranged) family. From the rebel's perspective, provisions for personal safety, and not the lure of economic incentives or political participation, are the necessary conditions for them to quit extremist groups.

Rebels frequently experience disillusionment with their organization, its ideology, or their comrades. But episodes of self-doubt are often not enough to propel them to the next step, where they must desert their comrades and permanently abandon their rebel lives. For whatever reason, once rebels decide to quit, they still cannot do so as long as they believe that (a) they could be killed or their families would be exposed to retaliatory violence after they disarm, and (b) the state would not lose much if it failed to protect them and their families. This problem of credible commitment not only thwarts rebel retirement, but it also hinders a sustainable end to armed conflict. Policymakers should be asking themselves what kinds of institutional mechanisms might address this credible commitment problem.

Insofar as they can learn from bottom-up best practices evolving at the grassroots level, states and international actors working in postconflict settings can become more effective in facilitating rebel retirement and reintegration. But there is one normative and one practical consideration that get in the way of policymakers looking at the issue from the perspective of the rebels. First, states thrive on their assumed legitimacy vis-à-vis the illegitimate rebel challengers, which make them rigidly unwilling and incapable of looking at things from the rebel's perspective even when rebel retirement is the goal. Second, most of the research on this topic perpetuates the untested but established assumption that economic incentives can lure rebels back because it was economic deprivation that radicalized them in the first place. An important implication of this book is that we need to tap into the agency, tenacity, resilience, and resourcefulness of civilians in conflict zones to wean the rebels from extremism.

However, as discussed in this book, sometimes informal exit networks can enrich the project of state-building, and, at other times, working through latent coercion and corruption, they can either thwart it or reinforce a depraved feudal power structure. The same variation extends to other informal arrangements of rebel civilian governance, and this is a dilemma that future research must explore. A better understanding of the protracted process of rebel retirement and reintegration allows us to anticipate when, where, and how a state may effectively engage in building institutions that enable smooth rebel exit and stabilize postconflict peace, where nonstate actors are likely to embolden this process, and where they can obstruct it irretrievably.

Road Map

The book unfolds as follows: Chapter 2 introduces the deep historical context of the origin and growth of the Maoist insurgency in India. It compares Maoist organizational structures, political ideology, recruitment strategies, mobilization methods, and patterns of violence in North and South India. Chapter 3 builds on this historical narrative to show how ordinary people in conflict zones learn to live with one foot in the "extralegal" insurgency and one foot in the "legal" state, contravening the sharp normative juxtaposition between the realms of state and insurgency professed by policymakers and assumed by external observers. Although ordinary people find it quite unexceptional, the scholarly literature on conflict does not take much theoretical cognizance of this gray zone, where the informal networks of rebel retirement grow. That chapter also shows how insurgent mass mobilization, including recruitment drives in urban and rural areas; rebel cultural outreach programs; and forceful activism, which was more successful in the South than in the North, also deepened local democracy. By exploring the concept of this gray zone, I build on existing research as well as lay the groundwork for a future research agenda on rebel governance and its legacy in peacetimes as well as on the bargaining and implementation of peace accords when actors are not just elite or unitary but also local, divided, and multiple.

Chapter 4 traces the process by which former combatants, both men and women, from the rank of ordinary foot soldiers to top leaders, retire and reintegrate through informal exit networks in the South. It also analyzes the antecedent local conditions, like configurations of prewar social bases of insurgency and the patterns of insurgent organizational ties that led to the emergence of harmonic exit networks in the region. Chapter 5 shows why different antecedent conditions in insurgent social bases and organizational ties led to the differences in processes and outcomes of retirement and reintegration in the North. The underlying theory of this book is simple, and as such should travel beyond the current time period and beyond the borders of India. Chapter 6 evaluates the scope and conditions of the theory of rebel retirement through informal exit networks. It addresses the implications of this project for scholarship and for policymaking and sums up avenues for future research.

2

Inside the Insurgency

Maoist-led uprisings represent the most recent episode in a series of agrarian uprisings endemic to India throughout British rule and go further back to the Mughals (sixteenth and seventeenth centuries). There were 110 known instances of violent peasant uprisings in India in 117 years, from 1783 to 1900 (Guha 1999). Rural uprisings have erupted in many forms, ranging from local riots to warlike campaigns that spread over many districts. During British rule, violent uprisings like the Chotanagpur tribal revolt (1807– 1808), Munda rebellion (1832, 1867–1890), Kol rebellion (1831–1832), Santhal rebellion (1885–1886), Rampa rebellion (1879–1890), Madri Kalo revolt (1898), and others posed a major threat to the British administration. What makes the Maoist insurgency distinctive in this long line of peasant uprisings is not the use of violent means by ordinary peasants, but its unified organizational structure and the ideological commitment to overthrowing the state as the ultimate solution to problems of landlessness, rural indebtedness, and inequality.

This chapter presents the entangled historical narrative of the Maoist insurgency in India, its ideological origin, military strategy, organizational characteristics, recruitment mechanisms, and ties to the local communities, with emphasis on the similarities and differences between the North and the South. It analyzes the social terrain on which the insurgent organization operated, which were the jumping-off points for the research presented in this book. It shows how the distinct pre-existing social and political context that the Maoists faced in the North and the South of India determined their mobilization strategy and organizational ties.

It also raises two analytically interesting puzzles. First, how do armed rebels shape their surroundings? In the next chapter, I discuss how the Maoists, given their distinct prewar social bases, created postwar conditions marked by strong grassroots civic associations in the South but not in the North. Interestingly, the same insurgent group produced very different postwar outcomes in two parts of India. This discussion flips the question state-centric theorists and cross-national studies of insurgency have asked

Farewell to Arms. Rumela Sen, Oxford University Press (2021). © Oxford University Press.
DOI: 10.1093/oso/9780197529867.003.0002

on how insurgent groups are shaped by their sociopolitical and economic contexts. For example, Skocpol argued that sustained peasant rebellion occurs when the state is in crisis, and Goodwin showed that insurgent groups will be cohesive when they face weak and exclusionary states (Collier and Hoeffler 2000; Fearon and Laitin 2003; Goodwin and Skocpol 2000; Skocpol 1979). But the reverse is also true (a process discussed further in the next chapter on the creation of the gray zone of the insurgency-state interface).

The second puzzle that follows from the first is the dramatic differences in the nature of insurgent organizational ties with the local community in the North and South of India, despite being part of the same insurgent organization, united by one ideology and a highly centralized command structure, fighting the same state and at the same time. The origin of these differences, rooted in local caste-class dynamics, is discussed in this chapter. The impact of these differences on retirement processes and outcomes is continued further in Chapter 3.

To begin the story of the Maoist insurgency in India, in the first section (Emergence of Maoists in India), I briefly introduce the socioeconomic and political context and the recurring agrarian miseries that led to the furious ideological debates within the Indian left and the eventual consolidation of Maoist movements in India. I draw upon extensive archival research of Maoist documents, party publications, vernacular newspapers, theoretical treatises, published and unpublished memoirs of Maoist leaders, and interviews with leaders and activists involved with Maoist organizations in India.[1] The distinctiveness of the Maoists lie not in their discovering a new agenda for agrarian struggles or in the use of violence; rather, they distinguished agitation violence from revolutionary violence and advocated for the latter, which required targeting not just local enemies of the poor but also the entire democratic apparatus of the Indian state (Sanyal 1968).[2]

The second section (Unifying Elements of Maoist Ideology) highlights the unifying elements of ideology and organizational structure shared by the Maoists both in the North and the South of India. The third section (Pre-War Social Bases of Insurgency) examines the processes of insurgent mass mobilization in the two regions. It introduces two criteria that determine the relationship of insurgents to their local communities: First, polarization of the social bases of insurgency, and second, militancy of the local authority. The subsequent sections introduce a comparison of the recruitment, outreach, and mass-mobilization strategies of the Maoists in South India versus those in North India. These sections develop the concepts of horizontal and vertical ties of the Maoists with their local communities and shows how variation in the strength of these ties influenced the capacity of the insurgent organization to shape their political context. This chapter concludes demonstrating how insurgent organizations, despite organizational and ideological unity, are locally embedded. Distinctive local dynamics are derived from the prewar social bases of insurgency, specifically the polarization of identities and interests and the degree of militancy, which affects the horizontal and vertical ties of insurgent organizations.

Emergence of the Maoists in India

The rural poor, comprising marginal farmers and landless laborers, tenants, sharecroppers, and small landholders, formed an essential part of the mass base of the Indian National Congress in its struggle for self-rule and independence. Independent India (post-1947), born agrarian and democratic, compelled *all* its political parties competing in the electoral arena to constantly negotiate farmers' demands for higher crop prices, lower farm-input processes, a waiver of agricultural loans, and high rural investments. However, while the rural poor was very much active in mainstream political parties, the most militant peasant movements in India have all operated within the ideological framework of Marxism-Leninism-Maoism (Herring 1991; Gough 1968; Gough 1974; Panikkar 1989). Among them the three most notable agrarian uprisings, occurring in the1940s and 1950s, were the Tebhaga uprising in the East, the Warli uprising in the West, and the Punnapra-Vayalar and Telangana uprisings in the South. The *Tebhaga* (literally, three parts) movement of 1946 was a struggle of sharecroppers to keep two-thirds share of their produce instead of just half, an idea born from the 1940 recommendations of the British government's Land Revenue Commission (Dhanagare 1976; Bandyopadhyay 2001; Sen 1972). It was concentrated in the Jessore and Khulna districts of undivided Bengal that eventually became Pakistan after the partition of India (Panjabi 2010).[3] The Bengal branch of All-India Kisan Sabha (Communist Peasants' Organization) adopted the idea and quickly mobilized sharecroppers in 19 of the 27 Bengal districts, involving 6 million peasants within the span of four months (Sen 1972; Rasul 1969).

During the same time, Kisan Sabha led the Warli tribal movement of 1945–1947 in Maharashtra in western India. The organization mobilized

Warli tribal communities against bonded labor, unpaid labor, surrender of half-share of produce to landlords, perpetual indebtedness, and exploitation like abduction and rape of tribal women (Parulekar 1975).[4] The Punnapra-Vayalar revolt, organized against the princely state of Travancore in the southern part of Kerala during 10 days in October 1946, was one of the few instances of the Indian working class setting up armed enclaves and fighting pitched battles.[5] However, despite communist mobilization led by agricultural workers against the corrupt nexus of a feudal landlord and national bourgeoisie, there was no organized attempt at forcefully altering the existing agroeconomic structure, property relations, or the nature of the state. In fact, the demand never shifted beyond wage reforms, and success was measured in terms of electoral achievements of the communists in the *panchayat* (village self-government) elections (Bouton 2014). In fact, the Communist Party was so weighed down by tactical adjustments and confusing signals emanating from the Soviet Union that their leadership refused to take a more determined stand on violence and violently changing the status quo (Herring 1986).

Illustrated in both the Tebhaga and Warli uprisings, violence was not part of the early communists' conscious strategy in confronting landlords and moneylenders, though incidents of violence did occur. In Warli, for example, the farmhouses of landlords were often burned down because tribal women were routinely raped in these houses. These acts of violence against the landlords' property were more used to confirm the activists' self-respect and dignity than an organized expression of their revolutionary zeal to reject the unequal relationship with the landlord, question his moral authority, and overthrow the system and the state. In Tebhaga, as well, the struggle was agitational not revolutionary in character, and communist activity was concentrated on enlisting new members; founding local chapters of Kisan Sabhas; holding provincial conferences and meetings at the district, *taluqa* (block), and village levels; organizing marches, mass demonstrations and rallies, and so on. When they resorted to more direct action, the "action" was very similar to the one adopted by the avowedly nonviolent, non-communist Gandhians, which included refusal to pay government taxes, land revenue, and willfully getting arrested.

Among the agrarian uprisings later in the 1940s, the Telangana movement (1946–1951) stands out as an exception in its use of organized violence against the state, not just the local faces of feudal exploitation. The movement transitioned from being opposed to local landlords to becoming a resistance against the *Nizam* (king) of the kingdom of Hyderabad,[6] and eventually against the newly independent Indian state. The Telangana communists in the 1940s were convinced that a Maoist uprising was well suited to the conditions of India where democratization preceded industrialization, creating a political economic condition they characterized as "semi-feudal, semi-colonial." Since the industrial working class was either too weak or absent to lead, armed peasants' rebellion was considered necessary to spearhead the revolution. For the first time, the communists organized people into village defense squads to protect themselves from the attacks of the Nizam police. Eventually, about 4,000 villages in three districts (Nalgonda, Warrangal, and Khammam) became "liberated areas" (called *gram rajyams*, meaning village republics) administered outside the control of the Indian state. Local communists redistributed land to the landless, raised guerrilla squads, attacked police camps, prosecuted rape convicts, and expounded women's equality and the abolition of untouchability. However, as soon as the Indian army occupied the kingdom of Hyderabad, the communists withdrew from the struggle abruptly on grounds that they shared rather than opposed the ideological proclivities of Prime Minister Nehru.[7]

Some of the leaders in Telangana upheld Mao's idea of "New Democracy" in opposition to the 1948 "Calcutta Thesis" that represented the dominant view of the all-India leadership of the Communist Party of India (CPI) (Sen and Teitelbaum 2010).[8] The "new democracy," free of feudal and colonial vestiges, would replace the old, Western-style parliamentary democracy that India adopted in 1947. During this time, CPI General Secretary B. T. Ranadive and peasant leaders of the Andhra region were among the first in the world to debate the legitimacy of Mao's contribution to Marxism-Leninism. The pro-Mao faction strongly resented the party's abandonment of the revolutionary struggle and its squandering gains in Telangana to join parliamentary politics (Ghosh 2009). Inner-party resentment became more intense as the Communist Party leadership adopted a resolution condemning "Chinese aggression" during the Sino-Indian War in 1962. The radical left faction within the party decried the war as an aggression by the capitalist Indian state against socialist China. The Nehru government promptly arrested several of these pro-Chinese communists, who conferred in prison to form a separate breakaway communist party. The Communist Party of India (Marxist), or CPI(M), soon became the dominant left party in India.

However, the formation of CPI(M) carried within it the seeds of further splits. The small pro-Mao faction in the new party soon began distancing themselves from the rest. The disagreement within CPI(M) was primarily on the class character of Indian bourgeoisie, which boiled down to whether communists should knowingly co-operate with other political parties in India that represent bourgeois interests. The Maoist radicals within the party argued that the Indian bourgeoisie was *comprador* (agents of foreign imperialists) in character, which rules out any co-operation with other political parties representing bourgeois interests. However, the mainstream Left argued that the Indian bourgeoisie was nationalistic with limited progressive and anti-imperialistic characteristics, which makes co-operation with them plausible. The radicals suspected that such co-operation would require that the Left eschew militant mass mobilization and adopt peaceful parliamentary politics, which would permanently undermine class struggle and the goal of revolution in India.[9] Eventually the party split and a section of prominent radicals within CPI(M) began organizing peasants to forcible seize lands and confiscate food grains in Naxalbari region in northern part of the state of West Bengal. They fought pitched battles with both the private militia of landlords and the police, inspiring an avalanche of agrarian uprisings in other parts of India. Half a century later, polemic on Naxalbari continues with great vigor in India. Naxalbari is still considered by many Indian political activists as the epitome of people's struggle against injustice, perhaps too ambitious, but nevertheless a forceful attempt for change.

The Naxalbari leaders formed the All India Coordination Committee of Communist Revolutionaries (AICCCR) within the CPI(M) on November 13, 1967. Eventually, the AICCCR severed ties with the CPI(M) and categorically rejected its parliamentary path in a "Resolution on Elections" on May 14, 1968. One year later, on April 22, 1969, the leaders of the AICCCR in Calcutta decided to form a new communist party called the Communist Party of India (Marxist Leninist), CPI(ML), with support from some CPI(M) party members from the states of Andhra Pradesh (specifically, the Srikakulam District Committee), Bihar, Delhi, Karnataka, Jammu and Kashmir, Orissa, Punjab, Tamil Nadu, and Uttar Pradesh. The Communist Party of China formally recognized CPI(ML) in July 1969.[10] Eventually other radical left factions like Dakshin Desh in West Bengal and Andhra Pradesh Committee of Communist Revolutionaries (APCCR) left the CPI(M) too, but they did not join CPI(ML) over some ideological differences. These factions later converged to become part of the current-day Maoists. Figure 2.1 depicts the fragmentation of the Indian left and the most important factions emerging from it up to the 1970s.

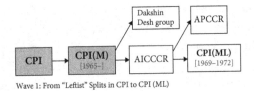

Wave 1: From "Leftist" Splits in CPI to CPI (ML)

Figure 2.1 Wave 1: Splits in the Indian Left*
* Shaded boxes denote currently active political parties.

Soon after its birth, the CPI(ML) party jumped into organizing armed uprisings in different parts of India. In the North, they started organizing peasants in the states of Bihar (Mushahari and Lakhimpur Kheri districts), and West Bengal (Debra-Gopiballavpur area in the district of Midnapore and in Birbhum districts) and in the metropolis of Calcutta). In the South they were strongest in western Andhra Pradesh (Srikakulam districts) (Mazumdar 1967, 2001; Mohan 1971). As the state unleashed police and paramilitary forces, successfully arresting or eliminating most of the top- and middle-level CPI(ML) leadership, the party disintegrated into several dozen bickering factions amid widespread desertions. When the surviving CPI(ML) leaders engaged in introspective meetings on what worked and what did not during the Naxalbari-inspired agrarian uprisings of the 1960s, the biggest split was on the question of secret organization versus mass mobilization. On the one hand, secret organization proponents wanted to keep the party and its activities entirely secret while they attacked their "class enemies" and state security apparatus. On the other hand, proponents of mass mobilization wanted to bring a part of party into the open to organize people for democratic protests and agitational politics and keep the other part preparing for armed uprisings hidden away in forests.

The factions that emerged from the splits of the undivided CPI(ML) can be grouped into three predominant trends based on their attitude toward (a) mass organizations; (b) elections; and (c) method of armed struggle. The first trend, concentrated primarily in the North of India, rejected both mass organizations and elections and upheld armed struggle—more through targeted assassination of class enemies than through a peoples' war waged by a guerrilla army. Although they had initially staunchly opposed the mass line, dominant leaders of this faction eventually made a complete turn around and returned to electoral politics in the 1990s.[11] CPI(ML) Liberation, the most prominent party in this faction, led the Bhojpur peasant struggle against landlords in central part of the state of Bihar, fought many bloody battles in the 1970s and 1980s against upper-caste militias of big landlords and garnered a massive following among lower caste Dalit peasants. But they changed strategy and abandoned armed struggle for electoral politics in the 1990s. Initially, this attempt was only moderately successful, and CPI(ML) Liberation could only manage to win a few seats as a marginal player in the state assembly elections in Bihar and in the North Eastern states. In 2020, the party changed its tactics further and joined a coalition of centre-left, socialist and communist parties for the state assembly elections of Bihar, which yielded 110 out of 243 seats for the coalition.

The second Maoist faction that emerged in the 1970s rejected the path of armed struggle advocated by CPI(ML) and chose mass organizations and electoral politics instead.[12] Over the years, this faction (often referred to as "trend" in left parlance) went through more splits, and some factions merged with the larger while others simply withered away losing both their support base and cadre alike. While the first trend made a full turn from rejecting elections to embracing it, the second trend embraced elections from the very beginning. The first two trends, representing electoral turn of Maoist factions, are concentrated in the North. There are some prominent third trend Maoist factions in the North as well, which eventually merged into the current CPI(Maoist).

The current-day Maoists in India descend from the third trend emerging from this tumult in CPI(ML) politics. The third trend rejected electoral politics but embraced mass organizations and armed struggle. They also rejected the idea of targeted assassination of class enemies and instead focused on creating liberated areas through a combination of an organized guerrilla army and agitational mass mobilization.[13] Of the two major factions in this trend, CPI(ML) Party Unity (PU) worked in the North, and CPI(ML) Peoples' War Group (PWG) worked in the South. The CPI(ML) Party Unity and People's War Group factions merged in 1998 to form the CPI(ML) People's War.

Another major Maoist group in the North was the Maoist Communist Center (MCC), which emerged out of radical left factions like Dakshin Desh that left the CPI(M) but never joined CPI(ML). Dakshin Desh (meaning Southern Land) named after a magazine started by Kanai Chatterjee, believed that India, the land to the south of Mao's China, will follow Mao's revolutionary footsteps. MCC operated in the states of Bihar and Jharkhand in the North and in small areas of West Bengal. The MCC categorically rejected electoral politics and was unenthusiastic about mass organizations.[14] It remained a largely underground organization, dreaded by the ordinary people who supported them. Other Maoist groups in the North, such as CPI(ML) Party Unity belonging to the third trend, was very critical of the MCC.[19] In fact, the North is witness to a decade-long bloody internecine turf wars between MCC and Party Unity, which left both sides heavily militarized (Louis 2000a).

Like Dakshin Desh in the North, APCCR was a Maoist group that operated outside the three major trends in the South. Unlike the MCC, the APCCR emphasized mass organizations and believed that it was possible to pursue electoral politics alongside armed struggle. All these groups, despite several internal disagreements, shared a common vision to overthrow the Indian state through insurrectionary means.[15] In 1998, Party Unity in the North joined hands with PWG in the South, forming in CPI(ML) People's War. This new organization initiated unity talks with MCC in 2000, eventually uniting Party Unity, MCC and PWG to form CPI(Maoist) in 2004. CPI(Maoist) combines the use of militant mass organizations alongside protracted peoples' war through a well-organized guerrilla army. Figure 2.2 illustrates the fractionalization and unifications in the Indian left that led to the formation of CPI(Maoist) in 2004.

This history of mergers and splits in Maoist politics in India has two broad takeaways: In the North, various Maoist factions vascilated primarily between secret assassination of enemies and complete rejection of electoral politics on one end to a transformative shift to electoral politics on the other end of the spectrum. In the South, on the other hand, the predominant tenet of Maoist politics was always strategic combination of mass mobilizations with a well-trained guerilla army. The PWG, as well as the APCCR that descended from the earliest Maoist uprisings in India in 1940s, emphasizes the need for robust grassroots organizations for a successful agrarian revolution. The overarching consensus in the South is that the Naxalbari uprising tried to engineer a revolution through a series of quick shock crippling attacks on class enemies, which quickly dissipated into disarray and devastation due to lack of support from mass organizations. Thus, first, the northern Maoists saw a zero-sum either/or dynamic between mass mobilization and violent revolution, while the southern Maoists historically considered them mutually reinforcing. Second, many northern Maoist factions have veered toward electoral politics, while southern Maoists have not embraced elections at the cost of revolutionary politics. The timeline of formation and disintegration of

Wave 2: Splits and Mergers Leading
to CPI (Maoist)

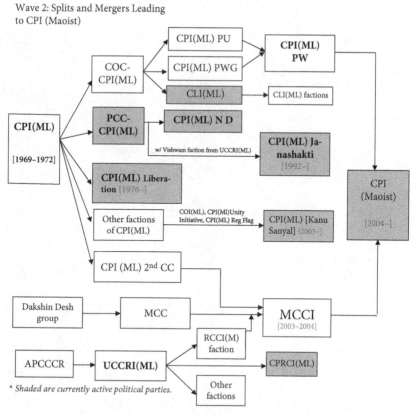

Figure 2.2 Splits in the ML Camp and Formation of CPI (Maoist)

various Maoist factions shown in Figure 2.3 further illustrate how the polar-ization between mass mobilition and secret organization progressed within the Maoist camp in North and South India.

Unifying Elements of Maoist Ideology:
State, Struggle, and Strategy

Despite differences between Maoist factions in the North and South (which I discuss in more detail in the subsequent sections), Indian Maoists united in 2004 under the overarching umbrella organization of CPI(Maoist) on the basis of shared commitment to three ideological pillars: (1) their

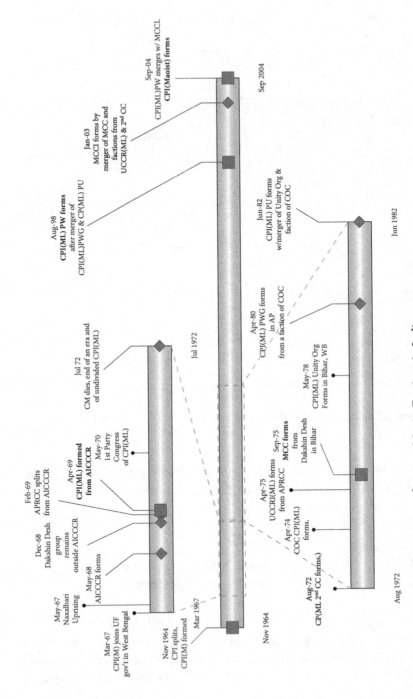

Figure 2.3 Timeline for creation of various Maoist Factions in India

understanding of the Indian state as "semi-feudal, semi colonial"; (2) their expectations about the protracted nature of struggle against the state; and (3) their choice of militant mass mobilization in this struggle.

The Maoists characterize India as a "semi-feudal, semi-colonial" country that lacks both real democracy and real independence. In India, unlike in the West, democracy preceded capitalism. Uneven, incomplete capitalist development was superimposed on feudal structures, most palpably in rural backwaters, where the Maoists built their bases, with a plan to eventually encircle the cities. In the minds of common people, it became impossible to differentiate state institutions from traditionally exploitative feudal agencies of landholding and money lending. For example, in the Maoist strongholds of Chhattisgarh and Jharkhand, local landholding families with control of forest and agricultural resources often evolved into elected representatives. In such settings, the Maoists attacked local landlords, moneylenders, forest guards, state police, and paramilitary forces, as well as bureaucrats who represent the abusive character of the Indian state.

The four observable implications of a semi-feudal system are sharecropping, perpetual rural indebtedness, landowner as moneylender, and inaccessibility of the market. Indebtedness is a consistent characteristic of a semi-feudal system, particularly because the landlord and moneylender rolled into one takes away a substantial portion of what the landless or land-poor peasant produces and then lends some back to that produce as consumption loan. This ties the peasants to a cycle of oppression, which worsens further when the landowner confiscates their small piece of land due to unpaid debt, reducing them to serfs. In this type of economy, peasants do not have much access to the market—they are not worthy of credit in the commercial banking industry because they have no assets to borrow against. Moreover, the peasant-tenant and his family members in such a semi-feudal system have to regularly render unpaid labor services to landlord/moneylender to compensate for unpaid loans and interest.[16] In contrast, in a capitalist system, production based on wage labor, is for the market and not for self-consumption, and surplus value gets invested back into production, guaranteeing new research and technological innovation (Bhaduri 1973; Bhaduri 1977; Thorner 1982). In capitalist agriculture, landless laborers can negotiate a high price for their labor when their demand is high. Small farmers have access to credit options other than the landlord, and since they are not tied to any particular landlord, they sell their produce to the highest bidder in the market.

By "semi-colonial" the Maoists imply that India is not fully independent of British imperial control despite official independence from Great Britain in 1947. They argue that the British transferred power to the *comprador* ruling classes who continue to advance foreign imperialist interests over those of Indian citizens. As a result, they advocate a "new democratic revolution" in India, a concept borrowed from Mao, which entails a struggle for "people's democracy" and liberation from both foreign imperialist and domestic feudal control (Ghosh 2009). Thus Maoists deem the current democratic institutions in India "as an outright fraud framed in the deceptive name of biggest democracy of the world" and build justification for armed confrontation as the only way to restore power to the people.[17]

Conceiving the Indian state as semi-feudal and semi-colonial has important implications for the Maoist mobilization. First, it indicates that the Maoists do not target industrial working class for recruitment and instead focus on a peasant-led agricultural uprising as the only path to revolution. In rural hinterlands and remote underbellies of India, where democratic institutions reinforce rather than replace the deep-rooted feudal structures of exploitation, the Maoists find the most favorable grounds to propagate.

Second, the Maoists advocate Protracted Peoples' War as the only appropriate strategy for dealing with a powerful enemy, the Indian state. If not in the short run, the Maoists believe that they can trounce the state in the long run because weak infrastructure in remote areas, internal conflicts in the ruling class, and a huge agrarian population in India would work in their favor. In military terms, the Protracted Peoples' War denotes an extended and fluid front that will bleed the ponderous war machinery of the Indian state dry under the strain of tortuous struggle in unfavorable terrain. It is analogous to overpowering an elephant by a thousand pin pricks. In political terms, the Protracted People's War stands for winning popular support in remote, neglected areas through extensive mass organizations.

Mao Zedong conceptualized Protracted Peoples' War primarily as a war of Chinese national resistance against foreign (Japanese) subjugation, but the Indian Maoists have applied the theory in the Indian context as a political-military strategy of long-term armed revolutionary struggle against the Indian state (Mao 1967). As long as hunger, starvation, inequality, unemployment, disease, and discrimination exist in India, the Maoists are confident in finding a steady supply of recruits in this "see-saw battle" with the state.[18] Further, given their mobile warfare strategy, if the state succeeded in clearing them out of certain pockets, the Maoists would proliferate to adjacent areas. Thus the Maoist battle call proclaims, "They can kill all the flowers, but they will not hold back the spring" (Mao 1967).

By emphasizing that the confrontation with the Indian state is likely to be protracted, the Maoists infuse optimism among the foot soldiers that even if the enemy enjoys strategic advantage at the beginning of an armed struggle, rebels must persist, consolidate their strength, and grow in battle experience to eventually force the enemy into a strategic retreat. Mao conceived Protracted Peoples' War in Clausewitzian terms as an extension of politics rather than its cessation.

The Maoists in India have a two-tiered organizational structure made up of military and political wings. The military wing is made up of the heavily armed People's Liberation Guerrilla army, consisting of full-time combatants, and part-time militia squads, supported by smaller village-level defense committees, made up of peasants and other supporters recruited primarily through mass organizations. The political wing relies heavily on mass organizations. The most well-known among them in South India are the Rythu Coolie Sangham (Agricultural Laborers Association), Singareni Karmika Samakhya (Singareni Collieries Workers Federation), Radical Students Union, and the Revolutionary Writers Association. The Lok Sangram Morcha (People's Struggle Front), Mazddor Kisan Mukti Morcha (Workers-Peasants Liberation Front), Jan Mukti Parishad (People's Liberation Council), and the Nari Mukti Sangharsh Samiti (Women's Liberation Struggle Association) operate in the North. Yet, there is an inherent tension in the coexistence of secret parties, trained guerrilla armies, and open mass organizations. Although mass mobilization and armed struggle are two complementary elements of Maoists' military strategy, the focus on armed struggle can sideline mass mobilization, without which insurgents cannot generate political consciousness and public opinion against their enemies.

The crucial steps in Maoist mass mobilization includes indoctrination of the masses, formation of village defense squads, people's militia groups, and eventually a professional guerilla people's army. The mass organizations that undertake mobilization efforts are distinct from the party, which remains underground and secretly directs mass organizations and the armed forces. Mass organizations are thus instruments for the revolutionary party to recruit people and raise their political consciousness for an eventual revolution (Mao 1967).

Prewar Social Bases of Insurgency: Polarization and Militancy

The Maoist political program lays out a plan to organize a socialist revolution in India via a two-stage process. The first stage, known as New Democratic Revolution, includes the overthrow of the current "semi-feudal, semi-colonial" state through a Protracted Peoples' War and founding the "Peoples's Democracy." This lays the foundation for the second stage, which establishes socialism, and finally communism. In order to progress through these stages, the Maoists offer a blueprint for recruitment, which identifies contradictions in Indian society and sharply polarize them into three groups—(a) Motive Forces that are most likely to lead and support the objectives of Maoists, (b) Enemy Forces which will most likely oppose their objective, and (c) Middle-of-the-roaders, who may not support the Maoists early on, but are likely to switch sides when the balance tips in their favor. Table 2.1 summarizes how the Maoists systematically categorize society in preparation for recruitment and mobilization.

The categorization of people into friends and foes is, however, simplistically based on economic interests of various groups as defined by class positions. Rural India is beset by crosscutting cleavages of caste, religion, and linguistic identities. The rural proletariat, made up of landless agricultural workers, for example, are singled out by the Maoists as their most potent motive forces because their economic interests are tied to ending the status quo and ushering a Maoist revolution. This analysis does not take into account how different caste, religious, and linguistic identities interact with their class interest. But faced with multiple rural groups in their social base, the Maoists are more likely to succeed if they achieve a neat overlap of ethnic and economic markers, which allows their sharp polarization into friends and foes. What are some of the characteristics of local context that can make such an overlap more or less likely?

The existing literature presents considerable evidence that various preexisting social conditions determine the kinds of social resources insurgent organizers have access to, which, in turn, determines the nature of insurgent organization (Staniland 2012). In fact, insurgent groups with similar ideology, ethnicity, state enemies, and, even, in this case, organizational unity can grow in dramatically different ways in interaction with their local contexts (Staniland 2014).In the rest of the chapter, I focus on the mediating role of the underlying social factors, specifically the interaction of caste

Table 2.1 Social Classes Identified by Maoists

Class Name	Class Composition	Position vis-à-vis Maoist Objective
Urban Proletariat	Class dispossessed of all means of production and compelled to sell physical labor to earn a livelihood. Includes wage earners in organized (public and private) sectors and unorganized sectors (typically, workers in small-scale industries, construction workers, and contract and casual laborers in large enterprises).	Motive
Rural Proletariat	Landless peasants including agricultural workers who do not have their own land and agricultural tools and depend mainly on selling their physical labor to earn a living.	Motive
Landlords	Rich and middle-class agricultural bosses who own significant amounts of arable land, do little or no farming by themselves, and rent or lease land and employ sharecroppers and agricultural workers. They often have additional means of livelihood as merchants, agro-based traders, usurers, quarry owners, and contractors to local and central governments or large corporations. They are the key backers of the current state.	Enemy
Comprador Bureaucratic Bourgeoisie	Indian "big" capitalists who benefited from British patronage. They are key supporters of a neoliberal world order. This class also includes the upper stratum of bureaucrats, leadership of major political parties, and some intellectuals and professionals.	Enemy
National Bourgeoisie	Middle and small capitalists who neither have a share of state power nor control over state funds. They are in conflict with and exploited by the *comprador* bureaucratic bourgeoisie. Politically a very weak and vacillating class.	Middle-of-the-roaders
Semi Proletariat	Class owning limited land and tools. Includes poor peasants, handicraftsmen, carpenters, masons, and mechanics. In urban areas, this class includes street peddlers (hawkers), rickshaw and auto rickshaw drivers, temporary construction workers, and domestic servants.	Middle-of-the-roaders

Continued

Table 2.1 *Continued*

Class Name	Class Composition	Position vis-à-vis Maoist Objective
Middle Peasants	Farming class owning land and agricultural tools. Does not sell physical labor but does not exploit others. May rent surplus land to landless and poor peasants and employ agricultural workers, but it is not their primary income.	Middle-of-the roaders
Rich Peasants	Class owns considerable amounts of land. Over 50% of their income comes from renting lands to landless and poor peasants, and they employ a large number of agricultural workers. They may have other means of livelihood, too. Unlike landlords, rich peasants are involved in day-to-day farming activities and do not necessarily support the agenda of globalization, privatization, and liberalization like the former overwhelmingly do.	Middle-of-the-roaders
Petty Bourgeoisie	This heterogeneous group is not a class. It includes small-scale producers, small traders, lower level intellectuals including teachers at schools and colleges, students, professionals (e.g., doctors, lawyers, and engineers), lower level management, and supervisory staff in public and private organizations—largely the middle class. It can be divided into three groups: (a) A "right-wing" section of the petty bourgeoisie benefits from the current state structure and policies of economic liberalization, privatization, and globalization. They generate surplus income. (b) A section of the petty bourgeoisie generates just enough income to support themselves, no surplus. (c) A third "left-wing" section of the petty bourgeoisie deals with declining incomes and related drops in quality of life.	Middle-of-the-roaders—the right-wingers will actively oppose the revolution, while the left-wingers will actively support it, especially when the revolution gains momentum. Intellectuals like teachers and students, professionals like doctors and lawyers, and artisans and traders may be left-wingers irrespective of their quality of life.
Lumpenproletariat	Urban and rural unemployed who are actively involved in petty criminal activities, the sex trade, human trafficking, and panhandling. While they can be natural allies of communist revolution, their hatred for the current state makes them anarchists, and they are often easily lured by the enemies to counter the revolution.	Middle-of-the-roaders—Maoists have a neutral/cautious outlook toward them.

and class structure, which shapes the cohesion, recruitment, organizational structure and militancy of the Maoists in North and South India. I argue that the Maoists' prewar social base in the South of India allowed for an emergence of a neat caste-class overlap of identities and interests that was not present in the North. The next section also shows how the extent of militancy in local clashes between the Maoists and their identified enemy classes varied between the two regions.

Underlying Caste and Class Structure in the North

A Sudra must never collect wealth, even though he is able (to do it).
A Sudra who has acquired wealth is a pain to Brahmanas.
                                    —*The Laws of Manu* (Bühler 1964, p. 430)

In the villages of North, the ancient Hindu legal text, Manu Smriti (The Laws of Manu) informally regulated ideas of duty, hierarchy, order, virtue, rights, justice, and sin to crystallize a way of life that served the rich upper castes at the expense of the poor lower castes (Bühler 1964). In the 1970s, when the Maoists entered these villages around central and South Bihar, the Sudras, or the backward castes, and the Dalits or the formerly untouchable castes, in the villages surrendered to the widespread custom that they deserved to be treated with contempt and prejudice because of their own sins in a past life that ranged from laziness and alcohol consumption to animal cruelty and atheism. In other words, caste inequality was not only a mode of exploitation from above, the fatalism and "other-worldliness" was deeply ingrained among the lower castes as well as means of justifying and reconciling them to preponderant inequalities (Kolenda 1964).

Despite being deeply entrenched in the everyday lives of the rural poor, electoral politics in North India did not mobilize along caste lines. Hindu-Muslim cleavage was historically the "master narrative" and Charan Singh and Ram Manohar Lohia were the only notable exceptions (Yadav 2010; Kumar 2010; Jaffrelot 2002; Varshney 2000).[19] The Maoists, for the first time, eloquently and systematically articulated the centrality of caste in perpetuating the grotesque disparities and injustice in the villages. Used to habitual capitulation, the rural aristocracy in the North was infuriated when they faced organized political and military challenges from the Maoist supporters among the lower castes. The upper castes in the North frantically activated their kinship networks to build barricades against any wave of defiance. They also raised private armies of upper caste militias, committed to kill and die in order to defend their traditional way of life from being inundated by a Maoist-led revolution. Economic anxiety of the feudal elites, threated by left-wing attacks on highly profitable traditional modes of surplus extraction, also intensified upper-caste resistance. But, as discussed later in this chapter, battle lines in the Maoist-affected villages of North India were mostly drawn along caste lines.

The local population in the rural North belonged to three broad caste groups: the upper castes at the top, the backward castes at the intermediate level, and the Dalits (formerly untouchables) at the bottom. Maoists identified the upper castes, or rural elites, as the ruling class, comprising about 13% of the rural population and owning over 80% of the land. Although the big landlords belonged exclusively to the upper castes (Brahmins, Bhumihars, Rajputs, and Kayastha), the majority of these high-caste households were small landlords with landholdings that might also qualify them as "middle peasants." Their economic status was very similar to the middle peasant households among the backward-caste (Bania, Yadav, Kurmi, and Koeri). Although the Maoists identified these backward castes as a sympathetic class, some landowning, backward-caste households actually had economic interests in common with the upper-caste farming families. For example, landowning families of both the upper and backward castes were equally engaged in wage suppression. They blamed the Maoists for raising daily wages and making Dalit hired labor unaffordable. On the one hand, despite such cross-caste shared interests, caste identity took precedence and inter-caste marriages between upper and backward castes remained a taboo in the villages. On the other hand, faced with demands for just redistribution from below, the upper castes banded together, embracing even the poorest of their caste men (Kunnath 2006), thereby validating caste as the dominant cleavage and the primary unifier in villages, overruling class interests. Adding further complexity to the caste-class conundrum, some backward-caste families worked as landless farm laborers alongside Dalits without much social interaction with them, such as dining or marrying across caste lines. The Dalits, who comprised 14% of the rural population, were the rural proletariat, who, due to their landlessness, were historically powerless in local social affairs and invisible in state politics and administration (Frankel 1989; Bandyopadhyay 2006; Corbridge 1987).

The Maoists, before any political party, targeted the landless/land poor Dalits as motive forces of agrarian revolution against the enemy class of rich, upper caste landowners. They also recruited many backward castes in this fight. However, some backward caste families, particularly among the rich and middle peasants, were anti-Maoist; driven by their better economic status or perceived caste superiority compared to Dalits, they maintained their distance from Dalits, and instead joined hands with upper-caste militias. The Dalits, in turn, remained suspicious of backward caste cadres who joined the Maoists, alleging that kinship ties of their backward-caste comrades with the landed co-ethnics would eventually trump their allegiance to the Maoist cause. Some backward caste cadres within the Maoist parties also asserted their superiority their Dalit comrades even within the Maoist organization.[20] 96% of the upper castes in Bihar in the 1980s and 1990s belonged to the landlord and rich peasant category; only 36% of the backward castes were found in this same category. Nearly all—some 93%—Dalits were landless agricultural laborers (Sharma 1994; Sharma, Singh, and Kumar 1994). The fact that 60% of the rural population—those who were predominantly Dalit and owned insufficient or no land—were pitted against the 30% who were predominantly upper-caste landowners, sometimes gave the Maoist conflict in North India the appearance of a caste and not a class struggle (Prasad 1994, p. 180).

What made the divided loyalty of backward castes a bigger issue within the Maoist parties was their rise in electoral politics, beginning in the 1990s (Chaitanya 1991; Witsoe 2012, 2011; Robin 2004). As the villages in the North were torn by caste wars through the 1980s and early 1990s, caste-based political parties were just starting to enter the electoral fray in the states of Bihar and Uttar Pradesh. For example, the Bahujan Samaj Party (BSP) was launched in Uttar Pradesh in 1984. The party won only 1.6% of votes in the 1991 elections, but steadily increased its clout for it's Mayawati to become a Chief Minister of the state by 1995. The Samajwadi Party, led by the backward castes (Yadav) in Uttar Pradesh, was formed by Mulayam Singh Yadav in 1992. In Bihar, Laloo Prasad Yadav formed another caste-based party, the Rashtriya Janata Dal (RJD), in 1997, which increased backward caste representation in state legislative assemblies in Bihar. The rise of backward castes in electoral politics of North India is often referred to as the "second democratic upsurge" in India (Yadav 1999) and even a "silent revolution" (Jaffrelot 2003). Between 1952 and 2002, the percentage of upper-caste members in state legislatures halved from 46 to 26% (still twice their share of population,

13.6%) (Jaffrelot and Kumar 2012). The symbolic significance of the rise of the backward castes was enormous: As caste became important in electoral politics, it was increasingly perceived as the most significant determinant of status and life chances in the villages as well.

Maoist cadres could hardly remain immune to the high-octave caste polarization in electoral politics. The sharp upsurge of political fortune of the backward castes within Indian democracy (Kumar 2013), made Maoist politics and its rhetoric of armed struggle relatively unattractive to their support base, particularly to the backward castes. The redistribution of land and jobs that the Maoists promised—in the distant future only after considerable bloodshed and inordinate sacrifices—already seemed like a plausible goal within the democracy. Since the electoral path virtually promised the same outcome as the Maoists within the limits of legality, the Maoist path lost some of its earlier appeal for the backward castes in the North.

As the backward castes got a taste of power within democracy, they used their kinship networks to crush Dalit economic aspirations with severity no less formidable than their upper caste predecessors. Not only did they oppose wage increase for the Dalit agricultural labor force, even the poorest among backward castes abandoned Maoist parties to align themselves with caste and kinship networks, overriding their distinct class interests. In this context, caste-based reservation, an affirmative action policy providing caste-based quotas to Dalits in education and public sector jobs, further stoked the fire of mutual animosity between Dalits and backward caste cadres, disrupting the cohesiveness of the Maoist organization at a time when it faced intense militarization of its campaigns against rural landowning classes.

Intense Militarization of the Maoist Movement in the North

The Maoist project of building a mass base in the North began facing increasingly militant resistance from the landowning, feudal upper castes who, having lost some of their political clout in electoral politics, were determined to protect their rural landed interests from Maoist mobilization of Dalits in the villages. In fact, every cluster of 10–15 adjacent villages in the North began raising their own upper-caste militias (locally known as *sena* or army)led by dominant landowning caste and devoted to attacking Dalit neighborhoods (Kumar 2008; Das 1986; Sinha 1978; Louis 2000a).[21] The most deadly and infamous of the upper-caste private militias in Bihar was Ranvir Sena (literally, brave warrior army) founded in September 1994 in the Belaur village of the Bhojpur district of Central Bihar following the merger of several private caste armies (Sinha and Sinha 2001; Louis 2000a; Chandran and Gupta 2002).

These upper-caste militias could not have operated with total impunity in the villages without active support of powerful caste-based patronage networks pervading political, administrative, and law enforcement circles in Bihar. For example, Bhumihar (part of the upper caste) landlords had the support of the Congress Party in raising their caste militia called Brahmarshi Sena.[22] The Rajput landlords in the Congress Party backed the Kunwar Sena, and the Kurmi landlords in the Congress Party backed the Bhoomi Sena, and so on. Every upper caste militia had ties to political parties via kinship networks. Even some backward castes, specifically the Yadav, had the support of the CPI, a prominent mainstream left party, in backing the Lorik Sena.[23] Sunlight Sena in South Bihar had the active support of the two-time chief minister of Bihar and former governors, as well as elected members of local and central legislatures who all belonged to the landholding Rajput caste.[24] A former prime minister, a defense and a home minister of India were allegedly among the patrons of the Ranvir Sena.[25] Prominent upper-caste politicians in various political parties joined hands to offer patronage and protection to these caste-based militias. Caste solidarity networks routinely trumped political and ideological divides in the rural North.

The Maoists did not back down in the face of escalating upper caste and state violence, a frenzied arms race, and a succession of devastating hate crimes in rural Bihar. The MCC asserted its military domination over upper-caste landowners in 500 villages in South Bihar by sponsoring massacres of upper-caste landlords, the most brutal of which was organized in the summer of 1987 (the Baghaura-Dalelchak massacre), killing 54 upper-caste men in a small village. The Maoist army identified every single upper-caste (Rajput) male in the village, including a six months old male child, threw some of them alive into a bonfire set up in the middle of the village, and chopped off the heads of the rest with blunt axes, forcing the women to watch. Then they drenched standing crops in their blood and burned down their houses. This gruesome incident terrified upper caste gentry everywhere in the North. Pervasive panic sent tremors of shock through upper-caste networks in political parties, police, legislature, and administration, setting off an avalanche of upper-caste retributive carnage across other parts of Bihar (Sinha and Sinha 2001; Jaoul 2011; Sahay 2008; Louis 2000b). In kneejerk response, these networks also mobilized unprecedented state resources for counterinsurgency against the Maoists in the North, both in the form of repression and development initiatives. It began in 1986, when the chief minister of Bihar, in a highly controversial decision, decided to arm landlords against the rebels (Chaudhry 1988; Chakravarti 2001). By the mid-1990s, every village in Bihar was armed to the teeth. Thousands of licensed guns exchanged hands in rural Bihar, creating a booming black market of weapons. The enormous and growing arsenal of both licensed and illegal arms spewed a deathly arms race between state-backed upper castes and the Maoist army of Dalits and other poor. Thus the democratic state in the North, including all major institutions from politicians, bureaucrats, and judges down to constables in rural police stations, became implicated in daily bloodbaths, orchestrated along caste lines. State counterinsurgency against the Maoists became indistinguishable from illegal rampages of upper-caste militias, particularly given the overlap of personnel, camps, and arms.

As illegal firearms became easily available, private gangs of arms smugglers, drug dealers, and traffickers also entered various Maoist factions. In this feverish escalation of armed confrontation in the countryside, parts of the Maoist organization started running protection markets, whereby they offered protection to isolated individual landowners in specific regions for hefty payments or in exchange for some land or guns. This tactic later took on the form of an extended protection racket, and competing Maoist factions clashed among themselves to protect landowners they took on as clients. Alongside caste militias and protection rackets, police and gang violence, political and administrative corruption vitiated rural Bihar and made a mockery of rule of law. Lawmakers and law-breakers were indistinguishable from each other (Jaoul 2011; Sahay 2008; Chaitanya 1991). The Maoists were frequently embroiled in fraudulent extortion and kidnapping networks of police-politicians-bureaucrats-smugglers, which made ordinary people wary of them. As the rebels lost their revolutionary credibility and the state lost its claim to legal and moral superiority, pervasive violence steeped into everyday lives. Jharkhand, unlike other Red Corridor states, currently has more than a dozen armed groups active in its forests, many of them breakaway factions of the CPI (Maoist). These splinter groups, dressed in similar battle uniforms as the Maoists, hide in dense forests, and extort a levy from mining and development projects. The police, instead of prosecuting these groups, allegedly use them to gather intel against Maoists, which worked initially but eventually backfired as leaders of these groups emerged as de facto warlords, operating with viciousness and vengeance reminiscent of the old MCC bloodbaths of the 1980s.This book argues that the underlying caste/class structure and pervasive violence permeating state, insurgent, and social spheres creates conditions for low retirement and discordant exit network in the region.

Underlying Caste and Class Structure in the South

The southern Maoists found a caste/class structure that was molded by left agrarian uprising in region going back to the 1940s. Before India became independent, the communists in Telangana built up Maoist-type guerrilla organizations across 4000 villages in Telangana. Although communists were forced to withdraw the armed struggle after India became independent, they had mobilized thousands of small and middle peasants in the countryside against upper caste big landlords demanding minimum agricultural wages, abolition of forced labor, protection of tenants, and abolition of landlords. A legacy of the 1946 communist-led agrarian uprising is its lasting impact on rural institutions like the *panchayat*. *Panchayat* (village local government) is a traditional institution in the villages of the Telangana region, where any petty dispute is publicly adjudicated with the landlord presiding over proceedings. Communist rebels publicly challenged upper-caste authority in *panchayats* and put some landlords on trial. Shaken by the strength of the movement, a lot of landlords fled to the cities (Balagopal 2006).

Another distinctive characteristic of the social landscape in the South is that the Hindu-Muslim cleavage has never been a "master narrative" in electoral politics of South India. When India became independent, the Nizam resisted integration of Hyderabad to India and dabbled with the idea of joining hands with Pakistan. He sent Razakars (a private militia that claimed Hyderabad as a Muslim state) to the countryside to brutally suppress communists. The landed upper class, upper caste Hindus in rural Telangana were terrified of Razakars. Some bought protection from communists, and many left the countryside en masse and migrates to urban areas and neighboring states. This further reduced their rural clout, which was historically not as strong as their northern counterpart, partly because they constituted merely 2% to 3% of the population (Elliot 1970; Kohli 1988; Vaugier-Chatterjee, Jaffrelot, and Kumar 2009; Srinivasulu and Sarangi 1999). On the one hand, Brahmins in Telangana did not have adequate numerical strength or political clout in Nizam's administration to emerge as a formidable adversary for Maoists. On the other hand, they got a head start in education, which allowed them to sever rural ties, divest their landholdings and migrate to urban areas since the 1950s (Irschick 1969; Ramaswamy 1978).

Therefore, resistance to the second phase of Maoist uprising since the 1970s came primarily from non-Brahmin caste groups that emerged as the new rural elite. These agricultural caste groups, such as the Reddys, Kammas, Kapus, and Velamas were the most important social groups in the state of Andhra Pradesh in terms of numerical strength, land control, and access to political power.[26] Their caste and economic status was comparable to that of rich peasants of the backward castes (Yadav or Kurmi) in the North. However, unlike their northern counterparts, the Reddys and Kammas are legally classified as forward castes in the South. The Reddys, who represented about 8–10% of the state's population, were the most prominent among the forward castes primarily because of their firm base in agricultural wealth their early exposure to European education, and substantial economic advancement. These factors enabled them to challenge Brahminical dominance and join the Communist Party in the Telangana region in the South as early as 1930s (Suri 1996; Ramakrishna 1993; Baker and Washbrook 1975; Baker 1975; Irschick 1969).

There were about 50 backward-caste groups constituting about 36% of the population in the South.[27] Much like the North, the motive forces of the Maoists in the South were the Dalits, who were the lowest in caste hierarchy, comprising approximately 16% of the state's population and working primarily as agricultural laborers. The Maoist support base in Telangana was primarily made up of the Malas and Madigas, the two foremost Dalit castes that constituted more than 90% of the state's Dalit population (Thirumali 2003; Rao 1979).

The class structure in Telangana is built on its landholding pattern, which was exceptionally unequal and exploitative. The region saw little agricultural advancement; very few landlords, even in the 1980s, had tractors or cultivated anything other than paddy and millets, which were of the traditional variety rather than the fertilizer-hungry high-yield variety. The surplus appropriated by landlords was not transformed into productive capital but instead was either consumed or "invested" in mercantile activities like public works department contracts, wine shops, and real estate. The *deshmukhs/dora* represented a combination of a landlord and a revenue official, who had control over land and land records, which made them powerful arbiters of the destinies of thousands of peasant-cultivators. Below them were the rich cultivator-owner class, who worked on land themselves and were financially well off but socially inferior to *doras* (Iyengar 1951). Majority of the landlords and rich peasant classes belonged to the same forward caste groups, Reddy and Velama (Iyengar 1951). There were a few brahmin landlords as well, but they were inconsequential in size and strength compared to the land rich forward castes. Caste and class categories overlapped more neatly in Telangana than in the North. The battle lines were drawn: Dalits, mostly Malas and Madigas, were poor and landless and they joined the Maoist camp. The rich Reddy landowners led the anti-Maoist resistance in villages. In other words, the Maoists were able to polarize villages in South into two camps: rich, forward caste landowners poor, lower caste landless peasants.

Paradoxically, the landowning Reddy peasants, identified by the Maoists as their class enemies in 1970s, were once the primary supporters of the communist agrarian uprisings in Telangana in 1940s. However, the Telangana Reddys were not as politically savvy as the Reddys in coastal Andhra Pradesh who dominated the Communist Party leadership. The Reddy communists sought recognition as liberal, moderate, reformist representatives of the non-feudal agrarian sector (variedly described as small landlords, rich peasants, or market-integrated rural rich) critical of upper-caste Brahminical domination. (Elliot 1970). When the first agrarian uprising in Telangana ended abruptly in October 1951, the Reddy communists exerted their political clout to arrest full-fledged land reform in Telangana. These moderate communists succeeded in retaining a very high landholding ceiling of 50 acres, which allowed redistribution of land from *deshmukhs*(feudal lords) to the cultivator-owners (mostly Reddy), but checked any further reallocation of resources further down the caste-class hierarchy. Therefore, the incomplete land reform pursued by Reddy communists in 1950s broke the backbone of the traditional feudal elite in rural Telangana and facilitated emergence of a new rural elite led by Reddys (Appu 1975; Khusro 1958; Pavier 1974).

When the radical factions within the communist party began splitting from the party in 1960s, the Reddy assumed leadership of moderate factions and defended their gains. By 1970s, the radical Communist factions reasserted themselves and advocated renewal of armed agrarian struggle in Telangana with an aim to complete the unfinished program of redistribution

of land all the way down to the landless Dalits. Since 1970s radical communist revolutionaries in Telangana were faced with resistance from Reddy
communists. The land poor and landless in the South were deeply resentful
of their former Reddy comrades, who abandoned communism for a greater
share in state and local governments led by the Congress Party. The Soviet
Union, which had considerable sway over the communist party, approved
this bonhomie between moderate communists and Prime Minister Nehru's
Congress Party because Nehru took pro-Soviet stance in macroeconomic
and foreign policies of newly independent India. As a result, Congress Party
rule in Andhra Pradesh became synonymous with "Reddy Raj" (rule of the
Reddys). In the first 13 of 16 years of Andhra Pradesh as a separate state
(1956–1972), the state was not only ruled by Reddy chief ministers, but the
most important portfolios in various state departments were also distributed
to Reddys (Bernstorff 1973). As Reddy political capital was on the rise within
the democracy through the 1980s and the 1990s, the backward castes and
Dalits felt increasingly forsaken by the state.

The Maoists tapped into the growing sense of alienation among the rural
poor and built a potent movement around the abolition of feudal practices,
including caste and economic atrocities against of the Dalits, who were
exploited relentlessly as feudal farm-servants and bonded labor. In addition, the landlords frequently sexually abused Dalit women. The Maoists
encouraged Dalits to begin a social boycott of upper caste landlord and police camps in villages, which resulted in the entire village stopping services to
upper-caste families. These families that relied on Dalits as wet nurses, cattle
feeders, agricultural labor, washermen, barbers were suddenly left to fend
for themselves. A social boycott was often sufficient to bring the landlords
to their knees and was generally the first tactic employed in most villages.
To the poor low-caste villagers, social boycott was the revolution. They were
accustomed to accepting a hundred shoe-floggings if they as much as held
their heads up in the presence of upper-caste landowners. By challenging
entrenched social norms of caste domination, the Maoists enlisted the loyalty of the majority of backward-caste and Dalit villagers. (Thirumali 2003;
Pavier 1974). Thus the underlying caste divisions as the Maoists found them
in the 1970s reinforced and further accentuated the class polarization they
were trying to achieve. This sharp polarization of caste/class identities, however, did not result in intense military confrontation between the two sides.
The local political economy in the South, as clarified later in the chapter,
explains why that was the case.

Low Militancy in the Maoist Movement in the South

In Telangana the rural elite was neither able nor willing to match the Maoists in militancy. Whether peasants become revolutionary depends as much on the interests and capacities of their class opponents as it does on the interests and capacities of the peasants themselves (Wolf 1969). Unlike the landed classes in the North that raised private militias and fought pitched battles with the Maoists, the adversarial classes of Reddy landlords in the South were unwilling to get trapped in violence and bloodshed to maintain their rural domination. Instead they preferred to migrate to urban areas and invest their agricultural income in profitable enterprise in entertainment, education, and real estate (Prasad 2015; Simhadri and Rao 1997). They also started divesting funds to other agribusinesses in seeds, fertilizers, pesticides; engaged in usury and moneylending (*girgir* banks in Telangana); invested in urban institutions like schools and colleges, hospitals and pharmaceutical enterprises, as well as in information technology and real estate. In addition, the Reddys, given their early adoption of higher education and English language and political patronage of co-ethnics in political parties, also established dominance in civil administration and enjoyed control over the regional power structure (Srinivasulu 2014). They earned considerable income by acting as brokers in various government development projects. Some landlords reinvented themselves as "village elders" who negotiated with government and international development agencies and graciously accepted what are modestly called "expenses" in return for their services (Balagopal 1990, 2007).

In addition, the upper-caste elite in Telangana was divided, both in interests and identity. The roots of the divide go back 200 years, when most of Andhra Pradesh came under direct colonial rule, but the western part of Andhra Pradesh, known as Telangana, remained a part of the territories of the Nizam of Hyderabad. When India became independent, coastal Andhra was annexed to the Madras Presidency, while Telangana, despite sharing the same language of Telugu as coastal Andhra, remained part of the princely state of Hyderabad. Eventually Hyderabad was annexed by India, and both Telangana and coastal Andhra were part of the Madras Presidency, dominated by Tamil elites in politics and administration. The Telugu-speaking Brahmins in coastal Andhra resented Tamil domination and led the movement to create a Telugu-speaking state separate from the Tamil-dominated Madras Presidency. The Telangana elites, however, remained marginal in the Telugu renaissance. Two hundred years of Nizam rule gave Telangana a cultural, political, and linguistic distinctiveness, and kept it relatively back-ward in education, administration, and political mobilization compared to the coastal region. In addition, the upper-caste Hindus in Telangana were always relegated to secondary status compared to the Muslim elites under Nizam rule. Despite shared religious and caste rituals, they were also never completely integrated with the Telugu-speaking coastal elites, who despised the strong Islamic and Urdu influences on their language and culture. After successful creation of the Telugu-speaking state of Andhra Pradesh, there were massive and violent agitations by the Telangana elites (Mulkis), who were employees in the former princely state, against the coastal elites (non-Mulkis). The Mulki movement, led by students and non-gazetted officers in Hyderabad, demanded that as the sons-of-the-soil they deserved special protections in government jobs against the migrant non-Mulkis.[28]

The rural elite of Telangana, despite being co-ethnics, also kept their dis-tance from the Mulkis. Unlike the Mulkis, these rural elites spoke Telugu and earned their incomes predominantly as landowners. They had no history of cooperation with the urdu-speaking rich Muslims in the court of Nizam in Hyderabad. The urban upper-caste Hindus in Hyderabad (Mulkis) never sought to unite political forces with their rural co-ethnics (Leonard and Weller 1980). Even when the Nizam threatened to overrun the Hindu estate of Gadwal, a symbolic patron of Hindu culture in the region, the rural and urban upper-caste Hindus did not unite. Urban Hindus disliked the feudal ways of Reddy rural notables as much as they despised the Muslim ruling class. Thus the upper castes/upper classes in Telangana were unable to forge a united front.

In addition, the rural Reddys, who emerged as the predominant caste in Telangana, were also divided. Both the Congress Party and the Communist Party in Telangana were dominated by the Reddys from coastal Andhra Pradesh (Forrester 1970). These Reddys took leadership positions in Andhra Mahasabha and eventually the Communist Party of India (Sundarayya 2006; Leonard 1967).[29] The land reforms in the early 1950s broke the power of the traditional landed elite in rural Telangana (Appu 1975; Khusro 1958; Pavier 1974). But the Reddys were the primary beneficiaries of the seized land, and they became the new face of rural oppression over the next two decades. This is the classic conundrum in agrarian uprisings: transferring land to agrarian underclasses through successful land reform then leads to conserving pre-cisely those underclasses who had formed the tactical roots of mobilization (Herring 1997).

With the concentration of land and political power, the new rich capitalist farmers mostly within the Reddy caste in Telangana found increasing opportunities for accumulation outside agriculture. In the literature on agrarian mobilization it has been argued that unless the upper-class non-cultivators derive their income exclusively from land they are unlikely to get locked in a zero-sum game in an agrarian conflict (Paige 1975). As the upper class in the South were willing and able to enter capitalism, anti-Maoist resistance here, unlike that in the North, did not escalate into entrenched battles of life and death over control of land. One important consequence of this was the increase in absentee landownership, higher tenancy, and increased land rents, which have all complicated class–caste relations.

Summing up, the upper caste elites in Telangana were divided along rural-urban, coastal-local lines. They were absent in villages owing to earlier communist mobilization, and the Reddys who dominated rural landholding had the political clout and social networks to seek higher profits and alternative employments in urban areas. This made them unwilling to stake their lives in pitched battles with Maoists. As a result the degree of militancy in the South never reached the frenzied levels of caste wars in the North, which allowed the southern Maoists to focus on building mass movements and dense organizational ties.

Ties with the Local Communities: Maoists' Horizontal and Vertical Ties

As insurgent organizations navigate pre-existing social landscapes, they also proactively forge vertical and horizontal ties (Staniland 2014). Horizontal ties, embedded in formal or informal relationships or a mix of both, link rebel leaders and organizers in various locations and to a broad support base across the country and beyond. Vertical ties, in contrast, refer to bonds of trust, information, and belief that connect the leaders of an insurgent organization with their local communities where they recruit and operate (Staniland 2012). Unlike horizontal ties, vertical ties are geographically rooted. Thus vertical ties are social anchors for the Maoist movement that galvanize mass action, and horizontal ties are the sail that steers the organization to broad goals of social and political change. I argue that both horizontal and vertical ties were strong among the Maoists in the South of India. In the North, the Maoists built strong vertical ties, but their horizontal ties were weak. As a result, deep vertical ties connected the Maoist leadership to its localized support bases in both regions. But in the absence of countervailing horizontal ties, the northern Maoists became so deeply entrenched in local factionalism that they lost organizational autonomy to pursue broader revolutionary goals.

Vertical Ties

In the early days of Maoist mobilization, their mass organizations, also referred to as frontal organizations, played an important role in establishing the top-down vertical ties between the leadership and local communities, both in North and South India. Mass fronts have traditionally had two layers. First, secret armed mass organizations were created to propagate revolutionary goals and recruit rebels. Second, open mass organizations were unarmed and designed to build pressure on the state through legal-constitutional struggles on progressive issues. Open fronts offered a fertile recruiting ground for a large number of students, agricultural laborers, mineworkers, tendu leaf collectors, writers, intellectuals, and teachers to join the support base of Maoist movement. A select few among them eventually became inducted into secret mass organizations or into guerrilla army and even fewer were given party membership. For example, many former Maoists from the forested areas of the Palamau, Latehar, and Chatra districts that I met in the North referred to Mazdur Kisan Sangram Samiti (MKSS), a mass organization of agricultural laborers launched by the PU in 1980, as their first point of contact with the rebels.[30] In the South, the former Maoists I met mentioned Radical Students Union (RSU) on urban campuses or the Radical Youth League (RYL) activists in rural areas as their first points of contact.

Strong vertical ties mattered most during the early stages of mobilization when Maoists were most vulnerable and their enemies strong. In the villages, ordinary people either personally knew the local Maoist organizer or knew them through someone they knew closely. PWG formed mass organizations in the South across every profession, from medical doctors, college professors, schoolteachers, artists, writers, journalists, students, mine workers, factory workers, construction workers, farm workers, and so on. Open mass organizations aligned to the PWG were eventually banned by the Indian state. Though not armed and possessing little knowledge of the military strategy, open mass organizations were, as one Maoist leader put it to me, their "eyes and ears on the ground." They adopted unique, locally suited strategies of mobilization that further reinforced vertical ties of the insurgent organization to its local community.

As the landlords in the North entered an arms race with the insurgents, the death spiral started choking the mass fronts in the North. For example, Dr. Vinayan, the popular mass leader of MKSS, who was instrumental in recruiting many top Maoist leaders in the North, was suspended by PU by 1986 for criticizing the "meaningless violence and undisciplined manner of peasant struggle" that hijacked mass mobilization and exposed ordinary people to unnecessary police harassment and upper-caste retaliation.[31] As violence escalated, the Maoists in the North scrambled to recruit more fighters and they relaxed selection criteria, induction process, and training requirements. The biggest challenge was that local leaders were slow to emerge in the North. A constant struggle to up the ante against entrenched "landlordism" became the key element in identifying leadership, and this cumulative raising of the stakes in the conflict created further violence. In a context where police refused to register complaints against their caste brethren and the Dalit/Maoist activists, even social workers and lawyers, were arrested for legal political activities, northern Maoists abandoned political activities and shifted more and more to militancy and ruling by fear and hate.[32]

Under such circumstances, more and more people wanted to possess a gun to feel safe and powerful. By supplying guns and a license to kill, the Maoists in the North recruited mafia and criminals into their ranks, who then took control of the Maoist arsenal and considerable funds, and some eventually turned against the Maoist Party (e.g., the Jagnandan Yadav group in Bihar). A former rebel I met in the Palamau district described the trend with the following example. A local Dalit youth, known for his temper, aggressive personality, and intense hatred of Yadavs, joined the PU peasant organization. He displayed great militancy and leadership, and he eventually came to exercise a strong influence on the organization. Subsequently, the local Maoists detained a villager who they suspected as police agent responsible for the death of three comrades, and demanded that the armed unit execute him. The commander of the armed unit refused to penalize the suspected informer due to lack of evidence and chastised his unit to concentrate on the land struggle. The local unit, however, condemned the commander as a coward, and with tacit approval of the upstart Dalit leader went on to brutally assassinate that person. As it became known that they had killed an innocent man, it sent a shock wave through the village, that willingly shared their meagre resources with Maoists and sheltered them from law enforcement. Many seasoned Maoist cadres complained that incidents like these have hurt their larger goals of militant agitation for land redistribution. However, the wild, violent and dangerous recruits, like the Dalit youth who organized this wrongful assassination, rose quickly through the organization in the North. They committed other blood-curdling excesses during their long rebel careers. These excesses added up to contribute to the intense militarization of Maoist movement in the North. Often local commanders, empowered by guns and cash, went against central party leadership. But the leadership failed to rein in their local agents because even though they instigated un-principled hate crimes they also served the party by scaring landlords and establishing control over upper-caste arms, grains, and land. (Shah 2006; Witsoe 2012; Sanchez 2010; Mahadevan 2012). This made the Maoist organization in the North more locally, but the anti-social nature of vertical ties also permanently alienated Maoists from a broader support base. In the South, in sharp contrast, vertical ties to local community were pro-social, facilitating strong grassroots associations that advocated for civil liberties, human rights, further increasing the appeal and credibility of the Maoist organization and platform.

Horizontal Ties

As the Maoists in the North got more and more caught up in the vortex of violence, their horizontal ties to broader social forces, actors, and networks outside the epicenter of conflict deteriorated. Despite escalating violence in the South, on the other hand, the southern Maoist organization continued to uphold their strong horizontal ties across different geographic and social sites. It is a truism that deserves repeating that an armed insurgency, no matter how restricted to particular conflict locations, is seldom insulated from nonstate actors such as nongovernmental organizations, professional organizations, and religious institutions. Various state actors, including national-level politicians and bureaucrats, also intervene in conflict zones pursuing their own diverse agendas. Insurgent organizations, particularly ones like the Maoists in India, that govern the territories they control, pay attention to forging cross-class horizontal ties with these different sections of the population outside their immediate geographies of conflict.

Horizontal ties link insurgent organizations to students, activists, artists, intellectuals, professionals, workers, government officials, politicians, and business elites drawn from diverse social and geographical locations. Some of these groups joined marches and public meetings organized by Maoist frontal organizations, and others did not. But they were broadly sympathetic to the political goals of the insurgent organization, while also being occasionally critical of insurgent methods, actions, and policies. In the Maoist typology of social classes, those connected through horizontal ties typically do not belong to the enemy classes or the motive forces but to the middle-of-the-roaders who may oscillate between being supportive and critical of the insurgent organization. Maoists' horizontal ties also included clandestine ties to local leaders of various political parties. It is widely known that Maoists, despite denouncing electoral politics, maintain close ties to the local political parties in their areas of operation. They are known to show their support for a political party in three ways: they encourage people to vote for their preferred candidates; they prevent them from voting for the adversaries of their preferred candidates or they encourage people to not vote at all.

Horizontal ties can be strong or weak depending on the flow of information, terms of reciprocity, bonds of normative obligations, shared political preferences, and capacity for collective action. Strong horizontal ties help a movement get off the ground: They bolster communication, coordination, and cooperation on movement issues; generate publicity; create a narrative of (in)justice around popular discontent; give legitimacy to anti-state uprisings; and drastically undermine the ability of the democratic state to crackdown on local rebellions.. Within the insurgent organization, strong horizontal ties amplify the outreach and appeal of an insurgent organization and act as a countervailing force to vertical ties which lock it to the acrimonious interests of its local constituencies. In other words, strong horizontal ties increase relative autonomy of the leadership from various crosscutting cleavages that divide the social context of the insurgent organizations. Weak horizontal ties, on the other hand, isolate insurgent organizations and make them vulnerable to state repression.

Similar to vertical ties, Maoist front organizations play an important role in forging horizontal ties with social constituencies that play important roles in shaping public opinion about the Maoists. But horizontal ties are also forged at the level of top leadership of the central committee. The RSU of the PW in the South is an example of a mass organization that played an important role in forging horizontal ties in the region. In the 1970s and 1980s, it recruited

many students at various college and university campuses and created powerful mass mobilization on wide-ranging issues, such as transparency in college examination systems, being raped in police custody, workers' strikes,
improving safety standards for miners, abolition of unpaid labor, land inequality, increased wages for agricultural laborers, boycott of elections, and
protesting the Soviet occupation of Afghanistan. Many people attended their
meetings and marches as the issues resonated with a broad cross-section of
society and generated popular interest in the Maoist program.

The Maoists also built strong horizontal ties by either supporting or
joining forces with various popular movements by mobilizing meetings
and marches on police reform, human rights violations, (un)democratic
political culture, caste-based reservation, patriarchy, secularism, and
freedom of expression and assembly. When the non-gazetted officers' association in the South took to the streets to protest changing the retirement
age of government employees from 58 to 55, the southern Maoists declared
their support for them. In this way, they connected local movements to
broad issues of citizens' rights, drawing supportive statements from poets,
noted lawyers, and civil liberty activists. The Maoists were able to integrate
tens of thousands of miners and many trade union organizations into their
working-class movement by mobilizing on issues that resonated with the
general public.

Faced with the upsurge of "demand politics" in various parts of India since
the 1970s, where angry and disappointed Indian masses took to the streets
to assert their rights, the Indian state started responding to mass uprisings
with police action that included unlawful detention, torture of political
prisoners, destruction of houses, desecration of drinking water wells, van-
dalism, burning crops, and framing rebels for serious crimes. "Encounter"
killings by police were no longer exceptions—they became the norm
(Venugopal 2007; Balagopal 1981).[33] Public outcry against police oppression
also consolidated horizontal ties between Maoist frontal organizations and
civil liberty activists and lawyers, who constituted the most vocal citizenry.
These urban auxiliary support bases not only critiqued the police excesses
but also documented other Maoist demands that could be negotiated within
the limits of legality. These activists, in turn, had school, college or kinship
ties with journalists, editors, filmmakers, poets, academics, bureaucrats, and
democratic politicians. Various Maoist demands, including restructuring
landholding, abolition of feudal caste inequality, and the need for organized
lending in rural areas to end usury, generated considerable debate within

these urban circles. As Maoist issues gained more visibility, the Maoists invested in a robust horizontal network of supporters and sympathizers who would write, debate, and publicize the movement to the general public.

During my fieldwork in the North, former rebels recounted how they invited bureaucrats to inaugurate free private schools they had set up in rural areas to compensate for the lack of access to public education. District magistrates were present at handicraft fairs organized by Maoists in collaboration with other tribal organizations. These events were covered in local and state newspapers, and elected politicians, even from non-local constituencies, were pictured at the fairgrounds. However, these horizontal ties were devoid of any ideational convergence between the urban elites and the Maoist commanders and were based on some quid pro quo of financial gain or trade of influence and territory control.

In the South, on the other hand, bureaucrats personally knew and admired the courage of some rebel leaders.[34] Journalists and editors were former guerrillas.[35] And current guerrillas had former classmates in the ministry and state secretariat. Some of the horizontal ties were built anew by the Maoists, but some were old ties that were reinforced by a broad solidarity around certain issues. This generated an embedded horizontal network of citizens within democracy in the South who selectively supported some aspects of the extra-democratic endeavor of Maoists while simultaneously working in their respective capacities to demand greater political and administrative accountability. Thus a robust interface between democracy and insurgency grew, which became more vibrant in the South and increasingly emaciated in the North.[36]

There are at least four reasons why the horizontal ties, always weaker in the North than in the South, became increasingly scrawny over the years. First, the Maoist mass organizations in the North were not as robust as in the South. This was primarily due to the pitched caste wars and consequent arms race that engulfed Maoist organizations in the North, which left little time and resources for Maoists to invest in their mass programs. Northern Maoists became preoccupied with saving their own lives and those of their supporters from frequent onslaughts of upper-caste militias. Open mass programs dwindled in the North not only because activists were targeted in open shootouts but also because activists and their political programs lost voice, visibility, and funding within the Maoist organization as military commanders gained ascendancy.

Second, the military commanders gaining ascendancy in the North as the public face of the organization were ill-suited to maintaining horizontal ties with the larger society. They stirred a mix of fear and disdain among members of civil society, alienating even the most sympathetic among them. Through most of 1990s, the three main factions of the Maoists in the North— PU, MCC, and Liberation— fought bloody turf wars against each alongside caste wars against their enemies. Their incessant preoccupation with factionalism and bloodshed inspired little public faith in the northern Maoists and caused many formerly supportive rights activists to sever ties.

Third, the availability of non-Maoist progressive platforms in the North also undercut Maoist horizontal ties. For example, Jayaprakash Narayan (popularly called JP) led a very popular socialist movement in the 1970s. Known as a fearless crusader against the emergency imposed by Prime Minister Indira Gandhi in the 1970s, JP, a Marxist turned Gandhian, called for a "total revolution." He was instrumental in forming the Janata Party that united all left-leaning anti-Congress forces in the North under one banner, and the leader of the party, Morarji Desai, became the first non-Congress prime minister of India, defeating Indira Gandhi. A credible, popular democratic platform mobilizing on similar issues of social justice and class mobility also undercut the Maoist support base in the North.

Fourth, through the 1980s and 1990s many factions broke out of the overarching left-leaning camp of the Janata Party in the North to carve out their own caste-based regional parties. As caste emerged as the primary axis of polarization in the North, even the Maoist support base divided its loyalty, endorsing commanders of their own caste over others, thereby fracturing loyal base and undermining broad horizontal ties with the insurgent organization.

Conclusion

In this chapter, I presented a historically grounded analysis of the origin and evolution of Maoist movement in two conflict locations in North and South India. There are three main takeaways from this chapter. First, the Maoists operated on distinct social and political terrains in the two regions. Second, despite being part of the same insurgent organization, united by one ideology and a highly centralized command, these pre-existing local conditions made (a) polarization of the support base partial (b) horizontal ties weaker and (c) militancy more intense in the North than in the South. Third, differences in pre-war social bases, polarization of support bases, strength of organizational ties and degrees of militancy between the two regions determined the distinct processes and outcomes of rebel retirement in the two regions.

The distinctive pre-war caste structure in North played an important role in explaining why retirement is much lower there than in the South. The backward caste in the North was divided in terms of their class interests. The poor and landless among them joined Maoist army because they found their class interests aligned to Maoist program. The better off among the backward castes supported the anti- Maoist landlords, because they cared about hiring agricultural workers at a lower wage than the Maoists demanded for them. Thus the backward caste in the Maoist party were often forced to choose between their caste networks and their class interests and affiliations. With the rising prominence of backward castes in electoral politics in the North since the early 1990s, pro-Maoists found new hopes of representation in electoral politics. The Dalits within the Maoist camps also started getting suspicious of their backward comrades, fearing that they were more loyal to their co-ethnics in electoral politics than to the Maoist agenda. Thus the underlying caste-class structure played a role in weakening the cohesiveness of Maoist organization in the North, This chapter shows that in the South the underlying caste-class structure divided and weakened the upper caste while further solidifying the interests and identities of Maoist support base. In other words, the southern Maoists achieved sharp caste-caste polarization of society into two antagonistic camps pitted against each other in a way that they did not have to choose between caste identity and class interests. This sharp polarization, desirable from the perspective of insurgent organizations, allowed southern Maoists to build strong vertical and horizontal ties, which led to high retirement through harmonic exit networks in the region. Incomplete polarization, along with high militancy in the North, stifled exit network and rebel retirement in the region.

In the rest of the book I show how high militancy and low polarization in the North eventually emboldened corrupt networks of bureaucrats-politicians-police-mafia in the gray zone of state-insurgency interface, which acted as an impediment to rebel retirement and reintegration. In contrast, low militancy and high polarization allowed southern Maoists to build massive mass organizations, which energized grassroots politics and civic associations in the grey zone of state-insurgency interface, leading to high retirement and reintegration. The primary contribution of this chapter is to demonstrate the structural constraints and social embeddedness of insurgent organizations. This does not imply that insurgents do not have any agency and autonomy. Insurgents can often defy organizational dictates, overcome structural constraints, and carving out new paths for themselves—an insight further developed in the next chapter.

3

The Gray Zone of
State-Insurgency Interface

A single image illustrated the difference in rebel retirement between North and South India for me. One October morning in 2013, I went to the legislative assembly building in the North Indian state of Jharkhand to meet Yadav, a former Maoist guerrilla turned politician. Yadav was meeting a few senior politicians of a major regional political party to convince them to nominate him as their party candidate for the 2014 Legislative Assembly elections. He came dressed in a long, all-white, starched collarless shirt, loose cotton trousers, and shiny white shoes, which is very much the typical attire of Indian politicians. I noticed that a group of young men, armed quite conspicuously, with their faces half-covered in checkered red-and-white cotton towels, were following Yadav everywhere. When I asked about them, Yadav quipped that they were family and friends from his village, who were visiting the capital city of the state for sightseeing. It took a few meetings before he confessed that they were actually his personal army of bodyguards, shadowing him everywhere, because his former comrades had taken out a death warrant against him and he feared for his life.

I had been meeting former rebels in various parts of South India for about a year at that time. I met them in the open courtyards of their homes in villages and small towns, often surrounded by family, friends, and neighbors who knew their insurgent past. In fact, many confessed to respecting them even more for it. I have seen them cooking for their families, dropping their children off at school, running roadside cafes (often referred to as hotels locally), working in cotton fields, attending weddings, making music, teaching in colleges, and selling moonshine. Among the roughly 50 former rebels I had met in the South until then, I had never seen anyone standing out in a crowd, surrounded by armed bodyguards, or felt the palpable fear and despondence that characterized my meetings with retired rebels in the North.

Though I could not have known it then, former combatants in the North are unable to return to their families. This is in sharp contrast to their

Farewell to Arms. Rumela Sen, Oxford University Press (2021). © Oxford University Press.
DOI: 10.1093/oso/9780197529867.003.0003

southern counterparts, whose prospects of reintegration, indicated by the likelihood of returning to "normal" life, are very high. Barred from entering their childhood homes by their own relatives and neighbors, retired rebels in the North are compelled to live in rented spaces in and around the capital city of Ranchi where they had surrendered their arms. They cannot go back to farming or any other family profession, even if they want to. Several former Maoists in the North told me that they would much rather return to their insurgent lives than be forced to live like strangers in a big city, separated from their loved ones and despised by their neighbors as dreaded criminals.

Their post-retirement employment options were limited to two: They were either aspiring politicians trying to win nomination by an existing political party for national, state, or local election; or they worked as other politicians' henchmen, employing extortions and other intimidation techniques to deliver votes, raise campaign donations, broker real estate deals, or cover up crimes along the way. Retired rebels were well suited to either role due to the control they had over territory during their insurgent careers, which guaranteed their ability to understand salient issues, mobilize men and capital, and sway votes in those areas.[1]

In contrast, former rebels in the South find it easier to return to the virtual anonymity of quiet "normal" life with their families, a fact illustrated by the diverse professions they pursue post-retirement. These range from farming and homemaking to university teaching to becoming a *goonda* (hired thug). Except for a handful who ran for office at local levels, retired Maoists in the South, unlike their northern counterparts, do not join electoral politics. Yet, many more Maoist rebels retire in the South. This correlation between high retirement and low electoral participation in the South is puzzling. In general, the existing literature on rebel-to-party transformation takes electoral participation of former rebels as a critical element of conflict resolution and democratization (O'Donnell et al. 1986; Shugart 1992; Söderberg Kovacs and Hatz 2016; Manning and Smith 2016). Such exit of former guerrillas directly into electoral politics is even more striking in the case of Maoist rebel groups that are ideologically opposed to electoral politics, viewing it as an unjust political system that perpetuates the majority status quo without mechanisms for radical change in power sharing between dominant and marginalized classes.

Yet, as shown in this book, northern Maoists who embrace electoral participation are less integrated than southern Maoists who do not. In fact, neither the retired rebels nor the voters that I spoke to in the North see such electoral participation by former Maoists as a condemnation of violent extremism. As some retired rebels explained during interviews with this author, they chose insurgency over democracy in their youth, and subsequently changed their allegiance to democracy over insurgency, based more on expediency than on any conviction in the superiority of democratic processes over violent or insurgent methods or vice versa.[2]

Politicians and activists I interviewed in the North argued that the voters, who cast their ballots in favor of former rebels over other candidates, focused more on their electability and ability to deliver public goods locally, like road or schools, than their past.[3] The ordinary people in the North shared that they have witnessed Maoists masquerading as politicians, riding their motorcycles and soliciting popular support in the same way as various other political party leaders with no insurgent past. Some respondents shared how they have also seen elected politicians with no Maoist past imitating Maoists, bearing arms, and running Maoist-style kangaroo courts from their front porches.[4] The outward and the moral divide between being a democratic and extra-democratic actor was lost to the people in the North, who found it difficult to tell the Maoists apart from law enforcement agents too, given that they were both known to disguise in the opponents uniforms and employ similar intimidating and interrogation strategies against villagers.[5] One illustration of the insurgency-democracy continuum in the North is encapsulated in the election slogan of Paulus Surin, a former Maoist commander who was elected to state legislative assembly in Jharkhand 2009 and 2014. The slogan proclaimed: *Jeetenge toh din mein aayenge, harenge to raat mein aayenge* (If I win, I'll visit you during the day, if I lose, I'll visit you during the night).[6]

In a context where the local state shares sovereignty with many nonstate actors, most notably the insurgents that have vowed to overthrow the state, this campaign slogan did not surprise anyone in his constituency. The existing literature on rebel electoral transition suggests that former members of armed groups do not participate in elections if they do not expect to win. On the flip side, groups that expect to do well in elections and see opportunities to shift policy in a favorable direction, pursue direct participation (Matanock and Staniland 2018). This implies that retired Maoists in the North, who joined electoral politics, expected to win, while those in the South, who eschewed electoral politics, did not. However, former Maoists who have run for office in the North have mostly lost. All well-known former Maoists, including one-time MP Kameshwar Baitha, Ranjan Yadav, Yugal Pal, and

Kundan Pahan, who ran for office had lost elections multiple times.[7] In the 2009 Assembly elections, six former Maoist leaders joined the electoral fray and only one of them won.[8] In the 2014 Assembly election in Jharkhand, six out of 19 former Maoist and Maoist-backed candidates won, and of them, only one was able to retain the seat in 2019. In other words, 60% of Maoists and Maoist-backed candidates who ran for office in Jharkhand lost in 2014 (Table 3.1). Moreover, according to politicians I interviewed in the North, some Maoists who wanted to run for office were not considered because political parties realized they did not wield any real control over votes, and it was more profitable to enlist underhanded support of active Maoist commanders who could coax and cajole voters in various ways, including with threats of violence.[9]

In fact, during interviews, all of the retired rebels who joined electoral politics, when asked about the reason for joining electoral politics, admitted, without being prompted, that they were motivated to run for office despite knowing they might lose because the paraphernalia of a door-to-door election campaign, the crowd surrounding the candidate, the media attention, and the hobnobbing with other political leaders generate media attention and legitimacy, which many former rebels welcome as a departure from their insurgent career. In addition, running for public office brings additional security and police protection, which former Maoists in the North greatly valued for allaying personal safety concerns.[10]

Thus, the normative divide assumed between electoral politics as legitimate, nonviolent, and desirable and insurgent mobilization as illegal, violent, and dangerous did not resonate as a realistic depiction of their lives among respondents in the North. Although the Maoist Party routinely threatens the general public to boycott polls, it is common knowledge in Jharkhand that local armed squads (*dastas*) often prop up some political candidates, sometimes indirectly, by allowing their campaign vehicles and personnel to enter Maoist-controlled areas, or sometimes directly, by instructing voters whom to vote for.[11] Political parties, both regional and national, and across the left–right ideological spectrum routinely prop up retired rebels as political candidates in the North.[12] Just as elected representatives of the state had previously done, the Maoists also sold protection in return for support (Shah 2006).

Approximately 65% of retired rebels in the North also told me that they did not necessarily choose political careers over other options, but running for office was the only choice available to them that would not have left

Table 3.1 Electoral Outcomes for Former Maoists and Maoist-Backed Candidates Running for Office, 2014 Assembly Election

Name	CPI(Maoist) Connection	Constituency	Political Party Affiliation	Outcome
Vinod Sharma	Zonal commander	Daltonganj	Independent	Lost
Nirmala Devi[a]	Wife of Yogendra Saw, CPI(Maoist)	Barkagaon	Indian National Congress	Won
Girija Singh	Senior leader, TSPC	Daltonganj	Navjawan Sangharsh Morcha	Lost
Manoj Nagesia	CPI(Maoist) Sub-zonal commander	Kolebira	BJP	Lost
Anosh Ekka	PLFI supported	Kolebira	Jharkhand Party	Won[b]
Menon Ekka	PLFI	Simedega	Jharkhand Party	Lost
Suman Bhengra	PLFI	Torpa	Jharkhand Party	Lost
Ganesh Ghanju	Brother of TSPC supremo Brajesh Ghanju	Simariya	JVM	Won[c]
Satyanand Bhokta	TSPC support	Chatra	JVM	Lost
Mahadev Pahan	Brother of Kundan Pahan, CPI(Maoist)	Tamar	JVM	Lost
Prakash Ram	TSPC backed	Latehar	JVM	Won[d]
Sabi Devi	Wife of murdered Shanti Sena soldier who fought PLFI	Barhi	JMM	Lost
Jagarnath Mahto	CPI(Maoist) backed, known as "Tiger"	Dumri	JMM	Won[e]
Jai Prakash Bhai Patel	CPI(Maoist) supported	Mandu	JMM	Won[f]
Paulus Surin	PLFI Zonal commander	Torpa	JMM	Won[g]
Saloni Tuti	Wife of jailed CPI(Maoist) commander Marshal Tuti	Tamar	JMM	Lost

Continued

Table 3.1 *Continued*

Name	CPI(Maoist) Connection	Constituency	Political Party Affiliation	Outcome
Rajkumari Devi	Wife of Guddu Ghanju, JPC leader	Simariya	JMM	Lost
Mohan Ghanju	Wife of Ravindra Ghanju	Latehar	JMM	Lost
Manorama Devi	Wife of CPI(Maoist) sub-zonal commander Gautam Pawan aka Arun	Chhatra	JMM	Lost

Notes: *JVM, Jharkhand Vikas Morcha

[a] She was not fielded as candidate in 2019. For further details see https://indianexpress.com/article/india/india-news-india/hazaribagh-firing-incident-police-arrest-congress-mla-nirmala-devi-3090174/ (accessed April 23, 2019).

[b] He won the 2005, 2009, 2014 elections and was sentenced to life in prison in 2018.

[c] He lost in 2009 on the JMM ticket, won in 2014 on the JVM ticket, and did not run in 2019.

[d] He won in 2004 on the RJD ticket, lost in 2009, and won again in 2014 on the JVMP ticket, and lost in 2019 on the BJP ticket.

[e] He won the 2019 Assembly election as well on the JMM ticket.

[f] This was a family seat, and two brothers, one on the BJP ticket and the other one on the JMM ticket, retained the seat in 2019 as well. For more information, see https://www.thehindu.com/news/national/other-states/jharkhand-election-brothers-pitted-against-each-other-in-mandu-constituency/article30265438.ece (accessed April 23, 2020).

[g] He won in 2009 and 2014 but lost in 2019.

them alone and defenseless in the face of death threats either from former comrades or from their former enemies of rich landlords that they had targeted as insurgents. Anticipating rejection from political parties, some former Maoists, below the rank of area commanders, reported that they did not expect to run for office. Instead they expected to be employed as henchmen (known as *goonda* or rowdy) of various politicians. Goondas are professional bullies who become local dealmakers for legitimate actors like politicians, banks, or businesses, who hire their violent services to coax the public into fear and submission. Former Maoists are highly employable as ruffians because their violent rebel past is particularly effective in spawning fear and bullying ordinary people into submission.

In the North, ordinary people reported witnessing state agents like police, politicians, and bureaucrats routinely and strategically using illegality and violence to maintain their authority. Through insurgents-turned-goondas, politicians settle local issues, enforce their authority, manipulate voting, capture voting booths, and generally get day-to-day things done. When their political masters do not need them, these insurgent-turned-goondas employ their terror infrastructure, made up of other unemployed, local youths, in many side businesses, from the black marketing of cinema tickets and smuggling weapons and drugs, to kidnaping and extortion. In all these corrupt enterprises, the politicians use their influence to protect them. Thus for northern insurgents who become politicians and political henchmen, retirement is often more of a continuity than a change: They are called upon to capitalize on their networks of money and muscle power to win votes either for themselves and their political masters, as they did in the insurgency.

In the South, by contrast, retired rebels have many other post-retirement livelihood options. The insurgent democratic transition in the South, which involves former rebels embracing the same democratic institutions that they had once tried to overthrow, transpires outside the arena of electoral politics. This effectively enables former rebels in the South to return to the peace and quiet of everyday lives, while the transition process in the North, due to its close ties to politics, often does not achieve this result. This difference is in part due to the emergence of robust informal exit networks in the South, which not only ensure the physical safety of former rebels but also create alternative livelihood options that allow them to break away from their insurgent lives. The question is why the informal exit networks are not as robust in the North as in the South.

The answer lies in the distinctive local dynamics of state-insurgency interaction that transpire in the gray zone of their overlap. This gray zone becomes apparent when we ease the assumptions of sharp breaks between war and peace, legit and illicit, state and insurgency in conflict zones, particularly in places where structural violence is pervasive and spectacular episodes of violence are also recurrent. Violence is often too diffuse and integral to routine politics for people to categorize an outbreak of one or another episode of violence as an exceptional phenomenon.[13] Marielle Debos highlighted these "discontinuities between war and peace" in her study of Chad. It is interesting how outlawed extremist fighters in Chad also often observe the law and abide by social norms and informal hierarchies, while the state agents, tasked to uphold the law, would often break the law with impunity (Debos 2016). This is much like Maoist conflict zones of North and South India. The conceptual lines between the state and insurgents, the lawful and the lawless, crimes and political acts, police action and rebel resistance were blurred.[14] Civilians were exceptionally aware of the web of interconnections that emerge between the two warring sides even when they exchanged fire. To them, Maoist rebels, police, Central Reserve Police Force (CRPF) paramilitary forces like the Border Security Force (BSF), thugs, gangs, vigilante groups, mafia, and private militias are all "violent specialists" (Tilly 2003) capable of inflicting grievous physical damage and viewed as interchangeable sources of danger by civilians.

In the lived experience of civilians, both the local state and Maoist resistance to it are infused with violence, lawlessness, and intimidation. The common people I interviewed in the North expressed acute awareness that it was only prudent to avoid any contact with both the state and insurgent actors. However, they also admitted that their families and friends actively developed secret and semi-secret linkages with actors on both sides whenever necessary to ensure their survival and success. This created an expansive gray zone of clandestine, semi-secret and open connections not only between the state and insurgent actors (Auyero 2013) but also among civilians and myriad violent specialists on both sides of the state-insurgency divide. The discussions of the gray zone in this book show that civilians in these conflict zones do not live their lives sandwiched helplessly between two sides but actively devise their own networks, straddling the legal-illegal divide.

The civil war literature, given its earlier focus on conflict onset and termination, often treated civil wars as black-and-white contests between two coherent, unitary actors—the "legitimate" state on the one hand and the outlawed rebel group on the other hand. The black-and-white characterizations of conflict zones has increasingly given way to thick accounts of the analytical quandary of gray zones of state-insurgency overlap where both sides develop a range of clandestine, semi-secret and open networks to collaborate and conspire despite being embroiled in internecine exchange of fire. Scholars studying messy conflict processes acknowledge how intergroup alliances in multiparty conflicts shift constantly and how many private actors in conflict zones sustain powerful semi-secret political and economic networks that can also emerge as an alternative "shadow state" in the midst of institutional decay.

The account of the gray zone developed in this book is partly similar to and partly different from Reno's conception of "shadow state" in Africa. The form of personal rule that undermines rule of law, weakens bureaucratic structure, manipulates markets, and impairs formal government institutions in

Reno's African shadow states resonate in the gray zone in the North steeped in the lawless order of "jungle raj" (Reno 2000). However, criminalization of the state that characterizes the northern gray zone in India is not contingent on international recognition as it seems to be the case in Africa. In addition, unlike Reno's case in Africa, the mining mafia and other murderous extortion and kidnaping rackets in the northern gray zone are hardly despotic challengers to the state. They are more a criminalized nexus of politicians, insurgents, bureaucrats, businessmen and law enforcement agents deeply embedded in the state, reaping benefits from the status quo.[15] In other words, the gray zone in the North is not a "shadow state" operating in juxtaposition to the sovereign legitimate state. In contrast, the dark Hobbesian lawlessness coexists with and is mutually constitutive of the legal state, overriding the conceptual contradiction between the alleged rationality and legitimacy of the state vis-à-vis the violent irrationality of extremists. Without conflating all forms of violence, therefore, this book sheds light not only on the blurred state-insurgency boundaries in the North but also on the ambivalent, cross-cutting, mutually nonexclusive linkages civilians build with myriad violent entrepreneurs on both sides of the war. The sharp divides between conflict and peace, legal state and unlawful insurgency, violence and nonviolence were largely alien to the people.

In ethnographic reflections on the Indian state, scholars have theorized a spongiform interface or blurred boundaries to capture the interpenetration of state and society in day-to-day politics (Fuller and Harriss 2001; Gupta 1995; Hansen et al. 2001). The insurgency literature also recognizes that conflict zones are not all bloodshed and mayhem, and order often arises locally within them, particularly where rebels establish control over a territory (Arjona 2014; Balcells 2012, 2017; Chesterman 2001; Mampilly 2012). In these territories, rebels govern by developing institutional capacity, enacting taxation, and providing local services (Staniland 2012a). However, these studies do not adequately account for the various secret and semi-secret ties between various state agents, insurgents, and other societal actors, including civilians and various civic associations, particularly in areas where rebels and the state share control.

In India, for example, the Maoists established base areas with their own governance institutions, taxation, and healthcare, referred to as Janatana Sarkar (peoples' democracy), in limited areas in the dense forests (*dandakaranya*) of Chhattisgarh (Gudavarthy 2017).[16] In the two epicenters of conflict compared in this book, rebel and state control varied over time, sometimes tilting the balance in favor of rebels, and at other times giving the state upper hand. Through all the changes, however, the secret and semi-secret ties among state agents, insurgents, and other nonstate societal actors continue to flourish and persist.

Scholars have documented that states tolerate shared rule in certain pockets and deliberately outsource certain functions to nonstate forces, flouting the fundamental assumption of the Weberian state (Bates 2008). But this chapter shows how the local state in India maintains multiple secret and semi-secret ties with the insurgents at the same time and place as they fight each other in pitched battles. As mentioned, civilians are not defenseless victims sandwiched between the state and the insurgents (Kamra and Chandra 2017; Shah 2013). They also establish multiple networks with both the state and the insurgents creating a sprawling gray zone of shared sovereignty where rebel retirement and reintegration transpires. The difference between the northern and southern gray zones discussed in this chapter are not conditional on rebel territorial control but on prewar social forces.

Researchers of civil conflict have admitted that states can collude with paramilitaries who do not have revolutionary or secessionist intentions (Saab and Taylor 2009). The Maoists, however, have explicit revolutionary goals of overthrowing the state and have fought the state at multiple fronts for 70 years. The Indian state has also unleashed massive repression through federal paramilitary forces, commando-style policing, and vast intelligence networks. Underneath these overarching confrontations, the state actors, the insurgents, and the societal actors (civilians and civic associations) maintained their range of clandestine, semi-secret, and open ties. The insurgency literature has not fully conceded these ties exist, straddling the leaky walls between the domains of legal state and an illegal insurgency in conflict zones.

There is an increasing interest in understanding the micro-level processes of how rebel institutions can transform state agencies or traditional social authorities. To do that, it is important to account for the expansive web of surreptitious linkages that constitute the ambiguous gray zones of state-insurgency interface. Armed groups can transform shared beliefs, stir new emotions, change social and political preferences, and offer new readings of local and national politics even in areas where their control is cyclical over several decades.

This chapter illustrates the various mechanisms of social and political impact of Maoist agitation on the state and society through the example of anti-Arrack agitation in the South through 1980s and 1990s. It changed social taboos regarding the role of poor Dalit women in the public space and forced political parties to bandwagon with the popular sentiment against liquor even when the state raised revenue from auctioning liquor licenses and the politicians took hefty donations from the liquor lobby to finance their campaigns. This chapter also defines the gray zone and highlights the mechanisms through which caste/class polarization in the prewar social bases of insurgency and the strength of insurgent organizational ties determine whether the emergent gray zone is likely to be virtuous (as in the South) or vicious (as in the North). (Table 3.2.)

The empirical evidence of various connections among state, society, and insurgency show that the gray zones are not restricted to the margins of the state but proliferate profusely to encompass various aspects of social and political life in conflict zones. It offers a "grounded theory" of the Indian state that, although it strives to establish order in the face of violence, does not always do everything in its power to eliminate challenges to its monopoly over coercion within its territory.[17] The central arguments are guided by what I found in the field, and by how diverse stakeholders reported their experience in conflict zones living their lives. In their experience, the state, instead of being a rigid leviathan, is actually a malleable sponge that sometimes concedes control and authority. It is this porous suppleness of the state that increases its capacity to withstand innumerable blows from many insurgent groups. It absorbs shocks and punches from many directions, yet eventually falls back into shape with little permanent indentation.

Table 3.2 Path-Dependent Account of Emergence of Two Different Gray Zones

Militancy of Local Struggles	Polarization in Insurgent Social Base	
	High	Low
High	A. High group cohesion; frequent clashes: No gray area	C. Low group cohesion; frequent clashes: Vicious gray area (North)
Low	B. High group cohesion; sporadic violence: Virtuous gray area (South)	D. Low group cohesion; sporadic violence: Unformed gray zone

The State in Conflict Zones

The India-based evidence presented in this book suggests that the blurring of boundaries between the legal (state) and the illegal (insurgency) creates the gray zone of their interface. This interface is not limited to the margins of a weak state, where state law and order is continually renegotiated (Das 2004; Das and Poole 2004); it is, in fact, ubiquitous. It is the normal condition of the lived experiences of people in postcolonial, underdeveloped countries, particularly in the conflict zones (Chakrabarty 2000; Gupta 1995). The conception of the state in a conflict zone adopted here is distinct from the Stalinist view of the Indian state as an irreversible exploitative engine of oppression, as adopted by the Maoist insurgents. It also questions the Weberian view of a rational, legal state with centralized control over legitimate coercion within determinate territory promoted by the counterinsurgency forces. I use these two frameworks as benchmarks to show that the state is neither as completely exploitative nor as perfectly rational as the dominant orthodoxies of state and insurgent camps suggest. During my fieldwork, it became increasingly clear that the available conceptual tools, particularly the focus on a monolithic, unitary state and large-scale structures of state, epochal events, major policies, and important people (Evans, Rueschemeyer, Skocpol 1985; Skocpol 1979) does not completely capture the protean duplicity and suppleness with which the state can present itself. It is this non-monolithic state, sometimes benign and sometimes brutal, that defeats an insurgency. The rest of this chapter offers evidence how the Indian state in the conflict zones often behaved contrary to the expectations of both Stalinist and Weberian theories, and, in the process, I question the analytical utility and descriptive adequacy of these theories.

Ideationally, rejection of the Weberian state amounts to accepting that the state may not always want to exert complete monopoly over legitimate use of force within its territory. The dominant narrative in policy circles in India and elsewhere, in academic writings as well as among insurgent organizers, is that the state and insurgents are locked in a zero-sum game. The social science literature usually assumes that states seek to be monopolists over the means of organized coercion through physical violence within their territorial borders. Insurgents, particularly of the Maoist variety, also identify the state, and not the local faces of exploitation, as the real enemy. Therefore, there is a dearth of conceptual language to conceive of the coexistence of both conflict and collaboration between the state and the insurgency that takes up arms to overthrow it.

A logical corollary of the Weberian state is the associated analytical construct of "state capacity" that has acquired central importance in both policy and academic literature around civil conflict. Since some states successfully monopolize violence while others fail, it is argued that when a state capacity is low and its status as monopolist of violence slips, insurgency occurs (Skocpol 1979). As post–Cold War security intellectuals became increasingly interested in weak states, failing and failed states have been held responsible for the maladies of terrorism, famine, corruption, and general failures of development (Bilgin and Morton 2002; Gordon 1997; Gourevitch 2004; Hill 2005; Hironaka 2009). However, applying this argument of state capacity to the resurgence of Maoist insurgency in India since 2005, it would seem that the insurgency broke out because the Indian state lacked the capacity to prevent it. However, also if we define state capacity by its outcome, it leads to the following tautology: Insurgencies occur in states with low state capacity, and state capacity is low when outbreaks of insurgency occur.

The analytical utility of this circular argument is further challenged by use of numerous variables underlying the theoretical construct of state capacity, ranging from autonomous bureaucracy, military and police capabilities, and centralization of institutions, to per capita income and population size (Kocher 2010). All these underlying factors are popular explanations of conflict in the literature (Blattman and Miguel 2009; Collier 2000; Collier and Hoeffler 2000; Fearon and Laitin 2003), which robs "state capacity" of genuine explanatory power by making it virtually unfalsifiable. In addition, it is unclear whether the underlying mechanisms of state capacity work as clusters or if some undermine others. For example, if low per capita income and low police capability both indicate low state capacity and increase the likelihood of insurgency, we do not know how they are correlated with each other because there is no differentiation in outcome.

The idea of a monolithic state as either good or bad does not resonate with the people I spent time with in Maoist territories in either the North or the South. They see the Indian state as both a benevolent benefactor, offering relief and services to the poor citizens like themselves, and an abusive entity inflicting violence on them. On the one hand, the people opposed the police or forest guards, who are the proximate faces of the Indian state, when they harassed, threatened, wrongfully arrested, or otherwise abused civilians. On the other hand, they were grateful to the state for offering rural employment guarantee (NREGA) or providing much-needed childcare (*anganwadi*) workers.[18]

The state does not always see the insurgents as an embodiment of unadulterated evil, either. This chapter offers accounts of bureaucrats of the Indian Administrative Service, keeping secret and open channels of communication open with insurgents, and acknowledging the legitimacy of some of their demands. In other places, bureaucrats turn a blind eye to rebels extracting taxes from big corporations and small businesses, sometimes in return for a share of this illegal income. The state also regularly practices passive tolerance of various activities that strengthen insurgents. For example, the Indian state has always allowed insurgent spokespersons (it is common knowledge who they are) to live and work freely in urban areas. In fact, some of them, particularly academics and public intellectuals, known for deep ties to the Maoist organization, speak and write about the insurgency in national and international forums. Some of them are invited to police headquarters to lecture new classes of police officers on various aspects of Maoist insurgency. The state has also turned a blind eye to politicians who recruit insurgents to sway electoral outcomes right under its nose. It is common knowledge that some bureaucrats and police routinely receive payoffs from insurgent groups, and the state often allows private entrepreneurs to pay protection money to Maoists. Additional examples abound.

Regardless of the state and the kind of insurgency, states in conflict zones simultaneously accept and resist insurgents. This paradoxical coexistence of collaboration and violence between the state and the insurgency, illustrated by additional empirical evidence later in this chapter, is more the norm than the exception. The ever-changing, multifaceted state theorized in this book is a necessary ingredient for this coexistence. This chapter also shows that, depending on the nature of the interaction between the protean state and the insurgent group, the gray zone of their interface is either virtuous or vicious. This, in turn, shapes exit networks and retirement outcomes.

Policymakers do not adequately internalize the implication of this porous state in conflict zones in India yet. Once the state is not seen as a monolith, it is also possible to imagine policy responses to insurgency that go beyond the counterinsurgent leviathan. Instead of launching an all-out offensive of paramilitary and state forces against its own citizens (Kennedy and Purushotham 2012; Sundar 2012), like Operation Green Hunt against the Maoists, for example, the state can work under the radar through labyrinthine, covert, and semi-secret linkages to the insurgent organization with an

aim to identify and address the grievances that initially fueled Maoist popularity in the South. This chapter shows how the core issues - of the Maoist
insurgency along with their largest recruitment and support base (the Dalits)
migrated to democratic platforms via these prolific ties among state, society,
and insurgent actors in the South. Although such ties might be interpreted
as indicators of weakness of the Weberian state, they end up strengthening
democracy vis-à-vis an insurgency. I also argue that the only peace talks between the Maoists and the Indian state could be organized in 2004 in the
South by the Committee for Concerned Citizens, which embodied these
prolific ties. Even though the peace talks failed, the state-insurgency-society
ties that led to it eventually generated the impetus for rebel retirement by
supplying movement entrepreneurs (MEs) who coordinated with grassroots
reintegration stewards (RSs). In other words, the vigorous prosocial ties
among state, societal, and insurgent actors in the southern gray zone created conditions for democratic deepening in the South, which led to rebel
retirement and concomitant insurgent weakening there. The northern gray
zone, on the other hand, is also full of ties among insurgent, state, and societal agents. But these ties breed vicious protection rackets, which use their
money and muscle power with impunity, weakening the state and alienating
common people. These ties also exacerbate the insecurities of retiring rebels
and discourage rebels from quitting the insurgency.

In 2018, the Indian state, for example, launched a witch-hunt to identify and arrest anyone they suspect of having ties with the insurgents. The
use of an anti-terror law against activists and intellectuals who are allegedly
Maoist sympathizers and co-conspirators is a determined assault on the gray
zone and its bulwark of crosscutting ties that facilitate rebel retirement tin
the South but not in the North.[19] The discussion of the gray zone of state-
insurgency interface presented here makes the case for encouraging rather
than eliminating these go-between actors in the gray zone, which can only
follow if we appreciate the non-zero-sum relations among state, society and
insurgency.

State-Society Interactions

As civil conflict researchers began to move away from explaining conflict in
terms of just structural factors, they also realized that those factors are not
all independent variables. Conflict changes demographics, destroys assets,

polarizes underlying social cleavages, toughens police forces, and leaves its imprint on institutional structures of the state and on society. The state can hardly be treated as autonomous of society, which in the context of this book refers to civilians and various civic associations that inhabit the conflict zones.

In policy circles, improving state-society relations often requires coordinating formal (state) and informal (societal) governance structures. In order to achieve this coordination and improve state-society relations, policymakers assume that they should extend the state into so-called ungoverned spaces. Strong societal governance structures are, in fact, considered counterproductive to a strong state, particularly in postcolonial contexts, for two reasons (Midgal 1988, 2018): First, the state needs prompt integration into world capitalist systems, which requires complete evisceration of existing social institutions, which, in turn, is harder to achieve the stronger society is. Second, where colonial power channeled resources to local chiefs and landlords, it created strong societies, where the bureaucracy, mired in kinship ties, encouraged clientelistic and patronage networks. Lack of rational bureaucracy results in a capture of the state by sectional interests and the creation of predatory, patrimonial states (Bach 2011; Evans, Rueschemeyer, and Skocpol 1985; Evans 1989). This literature also shows us how the past lingers in reconfigurations of political order, especially in India (Kohli 1997, 2002).

The subaltern studies literature, also portraying the postcolonial experience specifically, however, questions the utility of applying the analytical separation of state and civil society to non-Western cases. These scholars argue that the postcolonial state is not autonomous of society and the society was also dominated by the state (Chakrabarty 2000; Chatterjee 1991; Guha 2007; Guha 1982; Kaviraj 2010). In a 2008 report of the Planning Commission of India, a group of academics and activists also argued that the Maoist insurgency is a consequence of the penetration of the "developmental state" into the communal spaces of tribal society. They recommended legal protection of the jurisdiction of local communities over regulatory, social, and economic aspects of rural life, not as an exception or a concession but as the natural right of any community (Planning Commission 2008).

Recent scholarship on Maoist insurgency in India has also shown that state penetration into societal divisions along caste and ethnic lines, going back to colonial era determines the nature and intensity of the insurgency

(Mukherjee 2013; Verghese 2016). In the North, on the one hand, British indirect rule involved low penetration of the state into rural areas (Kohli 2004; Lange 2009; Mahoney 2010). The upper- and middle-caste landlords (zamindars) were protected by the colonial state in return for the fixed share of the land revenue they delivered to the British. They were allowed to keep the rest of the revenue for themselves, which encouraged them to exploit lower-caste peasants with high land-tax demands (Mamdani 1996; Banerjee and Iyer 2005; Boone 2003). Thus northern landlords, historically tied to their land as a source of their power, prestige and prosperity, have faced many peasant uprisings directed at them as the most proximate face of an extractive system of government. In independent India, the early Maoists also organized against local landlords. Given these historical antecedents, it was not surprising that the landlords in the North fought fierce pitched battles against the Maoists in the villages.

In the Southern conflict zone, on the other hand, colonial indirect rule occurred through various princely states, which produced lower state penetration into societies than that in the North. This also allowed substantial local autonomy in the spheres of administration, taxation, land revenue, and law, while keeping foreign policy under the direct control of the colonial administration (Fisher 1991) The rural, landed elites in the South were neither directly beholden to the colonial masters, nor were they tied to the princely state in day-to-day affairs, which, contributed to their ability to explore non-agricultural sources of income, send their children to cities for higher education, and eventually embrace modern, westernized cultural and political ideas, including communism. This does not imply that the landed elites in the South generously gave in to the Maoists without a fight. It only implies that unlike their northern counterparts, the rural elites in Telangana could afford to retreat from protracted confrontation with Maoists in the villages. Since the southern Maoists did not face intense militancy in the villages, they were able to build successful mass movements across Andhra Pradesh, which allowed the insurgent organization to forge strong vertical and horizontal ties with state and societal agents. The trajectory of the anti-Arrack movement (against the sale of liquor), discussed in the next section, illustrates how these vigorous ties were forged among various state, society, and insurgency actors. The ambiguity of the state in the South, simultaneously repressing and embracing insurgent-led popular uprisings, is also well illustrated by the anti-Arrack movement.

Anti-Arrack Agitation and Insurgent Organizational Ties

The anti-Arrack agitation was a grassroots drive against the sale of Arrack (a low-cost country liquor consumed by the poor), which began in coastal districts of Andhra Pradesh in the late 1980s and spread to Telangana in the early 1990s. It was successfully framed as a class and gender issue by the Peoples' War (PW) faction of the Maoists.[20] Rural Dalit women from the poorest landless families were at the forefront of this movement. These women claimed that alcohol poisoning not only killed their husbands and orphaned their children but also contributed to the problems of household debt and alcohol-induced domestic violence.[21] In the early days of the movement, local Maoist organizers led the attacks on liquor contractors, setting fire to liquor shops, and effectively channeling popular anger in ways that consolidated public opinion against the consumption of liquor (Reddy and Patnaik 1993). As more men and women in villages and small towns joined the popular demonstrations, the use of violence by the Maoists was either unnecessary or went unreported.

With the rising momentum, the anti-Arrack movement permeated local state institutions and social life to such an extent that many within the local police, bureaucracy, and political parties, encouraged by a newspaper company (Eenadu), became sympathetic to its demands. Maoist organizers, via their horizontal ties to academics and activists, broadcast the goals and successes of the movement in academic seminars and political conferences.[22] Prominent English-language newspapers also began regularly reporting on the movement. Thus the anti-Arrack agitation emerged as a ready platform for political parties like Telugu Desam, the Congress Party, and the parliamentary left to band behind it. On January 16, 1995, despite opposition of the rich and powerful liquor lobby who donated generously to various political parties across the spectrum, sale of Arrack was banned in the state of Andhra Pradesh. The significance of this political consensus on the liquor ban in course of a few years cannot be fathomed without reference to the previous opposition to a liquor ban among political elites.

The opposition stemmed from the elaborate ties that the liquor lobby in Andhra Pradesh built with the police, politicians, and bureaucrats in the state. The state government of Andhra Pradesh was strongly opposed to anti-Arrack agitation, citing loss of revenue from liquor sales. However, there was more to it. Post-independence, most states in India either wanted to impose complete prohibition or levy very high excise duty on manufacture and sale of liquor, which not only crippled liquor trade but also resulted in prolifer-ation of illicit liquor business by criminals and bootleggers.[23] As a result, politicians were also keen to avoid any association with liquor traders up until the 1960s.[24] Liquor trade became mired in smuggling (to avoid high excise taxes), a corrupt auction system for liquor licenses emerged, and there was an intense black market of distilling. Liquor contractors in the South maintained their own criminal gangs for protection of their trade interests and for their personal safety.

As political elite in India became more and more dependent on money and muscle power to win elections in the 1970s, they no longer hesitated to accept the hefty donations liquor contractors offered in return for the willingness of the state to turn a blind eye to their semi-unlawful activities (Pande 2000). In fact, faced with growing resource needs to finance their political careers and remain in power, many politicians became liquor contractors. On the flip side, some liquor contractors also became politicians. Thus, by the end of 1970s, the criminalization of the political process in the South was firmly rooted in the liquor trade, and all political parties met the mention of regula-tion or control of liquor, let alone prohibition, with ridicule and skepticism.

However, the groundswell of popular opposition to Arrack led by Dalit women and supported by Maoists turned the tide against the formidable liquor lobby. The women activists, encouraged by Maoist organizers, attacked the unholy nexus among police, politicians, and bureaucrats, on the one hand, and the Arrack contractors, on the other hand, as public enemy number one. They explicitly highlighted the ill effects of this nexus on the moral fabric and family values of Indian society in street plays, door-to-door-campaigns, pamphlets, wall writings, and public meetings. Women agitators argued that although Arrack was the immediate cause of their miseries, the nexus between state agents and liquor contractors was their real enemy. Women activists identified politicians and district collectors of the Indian Administrative Services with ties to the Arrack contractors and demanded that they sever those ties.[25]

Women attacked liquor contractors with brooms, chili powder, and cooking utensil. They threatened to set illicit liquor on fire, alleging that liquor was responsible for their broken homes, dead husbands, and orphaned children. Women also came in large groups and stalled the auction of liquor licenses by the Excise and Revenue Department of the state, holding gov-ernment officials responsible for the same maladies. As the police began to make arrests for disruption of government business, all major newspapers covered the spectacle of poor women courting arrest reminiscent of Gandhi's Satyagraha-style for their rightful resistance. This generated a huge public outcry in urban areas, which politicians could not remain immune to for long.

The most crucial social impact of this movement was drawing low-caste women into the public space. Rural women formed "battalions" and took turns staking out liquor shops. Some men, both sellers and consumers of liquor, who violated the ban on liquor consumption were paraded through the villages with drums playing and slogans. The public shaming was supplemented by intense "broom treatments" behind closed doors, followed by refusal of women to serve food to those husbands who would come home drunk (Larsson 2006).

In the face of swelling demands for a liquor ban, the Congress Party, challenged by the rise of Telugu Desam (TDP) in the villages, hitchhiked on the popularity of the anti-Arrack mobilization.[26] The TDP realized that it would lose votes if it were seen as pro-Arrack and joined the fray.[27] Anti-Arrack Coordination Committees were formed at the district level to continue the struggle. These committees drew support and participation from across the political spectrum.[28] The literacy program of the state government (Akshara Jyoti) included a ritual in which the neo-literate women in the villages, upon completion of the program, pledged to fight the "Arrack-demon" with all their might. Soon the anti-Arrack mobilization was tied to other ongoing discourses on dignity of labor, adult literacy, and the welfare of women and children, creating a massive confluence of community organizers, civic associations, administrators and politicians of diverse political persuasion, who rallied on overlapping issues. They borrowed mobilization tactics from each other and attended marches and demonstrations together. This gave rise to a dense network of ties among the state, societal, and Maoist agents, often obfuscating the rebel-state divide in public perception. In fact, anti-Arrack activists I spoke to reminisce that the lines between state, societal, and insurgent agents were first blurred in the district-level anti-Arrack Coordination Committees. Many democratic civic associations and bureaucrats in state welfare projects developed deep ties with PW members and sympathizers. PW recruited from among them. Some members of PW mass organizations became active in other grassroots civic associations and developed ties with political parties as well. Bureaucrats sympathetic to the agitation admitted that they could not distinguish between party workers of parliamentary parties, PW members, and activists of various civic associations.

The anti-Arrack agitation was not the only grassroots movement in the South that coalesced broad consensus among multiple state, societal, and - rebel actors and created new ties that trumped older alliances, like the ones between the liquor lobby and political parties. The Dalit movement and the civil liberty movement, both born out of the Maoist mobilization, later migrated to democratic platforms. The next sections analyze how overlapping membership of insurgent mass organs and democratic civic associations forged the virtuous gray zone of state-insurgency interface in the South but not in the North.

Gray Zone

Previous research on civil conflict has argued that conflict zones are not landscapes of lawlessness (Arjona 2014), a fact also borne out by my field research in the two epicenters of conflict in India. In the experiences of people living in conflict zones, I encountered a sprawling gray zone where the licit/state and the illicit/insurgency coexist and collaborate while they also exchange fire. The existence of this gray zone refutes the zero-sum relationship between state and insurgency. It also shows that outcomes in conflict zones are not theoretically contingent on which side has how much territorial control and where. It is more useful to focus on the key actors and the web of connections they weave, sometimes for survival, and at other times for political or economic gain. Gray zones, from the perspective of civilians in conflict zones, are sites of partial resistance (Arjona, Kasfir, and Mampilly 2015; Scott 1987) where expressions of discontent with either the state or the insurgents coexist alongside collaboration with one or both of them. However, these acts of collaboration, as illustrated in this section, although pervasive and constant, are not necessarily at the level of elaborate collective action that has high costs, which no one wants to incur without considering the odds of success and the issues at stake.

In the summer of 2013, I came across an organization in Telangana called Association for Friends and Relatives of Martyrs (Amara Veerula Bandhu Mitrula Sangham, ABMS). When Maoist cadres died either in police custody or during exchange of fire with security personnel, ABMS activists would swing into action locating the police station, assisting family members with all necessary paperwork, and recommending legal actions, where necessary, to ensure that the grieving family members received the bodies of dead rebels (martyrs) to perform last rites. ABMS activists, both men and women, held various day jobs. Sometimes a dead rebel's family would contact them for help, but most of the time ABMS received information from someone in the insurgent organization or in the police, mostly through unidentified phone calls.

I met an ABMS activist, whose day job was in a public sector bank.[29] She shared how, in order to liaise effectively between the bereaved families and the state in a timely fashion, she and her fellow activists maintained a vast network of ties to the police stations, lawyers, politicians, local activists, and bureaucrats, as well as to insurgent spokespersons and sympathizers.[30] It is difficult to explain how ABMS would work successfully over many years without the cooperation of both state and insurgent camps.[31] While casualty numbers are documented and cited frequently as measures of conflict intensity, many hidden but frequent instances of cooperation among state, rebel and societal agents, as in the case of ABMS, go mostly undocumented.[32]

Research has documented how social networks of reciprocal help abound in poor neighborhoods, functioning as surrogate social security systems that provide care and subsistence when formal institutions addressing those needs are unavailable (Auerbach 2016; Burns, Godlonton, and Keswell 2010; Katznelson 1982; Levitsky 2003). Local networks of civic engagement between communities have been shown to reduce the frequency and intensity of violence in the area. However, the cumulative impact of these social and political networks on conflict processes and outcomes remain largely unstudied. This book argues that this cumulative impact results in a gray zone—an idea this book fleshes out by paying rigorous empirical attention to clandestine, semi-secret, and open connections among the state, insurgents, and civilians.[33] As a first step toward that, it offers a four-way classification of secret and semi-secret connections, as follows: (I) Concealed connections between established actors belonging to state and insurgent camps. (II) Semi-secret ties between actors belonging to state and insurgent camps. (III) Concealed connections that civilians have with the state and insurgent camps. (IV) Semi-secret connections that civilians have with the insurgents. In addition, there are open, unconcealed connections (Type V) between the state, insurgents, and civilians in the gray zone, which directly challenges the monopolist zero-sum idea of territorial control.[34]

Whenever the bureaucrats, politicians and insurgents in the northern epicenter of Maoist conflict reached secret arrangements to siphon money from government road or dam construction projects, it was an example of a Type

I clandestine "political" network in the northern gray zone.[35] There are many Maoist splinter groups in Jharkhand that have secret ties to the police and are allowed to run their illegal businesses, which employ kidnappings, extortion, and murder, in return for anti-Maoist intelligence and violence.[36] In the South, there were mentions of one dreaded gangster-cum-real-estate agent whose services were regularly sought by police, bureaucrats, and politicians despite having gone "underground" in 2007.[37] Maoists have also maintained secret contacts with political parties helping one political party over another during elections (Balagopal 2011).[38]

In general, concealed connections, by their very nature, tend to be more unethical and abusive than the semi-secret and open ones discussed here. Clandestine connections are shrouded in mystery, and there is no definitive knowledge about the agreements and exchanges they comprise. While the locals have an inkling of Type I clandestine connections, one or both sides implicated in the connection deny its existence. Much like clandestine connections, semi-secret connections are also shrouded in mystery. However, they are distinct from clandestine connections in that locals and sometimes also people outside the conflict zone are aware of them. The public does not know the exact terms of exchange or how enduring the ties are. An example of a semi-secret political network (Type II) between the state and insurgents can be drawn from the South. Sankaran, a senior bureaucrat in Andhra Pradesh known for his contributions to tribal welfare and for ending bonded labor and other caste indignities, was kidnapped by the Maoists (Peoples; War Group faction, known as PWG) in 1987 along with five other highest-ranking officers in the state government. He is known to have expressed his admiration for the young men and women who kidnapped him, whose methods he found unacceptable but whose analysis of inequality and poverty he found useful for its relevance to policymaking. He was particularly impressed by their profound knowledge of the various challenges to social welfare (the government department he headed) and by their passion and commitment to overcome obstacles to improving public welfare.[39] Referred to as the "peoples' IAS" and the "insurgent bureaucrat," Sankaran played an important role in abolishing bonded labor in Andhra Pradesh. After retirement from the Indian Administrative Service (IAS) in 2004, he was instrumental in organizing the only peace talks that have ever taken place between the rebels and the state (Kannabiran 2013; Sarma 2010).[40]

The most common examples of Type III concealed networks between civilians and the state are informers. In the North, the mining and coal mafia have similar Type III secret connections with the insurgency, which both sides have denied. The relationship is inherently corrupt, with the two sides colluding to extort, kidnap, and collect rent from the local population. Civilians in conflict zones can also have Type IV semi-secret relationships with insurgents. Examples include professionals who have either personally participated in or benefited from local Maoist campaigns or know someone personally who did. They are the people who may or may not have families and friends in the insurgency but believe that at least some of the insurgents' demands are legitimate. For example, there is a highly visible group of poets and writers in Telangana who have tirelessly written about the sufferings of common people in villages and small towns of Andhra Pradesh and their 'glorious struggle' against inequality and injustice over the last five decades, creating a strong current of public opinion favorable to the Maoists.[41]

After the Karamchedu massacre of Dalits in Andhra Pradesh in 1985,[42] the new Dalit leadership in the South was known to be sympathetic to the politics of the PW faction of the Maoists.[43] They referred to themselves as "Dalit communists" and called for a New Dalit Democratic Revolution, both as a continuation of the Maoist goal of New Democratic Revolution and as a challenge to its exclusive focus on class character (Balagopal 2000; Haragopal and Balagopal 1998). Further, in a clear attempt to win Maoist approval, they defined "Dalits" not just as untouchable castes but also as all people subjected to various forms of social, economic, and cultural discrimination. As hundreds of Dalit PWG cadres quit and joined the democratic Dalit movement led by the Dalit Mahasbha (DMS), the Maoists also felt compelled to debate the caste dimension of class analysis. The DMS conducted statewide roadblocks, silent marches, and strikes, and fought many legal battles seeking justice for the Karamchedu victims. Ultimately, however, they failed to hold the Karamchedu killers accountable.[44] Four years later, a PWG squad killed the Kamma landlord who had masterminded the massacre.[45]

During these years in the eighties and nineties, the Type IV semi-secret relations between the Maoist organizations in –Andhra Pradesh and other democratic actors were further strengthened in the DMS cultural platforms and journals, most notably *Nalupu* (literally meaning "The Black").[46] Later the public discourse around synthesizing caste/class analysis shifted to another journal called *Edureetha* (Swimming Against the Tide), launched by the former general secretary of the PWG who was also a well-known Dalit poet.[47] The profuse cross-pollination of Maoist movement ideology and mobilization techniques across the democracy-insurgency divide was repeated following the Chundur caste massacre in 1991 and continued through many other democratic movements up until the movement for separate Telangana in 2012–2013.

Sustained cross-pollination of ideas and mobilization strategies across the state-insurgency divide in the South created a robust gray zone that nurtured three-way state-insurgent-civilian networks (Type V) that are absent in the North. For example, journalists, activists, and academics are connected to the state via their professional and social networks, as well as to insurgent organizations via the organizations' horizontal outreach. An example of this kind of three-way open network between the state-society and insurgency came to fruition during the only peace talks between the state government of Andhra Pradesh and the insurgents in 2004. The Committee for Concerned Citizens (CCC), convened by Sankaran, the IAS officer who was kidnapped by the Maoists, also included well-known civil liberties lawyers, professors, and journalists in the South (Balagopal 2005; Gudavarthy 2005, 2013; Mander 2004). All members of the CCC, formed in 1997, were uniquely advantaged due to their connections to both the state and the insurgents developed during the past decade or so. The CCC was an attempt to put civilians, who bear the brunt of state violence against the Maoists and Maoist counter-violence at the center of all discussions (Sankaran 2002). The CCC also initiated a debate among political parties, trade unions, teachers' organizations, and other legal platforms, holding meetings to press for a dialogue between the state and insurgent representatives. The Maoists (PW) and the state government agreed to join the peace talks mediated by the CCC primarily because of the Type V networks among the interlocuters, which gave them the clout and credibility needed for mediating peace talks in a civil war. A series of letters between the CCC and the Maoists was published in the regional newspapers, especially in *Vaarta*, with many ordinary citizens sending in letters to the editors to participate in the ongoing discussions. The process went through many ups and downs, generating moments of hope and despair (Mander 2004). The peace process ultimately failed, but it strongly energized the gray zone. The robust gray zone in the South is not a sign of state failure or weakness. On the contrary, it deepened democracy by making it more deliberative and accountable.

Virtuous and Vicious Gray Zones

Based on this typology of various state-society-insurgency connections (Table 3.1) in the gray zone, there are two types of gray zones that can emerge in conflict zones. In the South, semi-secret and open relations of Types II, IV, and V dominated the state-insurgency interface, creating a robust gray zone where early instances of collaboration among democratic and Maoist mass organizations created opportunities for an open platform like the CCC to flourish. As the CCC openly communicated with both the state and the insurgency via open letters in popular vernacular newspapers, allowing ordinary people to chime in, it reinforced a virtuous cycle of open communication and multiple linkages across the state-insurgency divide. These linkages are perceived so positively in the South that everyone from elected politicians and newspaper editors to poets and homemakers do not deny them. Instead, they are keen to proclaim their direct or indirect connections to a banned insurgent organization.

The trajectory of the Maoist movement in the South, in particular its emphasis on mass mobilization, and the existence of Maoist groups that pursued armed struggle alongside electoral participation,[48] carved out this robust gray zone. The term "virtuous" draws a contrast with the violent and vicious gray zone that developed in the North, where earlier participation in Maoist mass struggles reinforced positive attitudes toward the movement in future generations. For example, the Go to Village campaign was a meticulously planned training program started by the Maoists in the 1970s. During their summer breaks, hundreds of students recruited by the Radical Students Union (RSU) from various urban campuses in Andhra Pradesh attended an intensive one-week political school before visiting pre-selected villages in groups of seven. The students spent about a month in the villages, stayed with the poorest landless families, and tried to disseminate propaganda among peasants on specific agrarian issues and the larger politics of agrarian revolution. They noted the names of potential activists among the peasants and passed those names to local party organizers who followed up with the peasants.

By 1980s, the PW recruited many of these rural youth into the Radical Youth League (RYL), which along with the urban youth organization (RSU) supplied the leadership of historic peasant struggles in Karimnagar and Adilabad. Six years after it started, the Go to Village campaign had sent 150 propaganda comprising 1,100 students to 2,419 villages. The student-youth teams also recruited thousands of coal workers for the first State Conference of the Coal Miners Union (Singareni Karmila Samakhya) (Balagopal 2006, 2011). Two decades later, many prominent members in the Joint Action Committee that led the movement for a separate Telangana, for example, started their political career in RSU or RYL before joining electoral politics. They see no reason to deny this background, a fact that demonstrates the open nature of the state-society-insurgency connections that characterize virtuous gray zones.[49]

In the North, on the other hand, Go to Village campaigns were scarce, and the MCC only claimed one in 1992.[50] If the clandestine ties (Type I and III) between the state and insurgency are predominant, as in the North, the gray zone of state-insurgency interface is steeped in violence, mistrust, and sabotage. Despite the secrecy around the exact terms of exchange between the mafia and the Maoists in the North, ordinary people in the conflict zone are well aware of the myriad outcomes of their ties such as bloody vendettas, kidnaps for ransom, and the routine extortion of small businesses. Reacting to Maoist challenges in their own feudal turfs, rural elites recruited various militias and massacred Dalit men, women and children en masse, spreading terror and displacing families from their villages. In direct retaliation, the Maoists in the North recruited violent, criminal elements to maintain their area domination and to protect their Dalit support base from systematic genocide. As a result, the civil liberty groups and various fraternal activist and professional organizations that germinated in the gray zone of state-insurgency interface became gradually sidelined and lifeless in the North. Their exodus made the local military commanders more powerful and dominant within the northern organization. This created a vicious cycle of further militarization of the conflict between the Maoist squads and the upper-caste militias, attracting more criminal, mafia, and violent elements to the Maoist organization. Certain Maoist factions, like CPI(ML)Liberation in Bihar, sought to interrupt the spiral of violence and deaths by joining electoral politics. Other factions like MCC and Party Unity started decade-long bloody turf wars in the North. Thus, on the one hand, the predominance of clandestine ties among state, insurgent, and societal agents made the gray zone in the North vicious, which affected the architecture of exit networks, processes, and outcomes of rebel retirement there. On the other hand, the dense network of semi-secret and open ties among state, societal, and insurgent agents produced a virtuous gray zone and high retirement in the South.

Informal Exit Networks

It is in the virtuous gray zone of the South that harmonic exit networks created conditions for Maoist rebels to retire and reintegrate. The primary actors in the harmonic exit networks in the South are the highly visible, geographically and socially mobile opinion makers who share the political preferences and normative commitments of the insurgents to a just egalitarian society, but they remain firmly ensconced in the democracy with all the rights of citizenship. In contrast, the primary actors in the discordant exit networks in the North belong to the police-bureaucrats-politician-mafia who dominate the gray zone.

I call them movement entrepreneurs (MEs). These MEs emerge from the long history of symbiotic relationships built through a range of semi-secret ties among the state, insurgency, and society. In the South, MEs have lived one foot in the state and one foot in insurgency, carving out an influential middle ground that has ties to and credibility with both the state and the insurgency.[51] On the one hand, MEs in the South exposed the myriad democratic deficiencies of the Indian state evident in its inability to fulfill citizens' demands for basic services and in its extrajudicial treat Maoist political prisoners in accordance with the law. On the other hand, they critiqued the unjust and unfair violence by the rebels, even if the rebels used it for revolutionary goals. In doing so consistently over several years, the MEs collectively constituted themselves into the overarching upper level of the two-level informal exit network. By becoming the most visible actors known for straddling the state-insurgency divide for many years, the MEs in the South incrementally strengthened deliberative democracy at the local level. As they critiqued both the state and the insurgency, they also kick started a pervasive bottom-up stimulus for discussions and debates among citizens on state-insurgency, which, in turn, consolidated an informed public opinion that wanted to hold both sides accountable.

It was through this process of deliberative democracy, the MEs in the South paved the way for peace talks; and some Maoist rebels, taking advantage of the ceasefire, visited their villages after years of separation from their families; the issue of rebel return became the focus of discussion in local sports clubs, women's groups, reading clubs, and professional organizations. My respondents in the South confirmed that their awareness of the issues around the Maoist insurgency and the Indian state evolved through the everyday, informal tête-à-têtes among the chattering masses in roadside eateries and chai shops in Telangana and from following the columns and discussions among the MEs in various media platforms. From among these local men and women in the South, emerged what I call the reintegration stewards (RSs). RSs constitute the lower level of the two-level informal exit networks and help resolve crucial, lastmile problems in the process of rebel retirement.

RSs emerge in the South from the local social base of the insurgency, and, unlike MEs, are geographically embedded. Employed in diverse occupations, these everyday people are also entwined by overlapping memberships in various grassroots organizations. They weave a bulwark of interests with all local stakeholders in rebel return through two mechanisms—trust and side payments. The RSs were reluctant to describe themselves as political/politicized actors. The only real grooming they received to grow into their roles as facilitators of rebel retirement was from their participation in the extensive societywide deliberations leading up to the 2004 peace talks, which not only received daily coverage in local print media but also penetrated their professional associations, college campuses and casual neighborhood conversations. They were shaped both by the euphoria leading to the peace talks and the collective disenchantment following its failure. Paradoxically enough, the failed peace talks generated the hope for peaceful transition of rebels into democracy in small towns and villages across southern conflict zone. It is paradoxical because the RSs did not indicate any amplified normative commitment to democracy over insurgency that set them apart from the rest of the local population. They share the same ambivalence toward democracy as the rest of them, exhibiting indifference or skepticism about public institutions and elected leaders. Their driving force, in their own interpretation, was personal attachment to returning rebels. They found themselves buoyed into these roles by friends and neighbors because they were liked and trusted as do-gooders, although never quite as charismatic and outlawed as Robin Hood. At the local level, where people know each other, the RSs rely on word of mouth to carry out their mission. They elicit verbal commitment from all local stakeholders in prospective rebel return that the returning rebels and their families will not be targeted for any kind of retributive violence. Side payments, orchestrated at the upper level by MEs, supplement this trust mechanism.

In the North, in contrast, the MEs are themselves entrenched in violent and corrupt networks of mafia-police-ministers-bureaucrats, tied to the state and the insurgency via Type I and Type III clandestine links. They have little social respectability to inspire or develop lasting networks with ordinary people in the villages. As a result, RSs, who constitute the lower level of informal exit networks, are virtually absent in the North, and, as a result, unlike their southern comrades, retired rebels in the North are afraid of returning to their villages. This fear discourages northern rebels from retiring at all.

The connection between RSs and MEs in the South is weak, measured by the amount of time, intimacy, and mutual confiding, or reciprocity the two groups share. The locally embedded RSs are everyday people in villages and small towns and, as such, are very different from the geographically mobile MEs, who are socially prominent opinion makers, often with name recognition. But the weak ties between RSs and MEs, as Granovetter's (1973) theory on the strength of weak ties argues, serve as bridges that nonetheless powerfully link them through shared endeavors. Although weak, the ties between RSs and MEs are crucial in the diffusion of ideas because, intuitively speaking, through these weak ties the idea of securing the safe return of rebels traverses a much greater social distance than it would through strong ties, which are . . . among socially and ideationally similar groups (Granovetter 1973). If the motivation is to spread an idea, which is, in this case, ensuring the safe return of retiring rebels, moving through strong ties will likely restrict it to a few cliques (because friends share strong ties). It is through weak ties that the idea diffused widely and the problem of credible commitment that deterred rebel retirement was resolved locally.

Conclusions

The most important implication of theorizing the gray zone is that people in conflict zones forge ties with both sides, and they live one foot in the insurgency and one foot in the state. Theorizing the gray zone shows that insurgent activities can co-occur with a well-functioning state and that sometimes conflict between the two can continue alongside their semi-secret cooperation. The primary policy implication of this argument is conceding that the relations between the insurgency and the state are not zero sum, which opens up space for conceiving counterinsurgency outside the dominant paradigm of a monopolistic state.

This chapter also creates an argument for harnessing the semi-secret and open ties that grow among civilians, insurgent and state actors in conflict zones for the purpose of rebel retirement. This chapter shows how these ties, straddling the state-insurgency divide in the South, in fact, strengthen the democratic state rather than weakening it. This book offers an alternative reading to the Andhra model popular in Indian policy circles, which argues that the Maoists lost control over Telangana because the specialized commando-trained police forces (Gray Hounds) hunted them down across state borders. However, the North, despite conscious attempts to raise similar counterinsurgency forces for at least two decades, could not produce similar outcomes. If policing was the primary determinant, why has the North not been able to replicate the southern success rate in securing Maoist surrender over the last two decades? I argue that the insurgency became weak in their strongest pockets of influence in the South because grassroots civic associations, some born out of Maoist militant mass mobilization on socially relevant issues, evolved from being just rebel frontal organizations into genuine independent voices. In the cross-pollination of issues and protest repertoire across the porous state-insurgency divide, MEs became the neutral voice of conscience of the people in a vigorous gray zone. Through their sustained activism since the seventies, the MEs kick started a public culture of deliberative democracy in the South that held both state and insurgent agents to the same standards of justice and human rights. While the southern MEs energized grassroots democracy that eventually nurtured RSs and the two-tier informal exit network, the northern MEs remained mired in crime and violence unable to foster local RSs. The next two chapters present deeper, path dependent analysis of how harmonic exit network flourished in the gray zones of the South but not in the North.

4

Rebel Retirement in the South through Harmonic Exit Networks

Out of the 10 districts comprising the Telangana region (a separate state since 2014), only two (Warangal and Khammam) accounted for two-thirds of rebel retirement in India between 2005 and 2014. Eight contiguous districts of Telangana are also among the worst affected by the Maoist insurgency. The Andhra model was invoked repeatedly during my interviews with state officials and politicians in New Delhi and in both conflict epicenters to explain high retirement in the South. However, neither development nor repression, the pillars of the Andhra model, varies enough between contiguous districts to explain the district-level variation in rebel retirement. A recent study on the Maoist insurgency in India shows that, controlling for state and year fixed effect, none of the four counterinsurgency policies (surrender and rehabilitation program; adoption of elite forces; offer of peace talks; and development) has a statistically significant relationship to the decline of state-level violence across all eight states of the Red Corridor. In fact, adoption of the surrender program and elite forces was found to be associated with an increase in violence.[1] The evidence of the impact of the development program on violence is also mixed; scholars have shown that the pacifying effects of National Rural Employment Guarantee Scheme (NREGS), for example, on the Maoist movement is concentrated only in districts with pre-existing local state capacity (Dasgupta, Gawande, and Kapur 2014).

Investigating this empirical puzzle of the spatial pattern in rebel retirement, both between the North and South, and between districts in each region, I suggest an alternative Andhra model, where vigorous grassroots civic associations in the gray zones of the state-insurgency interface host informal retirement networks that facilitate high retirement in Telangana. The harmonic exit networks in the South weave together multiple stakeholders, who work to build momentum for rebel exit and manage myriad uncertainties of reintegration.

Farewell to Arms. Rumela Sen, Oxford University Press (2021). © Oxford University Press.
DOI: 10.1093/oso/9780197529867.003.0004

At the same time as many rebels in the South were retiring, the total number of retired rebels in the North between 2005 and 2014 was almost 20 times less. Ideally, we would have the total numbers of rebels recruited in the two regions to compute the percentage of retired rebels. But in the absence of data on total insurgents recruited by region, we can only argue that Maoist strength, measured using the frequency of Maoist incidents or rebel casualties as a share of total casualties, is comparable in the two regions (Ghatak and Eynde 2017).[2] And in fact, the Indian government applauds the Andhra model specifically because they accept the underlying assumption that the Maoist movement equally affects both regions and yet the South has been more successful in suppressing it than the North.

Drawing on discussions in Chapters 2 and 3, this chapter briefly analyzes the background of the Maoist movement in the South, particularly with reference to the role of civic associations in the virtuous gray zone of the state-insurgency interface. It offers primary evidence of the various processes and negotiations in the process of rebel retirement drawn from the personal experiences of retiring rebels. Based on the rebels' account of the protracted process of retirement, it highlights, both empirically and theoretically, the two mechanisms of trust and side payments that resolve the problem of credible commitment locally.

Setting the Context

Telangana is different from the two other regions (Rayalaseema and Coastal Andhra) comprising the state of Andhra Pradesh in terms of colonial legacies, levels of economic development, land relations, soil fertility, agricultural practices and irrigation methods, literacy, and healthcare standards (Figure 4.1). In fact, when Andhra Pradesh was carved out of the Madras Presidency as a separate state for Telugu-speaking people in 1953 under the State Reorganization Act, Telangana, including the princely state of Hyderabad, remained out of it until 1956 (Rao 1988; Rao 1972; Regani 1972; Venkatarangaiah 1965).[3] Despite having a shared language (Telugu), the 10 districts of Telangana separated again from Rayalaseema and Coastal Andhra to become the 29th state of India in June 2014.[4] There are many accounts of the backwardness of Telangana compared to the two other regions of Andhra Pradesh (Kannabiran et al. 2010; Rao 2014; Rao 2011; Simhadri and Rao 1997). Among them, the Maoists have noted the difference in land

Figure 4.1 Three Regions of Telangana, Rayalaseema, and Coastal Andhra

relations, a legacy of indirect colonial rule in Telangana, and a larger population of Dalit (scheduled castes) and scheduled tribes as the most important factors in making Telangana their ideal recruiting grounds. However, the capital city of Hyderabad has one of the best connected road and bus systems in the country, and the rapid urbanization of the adjacent districts worsened inequality in the region.

The Moghilicherla village in Warangal, where I met retired rebel Raju Anna in 2013 and 2014, is a remote hamlet and was a hotbed of Maoist insurgency until about 2 years ago. Many young men and women from the village had joined the insurgency during the 1970s, 1980s, and 1990s. Some of them retired and returned to the villages. Others have not: They are either dead or missing, and, in some cases, family members hope they are deployed in the neighboring state of Chhattisgarh and will return some day.

When I visited, it was cotton-picking season and there were many small trucks (called *trekker*, a little bigger than a pickup truck) on the dirt road to the village. Each trekker was packed with about 50 women from neighboring areas who worked as seasonal cotton pickers. The *pucca* (partially paved) road led me to the village center, when I realized that four men, faces partially covered, had been following the trekker in two motorcycles. One of them approached my research assistant, who showed them my papers (an introduction letter from the chair of my dissertation committee and another from the director of CESS, Hyderabad where I was locally affiliated). They demanded to see my earlier work on Maoists as further validation of my status as an academic researcher on the topic. I tried to look it up on my smartphone, but I was informed that they had used jammers to block my cell phone signal to prevent outside communication. The men never spoke to me directly but instructed my research assistant to bring the name of my paper in writing, which I did, so that they could Google it themselves. They said that they were not from the police but described themselves as an "interested party." I never saw them again.

I met Raju Anna, a 40-something retired Maoist, at his house.[5] When he asked me about the trip, I mentioned that the South has remarkably smooth roads and a cheap, fast, reliable bus service. I have traveled to far-flung districts and villages in Andhra Pradesh on those roads, a feat quite impossible in my other fieldwork areas in Jharkhand and West Bengal. The roads are integral to the fabled Andhra model of counterinsurgency, often praised in New Delhi and elsewhere in India, for its judicious mix of policing and development that stifles insurgency.

A road sign on National Highway (NH) 7 in the Aanantpur district farther south, another Maoist hotbed in the recent past, reads: "Roads Indicate the Culture of the Nation."[6] To many these shiny pitch-black roads bear testimony to the state's newfound culture of modernization, urbanization, and relentless pursuit of an "India Shining," where radical agrarian uprisings are merely bad memories best forgotten.[7] In fact, a bureaucrat in New Delhi, who was once kidnapped by the Maoists when he was posted in the Malkangiri district at the Andhra-Odisha border, told me that he knew he had crossed the border to Andhra Pradesh when the roads drastically improved. He posited that the elaborate, well-maintained road network played a key role in overcoming the "remoteness" of rural Andhra, by encircling the Maoist hideouts, and, in effect, eradicating the insurgency.[8]

Raju Anna, the shy, soft-spoken former guerrilla, who never looked me in the eye, as a customary sign of respect in some parts of rural India, and addressed me as *didi* (meaning, sister), however, dismissed unequivocally that some shiny malls or extensive road building compelled Maoists in Andhra Pradesh to retreat and surrender. He described how roads and malls lull the urban middle class and politicians into a false sense of progress when ordinary people in villages simply bypass new black-topped roads to walk in diagonal paths reminiscent of older dirt roads. In fact, inequality figures are on the rise in Andhra Pradesh, and the average per capita consumption expenditure of the state has been in the same range as BIMARU (Bihar, Madhya Pradesh, Rajasthan, and Uttar Pradesh) states considered the poorest in India (Krishna 2006; Deaton and Dreze 2002; Krishna et al. 2004; Rao 2011).

Raju Anna noted that roads gave a speed boost to the police and paramilitary in the remote jungles where insurgents were hiding. But roads also took the element of surprise out of police movement and made them vulnerable to rebels' premeditated landmine and bomb attacks. During his 25-year insurgent career, Raju Anna rose through the ranks before he was transferred to the neighboring state of Chhattisgarh to militarily organize the incipient tribal uprisings there. He reminisced how he was trained ideologically and militarily to persist, improvise, retreat, and resurge.[9] Shiny roads, ruthless policing, new schools, or token land reforms do not persuade seasoned rebels like him and others, hardened by decades of battling hunger, disease, and torture, to quit. Raju Anna remembered the hunger, disease, torture, betrayal, and deaths he had witnessed and endured before he joined the Maoist ranks as a 15-year-old, following the death of his brother in the Giraipalli massacre.[10] During our many subsequent chats, Raju Anna repeatedly affirmed his unshakable faith in Marxist-Leninist-Mao Zedong (MLM) thought as the correct political path. And yet he quit.

At each of our meetings, Raju Anna shared goat-milk tea with me as he told his story of retiring from the Maoist movement. The process of retirement was streamlined within the insurgent organization in the South. Raju Anna informed his immediate supervisor first, who escalated it through party channels. He had long debates with his comrades who tried to persuade him to reconsider his decision. Finally, he was asked to put his motivations for quitting in writing. The organization formally approved his request and, in return, expected him to guard the secrets that could potentially jeopardize the safety of his comrades and the future of the organization.[11] Interestingly, archival research of newspaper reports of rebel retirement shows that an overwhelming majority in the South of India cited ill health as a reason for quitting; this rationale does not blame the insurgent organization in any way and is consequently benign enough for them to accept.[12] But I found the process of rebel retirement far more intriguing than the rationale for retiring (i.e., why rebels quit).

Credible Commitment Problem

I was curious to know more when Raju Anna mentioned that after he received party approval, it took him around 28 months to finally surrender to the police. Based on interview evidence, respondents need anywhere from two months to three years after receiving party approval to finally surrender arms, and rebels higher up in the organization typically needed more time than ordinary squad members. While deciding to surrender, Raju Anna's primary concern was that his former enemies would target him and his family as soon as he disarmed and returned to his village. Nothing in the government surrender policy package of a job, cash, land, and vocational training, even if it were actually implemented, could persuade him to take that risk. Life before livelihood, he said. This, I theorized as a problem of credible commitment: While Raju Anna could lose everything including his life if he surrendered, the Indian state would lose nothing if it did not keep its side of the bargain and failed to protect him. It took him three years to set up the informal exit network that compensated for the lack of credible commitment locally, assuring him of his personal safety after he disarmed. In course of the fieldwork, it became clear that concern for physical safety was the predominant concern for all the retiring rebels I interviewed, both in the North and the South.

Despite his usually mild-mannered way of making light of his very eventful insurgent career, Raju Anna conveyed the grave sense of danger he felt while making the decision to disarm. In the 1980s, he had burned the standing crops of the landlord in his village and demolished his *gaddi* (palace), paraded the landlord to village court, and declared that he deserved the death penalty for his "crimes against the people," including highly exploitative bonded labor, rape, usury, and murder. Everyone agreed, and the landlord was hanged to death from a giant old tree in the village square. The tree stands in the same spot today. The brothers and sons of the slain landlord have since fled to a nearby city, where they set up new businesses. They have also married into politically influential families, which made Raju Anna even more fearful of their capability for violent retribution. It is well-known that the high and mighty in rural India (and in many other conflict zones) can kill with impunity. Not avenging their patriarch's brutal murder and allowing the rebel responsible for it to return to the village without any consequence could be locally interpreted as cowardice, something returning rebels know too well.

Movement Entrepreneurs and Reintegration Stewards

Raju Anna highlighted in painful detail why it was difficult for him to make contacts with the outside.[13] In an attempt to defuse the looming threat to his personal safety and that of his family in the event of his disarmament and return to the mainstream, Raju Anna reached out to his brother first, who, in turn, spoke in strict confidence to a renowned civil liberty activist and a local journalist in a vernacular newspaper in Warangal. The basis for selecting these people was the length and depth of the brother's acquaintance with them. An overwhelming majority of other former rebels in the South also confirmed that the length of acquaintance and local name recognition or reputation was often used as criteria for selecting the first two confidantes in the process. These initial overtures were made cautiously and secretly, and more members of the community were progressively added to the network. Somewhat surprisingly to me, ethnic and kinship networks were not the basis of selecting the early exit network, a point I discuss later in the chapter. On behalf of Raju Anna, the first three members of his exit network—his brother, the local civil liberty activist, and the local journalist—began to reach out to their own personal networks of prominent personalities, including elected politicians, police, administrators, and other journalists and civil liberty activists.

In theorizing the process of retirement, I call these prominent personalities movement entrepreneurs (MEs), who have strong ties to the state, the insurgency, and local society. In the course of my meetings with other retired rebels, I realized that a handful of the same MEs were named as common interlocutors in many cases of retirement in the Warangal and Khammam districts where retirement is high.[14] MEs are well-known opinion makers, who share a normative commitment to social justice with the Maoists, but who also have deep ties with both the state and society. They regulate the flow of information and coordinate collective action in conflict zones. They maintain one foot in democracy and one foot in the banned resistance movement but claim autonomy from both. Through the leaky walls separating them, political actors in both state and insurgent camps are tied to the MEs. For example, a politician who was roped into play a vital role in the process of Raju Anna's retirement grew up in the same village and went to the same school, from elementary school through college, as the charismatic rebel leader.[15] People knew that they worked together on pressing issues of student politics in college, before parting ways, when one of them joined electoral politics and the other took up arms against democracy. In this way, the MEs make their careers out of their assumed equidistance to the state and insurgency, forming the upper level of two-level exit networks.

Another ME in Raju Anna's case was a civil liberty activist (contacted via the local activist who Raju Anna's brother reached out to) who was also a lawyer. On the one hand, he was known for defending the rights of political prisoners accused of joining or helping the insurgents in courts of law. He wrote op-eds in newspapers and journals, led fact-finding teams, and filed public interest litigations, while also sharing the same social space as top bureaucrats, journalists, and politicians; these people valued his analysis of grassroots socioeconomic ills and consulted him on aspects of policymaking. On the other hand, he also critiqued rebel excesses, particularly their treatment of suspected informers who betrayed the revolutionary cause. In doing so, he represented the influential middle ground or voice of conscience between the state and rebels.

The MEs destigmatized the process of rebel retirement in the South. It was not easy for Raju Anna to leave his comrades, the only family he had known in his adult life, behind. But he was more worried that his return would permanently brand him as a deserter, someone who quit his family for a revolutionary goal, and then quit his comrades before achieving that goal. The MEs created a strong social opinion in Telangana that rebels were also legitimate political actors representing the most marginalized sections of the population. In 2004, thousands of people queued up to meet the rebel leaders who came to the state capital of Hyderabad for peace talks. They came with letters asking for the rebel groups' attention to their problems like the lack of electricity, high debts incurred for a daughter's dowry payment, pending court cases, and so on. Raju Anna explained that the peace talks in 2004 gave legitimacy and respect to the Maoists in the public eye like never before. The Maoist leader Ramakrishna, also known as RK, already a legendary leader to the youth in Telangana, was given a hero's welcome wherever he went.[16]

After the peace talks failed, the momentum for peace generated by it endured, and discussions about ending the conflict and welcoming the rebels back to the villages continued in sports clubs, reading clubs, trade unions, student unions, and women's groups at the village level. These discussions became fertile grounds for the emergence of village-level leaders, often from among the youth and women, who became vocal advocates of creating safe conditions for the return of rebels. I recognized these advocates as reintegration stewards (RSs) for their role in nurturing and overseeing the process of rebel retirement, forming the second level of the two-tier exit networks. RSs emerge from the local social base of the insurgency, and, unlike the MEs, they are locally embedded. Employed in diverse occupations in district courts, coal mines, village administration, primary school education, political parties, local mafia, or rural health centers, these everyday people are also tied to each other and the MEs by shared membership in local chapters of various civil liberty and other organizations in Telangana.[17] Only 15% of the RSs, as reported by the interviewed former rebels, were women; and a total of 45% belonged to the lower castes including Dalit.

The MEs and the RSs together form a multilevel informal exit network that facilitates rebels' return, including for Raju Anna (Figure 4.2). In his case, these networks were made up of some people personally known to him and others not, who worked assiduously to ensure that scions of former Reddy landlords whom he had attacked during his insurgent career as part of the political program of the Peoples' War Group (PWG) did not assassinate him as soon as he disarmed. His brother, along with the local civil liberties activist and the journalist, constituted the first three RS who involved three MEs: a well-known civil liberties lawyer; a member of the legislative assembly (MLA) who was a former classmate of the top Maoist leader in the region; and a superintendent of police, whose brother joined the Maoists.

At the village level, Raju Anna's brother persuaded the local Dalit leader Sanjeeva (not his real name) to gather local families and the sister of the

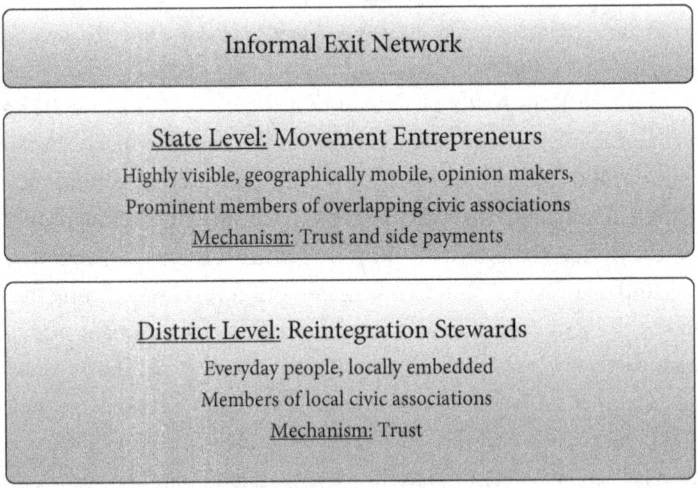

Figure 4.2 Two-level Harmonic Exit Network

landlord slain by Raju Anna to have long-drawn community dialogues highlighting the need for forgiveness. These meetings avoided the painful memories of gruesome deaths, police brutality, family's split apart by violence, and the destruction of standing crops in the 1980s and 1990s. In course of my conversation with him, Sanjeeva said that everyone understood the importance of the "practice of silence" by community members. To him, it was not denial of their past, but respect for the memories of the dead. Another RS in Warrangal, a woman in her late 40s, asked if there was anything to be gained by reopening old wounds, when the victims and the perpetrators have both suffered enough and are both eager to move beyond their brutal past. It was an ethical dilemma for this researcher to ask too many questions about the absence of truth and reconciliation recommended by international agencies as a necessary path to peace in postconflict societies. As community members agreed that they no longer wanted to regurgitate the losses and pains, almost as a protection/healing strategy, it eventually led to a consensus on the need to build peace locally through amnesty and reintegration of former rebels. For Raju Anna, Sanjeeva, assisted by a schoolteacher cum local civil liberty activist and Raju Anna's brother, emerged as the RS instrumental in driving these village-level discussions.

In these meetings, the RS and other villagers, particularly those who still had family members in the insurgency, impressed upon the landlord family that if Raju Anna or his family were harmed in hatred, anger, or retribution, it would create a reputation that would deter others from returning. The voluntary and sometimes spontaneous meetings often took place in the village library, built in the name of the well-known Dalit leader and primary architect of the Indian constitution, Dr. Ambedkar. The Dalit uprising in the village started with the Maoists but eventually found roots within democracy following the Karamchedu massacre and rise of Dalit Mahasabha in the 1980s (discussed in Chapter 3). Raju Anna, though not a Dalit himself, brought villagers belonging to different castes together around the local forgiveness project in hopes of facilitating more rebel retirement and reintegration. Interestingly enough, these horizontal trust and forgiveness networks evolved across caste divisions, with Reddy women commiserating with Dalit women, and young Dalit men taking leadership over upper-caste village heads. A consensus was built on the need to heal decades of loss, pain, and suffering afflicting these villages ravaged by inequality, exploitation, and then insurgency.

In the meantime, RSs met with some select villagers and representatives of the infuriated landlord family to discuss the importance of facilitating rebel return for the greater good of local peace, prosperity, and stability. The RS secured a verbal commitment from the family of the slayed landlord that she and her family would not seek retribution by harming Raju Anna or his family. In these villages, where everyone knows everyone else and expects to live together for the foreseeable future, trust is more of an "encapsulated interest" than a moral commitment. This trust, which facilitates local negotiations of rebel return, is restricted to the specific issue of rebel return and is locally embedded in the actors' intimate knowledge of one another's interests (Hardin 2001; Cook, Hardin, and Levi 2005).

The MEs ensured that the landlord family was also offered a very lucrative permit to run a gas station by an upcoming arterial highway. In other words, the RS, through trust, and the MEs, through side payments, ensured that Raju Anna would not be killed on his return. The connection between the RS and MEs is often weak, in terms of the amount of time spent together, intimacy or mutual confiding, and reciprocity. The locally embedded RSs are everyday people in villages and small towns, and, as such, are very unlike the geographically mobile MEs who are socially prominent opinion makers, often with name recognition. Although weak, the ties between RSs and MEs are crucial in the diffusion of ideas; through these weak ties the idea of securing safe return of rebels traverse much greater social distance than it would through strong ties among socially and ideationally similar groups or cliques (Granovetter 1977). This theory also provides a promising explanation of the process by which a behavior at the micro-level is linked to macro-level phenomena (Granovetter 1977). It was through weak ties that the idea diffused widely and the problem of credible commitment that deterred rebel retirement was resolved locally.

The primary incentive for both the MEs and RSs is social prestige and recognition as peacemakers that they highly value. The primary schoolteacher cum civil liberty activist, who acted as RS in Raju Anna's case, shared that he had little time for his own family and not a single day went by when he did not do something or the other for the community. He cited mediation in family or neighborhood disputes, transporting people to hospitals, prescribing medicines for minor ailments, planning festivals, and raising donations as some of the activities he led in the village. He added that he would feel anxious if a single day went by without anyone knocking on his door for advice or assistance.[18] Another RS mentioned that she may not be rich and famous, but her neighbors treated her with respect, and some day she might run for office in the village government.[19] However, they refused to describe themselves as activists, and admitted their general lack of interest in either Maoist politics or electoral politics.

The police, despite their knowledge of side payments and the semi-secret ties between the MEs and RSs on the one hand and the insurgents on the other hand, do not crack down on them or the rebels. They have significant career rewards tied up with their personal role in encouraging rebel retirement. The mechanism of reputation means that if the rebels knew or thought that the policy would kill them after retirement, the number of surrender cases would drastically fall, hurting the career-driven police and bureaucrats. Raju Anna and others were not as afraid of police retaliation even though they had attacked police stations and exchanged fire with them during their insurgent careers. I met one retired rebel after another who expressed incredulity when I asked if they were afraid that the police would kill them after disarmament. Politicians are also invested in encouraging as much rebel retirement as possible because there are high career dividends to being preferred interlocutors in rebel retirement both in electoral nomination and victory.

It took three years for Raju Anna to actually quit his 25-year rebel career and return to his village. He surrendered in Warangal at the height of CPI (Maoist) success in Andhra Pradesh in 2006. He was offered a monetary award of INR250,000 (about US$5,000) for his surrender, which he had to accept, as refusing would be considered a sign of continued allegiance to the party. However, he did not receive any land or vocational training as part of the surrender package. He decided to pursue agriculture along with his family who owned a cotton farm.

From multiple rounds of conversations with former rebels, the mechanisms of trust and side payments that made the informal exit network functional seemed most interesting to me. During subsequent interviews with police officers, it became clear that state surrender policies assumed that rebels would give up arms and accept the cash award in order to be considered officially "surrendered" and have the cases against them considered "closed." There was no policy response to the challenges of rebel integration. As I spoke to many other retired rebels in Andhra Pradesh, both men and women, from foot soldiers to central committee members, returning rebels reiterated the fear of reprisal from former landlords and moneylenders as the biggest deterrence from surrendering. Despite knowing this, policymakers have not been able to put in place intentional safety nets safeguarding the lives of retiring rebels. Under such circumstances, the following paragraphs further illustrate how trust and side payments compensated for these institutional deficits in the South but not in the North.

Trust and Side Payments

In the earlier discussion, three questions remain unanswered: First, in a place where social norms expect a son to avenge his father's death by killing the insurgent responsible for it are strong, how is trust generated and solidified? Given the long history of caste and class animosity, how do ordinary people in the villages trust the enemy—the representatives of landlord and/or moneylending families? The norm of reciprocity and trust are often weakened in conflict zones. Why was Telangana an exception? Second, how are the social inequalities of caste and gender reflected in informal exit networks? Are RSs recruited from higher castes? Do RSs mobilize depending on kinship ties—that is, Dalit RS for a Dalit retiring rebel, backward-caste RS for a backward-caste rebel, and so on? Do the informal networks challenge the social inequalities by putting a Dalit or a woman in a leading role, or do they merely reinforce social hierarchies? Third, how do we understand the role of side payments arranged by the MEs in the process of rebel retirement? From the experience of Raju Anna recounted here, which is representative of the general experience of other retired rebels I spoke to in the South, the process of retirement through the exit network hinges crucially on side payments. In one instance, a landlord family was offered a license to a gas station near an upcoming highway. In another case, a political party agreed to offer a party ticket to a family member of a killed landlord. If the MEs, tied by a range of open and semi-secret ties to the state and insurgent camps, did not facilitate these side payments, the informal exit networks might have faltered.

In answering the first question, it is important to reiterate that the exit networks in the South are harmonic due to the prosocial cooperation between RSs and MEs, which allows them to collaborate toward the pursuit of the common goal of grassroots peacebuilding. This prosocial behavior would be impossible if the MEs were not connected to each other and to the RSs via membership in various overlapping civic associations. A positive experience of prior collaboration creates a track record of reciprocity, which acts as the crucial building block of their synchronous cooperation in the exit network. The vigorous associational life in the South nurtures these norms of reciprocity. In addition, civic associations provide the physical space for RSs to meet and discuss the issue of rebel retirement even if it is outside the mandate of a library, a women's group, or a trade union. Without this formal social capital encouraging and pushing the deliberations forward, the quotidian interactions among neighbors in the marketplace, for example, or among parents outside a primary school would not be able to erect the informal exit networks that secure rebel retirement.

The long history of a symbiotic relationship between democratic movements and insurgent grassroots mobilization, as illustrated by the Dalit upsurge and the strong civil liberties movement through the 1980s and 1990s, for example, carved out the expansive gray zone where the civic associations that bring MEs and RSs together flourish. These civic associations are of two broad kinds—those born out of the Maoist mobilization and later evolving into a balanced critique of both the insurgents and the state (like the civil liberties movement and human rights organizations) as well as those born in the democracy and later co-opting many Maoist cadres into the democratic struggle (such as the Dalit upsurge in Andhra Pradesh).

The vigorous exchange between the overlapping memberships of these two kinds of civic associations created conditions in the South for the MEs emerging from them to live one foot in democracy and one foot in the insurgency. Their examples destigmatized such dual existence in the South. This creates an environment conducive to the appearance of RSs, who play a vital role in building a bulwark of trust locally. Many people openly claim their Maoist pasts and their associations with the Maoist movement in various capacities without fear of social sanction or legal repercussions. In their local settings, the RSs persuade members of landlord and/or moneylending families who oppose the return of rebels to sacrifice their personal vendetta for the greater good of the community. Not surprisingly family members of other insurgents joined the deliberations with RSs in hopes that their husband or daughter might return one day if they were able to build the reputation that retired rebels will be kept safe and respected in their communities.

The RSs achieve this objective through what I call the mechanism of trust. In a place where everyone knows everyone else, sometimes for two generations or more, the ritual of public affirmation by representatives of a landlord family carried enough weight for others to trust it. A representative of the aggrieved family, sometimes the widow of a slain landlord and sometimes a son or brother, came to the local community gathering of RSs and other stakeholders to affirm that they would not start a blood feud in the village. But the RS admitted that they could not have convinced the landlord families on their own if they were not backed by MEs who employed side payments to enlist their cooperation.

The RSs are active citizens who not only vote in various elections within the democracy but also exhibit other behaviors, including paying membership dues to professional and social associations, participating in street protests, attending political party rallies, and so on, in addition to being respected in their day jobs. Their reputation of public service, personal morality, and connection to MEs, the RSs act as the middle ground between two antagonist camps. And in turn, they earn additional social respect (instead of social sanction) for their roles in rebel retirement, which many confessed were their most valued possession. Thus civic associations create the conditions for the emergence of RSs as local interlocutors, build their reputation for leadership, and establish the first basis of public trust in RSs.

This discussion contributes to our understanding of the social legacies of conflict. What does a violent civil conflict do to the mutual trust in communities, particularly among antagonistic parties, in this case between landlords and the landless or land poor? Based on insights drawn from the post-traumatic growth literature (Tedeschi and Calhoun 2004), a conjoint survey experiment has shown that communities with high exposure to violence during the Liberian civil war were less biased against outgroup refugees (Hartman and Morse 2015). Conflict exposure, in fact, created higher potential for empathy-driven altruism among antagonistic groups in conflict locations. Scholars have argued that this is because when individuals experience hardship and trauma, their capacity to empathize with others increases, especially for those in need or suffering from similar afflictions. Empathetic concern transcends identity boundaries (Batson et al. 2016), and thereby motivates altruistic behavior toward both in-group and out-group others. Thus the mechanism of mutual trust, which sustains the harmonic exit networks in Telangana, is not much of an exception. However, the literature on post-traumatic growth does not fully explain how variation in the nature of conflict could create variation in the trust outcome. In the North, for example, as the conflict evolved differently, intra-community trust gradually depleted.

Interestingly enough, the trust is not built along pre-existing caste and kinship ties. Although the harmonic exit networks in the South are not entirely immune to local cultural norms and social hierarchies, they are rooted more in shared expectations than in shared cultural values (Tsai 2007). Unlike primordial institutions that tend to be too entrenched to accept incremental change, informal exit networks are more adaptive. Often the socially marginalized lowest castes in the villages play key roles as RSs, even when the retiring rebel is not their caste brethren. For example, Raju Anna, not a Dalit himself, recruited the help of a local Dalit journalist as one of his RSs. I have met and spoken with women RSs, who had first risen to prominence via their participation in the anti-Arrack (liquor) movement in the early 1990s. For example, an RS in Warangal, once beaten by her husband who spent his entire daily wage on liquor consumption, shared how she struggled helplessly to feed her children and buy necessary medicines. She found the anti-Arrack mobilization by the Maoist Peoples' War Group in the early 1990s a god-sent opportunity, participating in the movement not for the sake of ambition but for sheer survival needs. In the movement she discovered her courage to speak out and make demands in the face of rich, upper-caste men, which, to her, was a revolution in itself. Being part of a prior social movement gave her the name and reputation to act as the spokesperson for other women of higher castes, who wanted their husbands and daughters to be able to return to the village safely. As one of the RSs, she was able to overcome the subservient position associated with her Dalit caste and gender identity.

However, associational connections do not automatically explain why ordinary people or even the RS would trust the scions of rich, upper-caste landlords and vice versa when their relationship is fraught with violent confrontation and painful memories of loss inflicted on each other. Social norms of prosocial behavior and reciprocity serve as strong motivators of altruistic behavior within communities (Ostrom 2000) but may not operate as strongly outside the immediate community. How do the RSs convince the landlords? How do they elicit a verbal commitment from family members of slain landlords that they will not attack returning rebels? How is the landlord's word of mouth accepted by people who have learned to not trust the landed upper caste? The various RSs that I met readily admitted that they could not have persuaded the enraged landlord family all by themselves if the MEs also did not arrange for side payments to ensure that the returning rebels and their families were not targeted for retributive violence. Unwritten socially shared norms of trust that are created, communicated, and enforced outside of officially sanctioned channels of the state, could not coalesce to form informal exit networks that reduce the transaction costs of rebel retirement without side payments (Coase 1960).[20]

Theoretically, side payments play an important role when collective decisions are hard to reach because any party can veto the project as soon as it is not beneficial to that party. For example, there was a concern, among the MEs and RSs and in Raju Anna's mind as well, that the landlord family might still kill him even after committing to not do so. With the side payment of a lucrative gas station arranged, however, Raju Anna felt more secure in his decision to return. The side payment ensured that the winners of a collective project (Raju Anna, MEs, and RS) can compensate the losers (landlord family), such that they all benefit by implementing it.

Social desirability bias came in the way of my interviewees' willingness to elaborate on the nature of side payments. But they readily recognized that the side payments increased the likelihood of cooperation particularly when the uncertainty was large. My respondents, from the state and insurgency, did not view it as corruption, which is not unusual in the light of the research on cross-cultural studies on corruption (Hooker 2009). Even for international negotiations, linking one type of agreement with another facilitates side payments (Harstad 2007, 2008). Linking issues together in package deals can open the door to agreement by ensuring that there are prizes for everybody, and side payments are needed to reach the best result (Ruis and de Zeeuw 2010).[21] Side payments do raise ethical questions when they create conflicts of interest or provide incentives to break the rules, in the form of kickbacks, bribes, or commissions. But side payments can take many forms, some perfectly legitimate when it is offered in a multiparty agreement where some have much more to gain than others. In the informal exit networks that facilitate rebel retirement, side payments act as humanly devised constraints on individuals and organizations in pursuit of their distinct goals and bind them to the norms of prosocial behavior.

Conclusion

Harmonic exit networks in the South grew upon the seamless collaboration of various democratic and extra-democratic actors in the gray zone of the state-insurgency interface. Legal civic associations that have sprouted out of or existed symbiotically with Maoist politics invigorate this collaboration. Paradoxical as it may sound, the roots of prosocial behavior among MEs and RSs that grease the harmonic exit networks lie in the dense network of grassroots civic associations, many of which are created by the insurgency. Some of these legal associations are born out of the need to protect the Maoists from illegal excess of the democratic state (such as civil liberties associations). Others are Maoist fronts, furthering their agenda of radical redistribution within democracy (including cultural organizations, student associations, and trade unions). Still others are of democratic origin, but their eventual rise is embedded in their ability to co-opt Maoist cadres in their democratic platform (Dalit Maha Sabha, for example). There are also some that are formed within democracy but need semi-secret ties with both insurgent and state organizations to fulfill their organizational goals (for example, the ABMS discussed in Chapter 3).

The overlapping membership of various civic associations creates a virtuous gray zone where many actors and organizations live one foot in the democracy and one foot in the insurgency. Over the years, the gray zone has become more sprawling and all-encompassing in the South, as Maoists, despite rejecting electoral politics, started meddling in the electoral process by influencing election outcomes one way or the other. As highlighted in Chapter 3, insurgent leaders also have taken a public stand on significant issues in local politics, and their approval of or opposition to issues like the separate Telangana movement, commercialization of education, or retirement age of non-gazetted officers, for example, had considerable impact on the final outcome. In other words, the extra-democratic political clout of Maoists always played an important role in setting preferences and determining outcomes within democratic politics in Telangana. Successive generations of politicians in the South across all local and national parties are known to have courted the Maoists for support in their electoral battles.

Through rich, empirical evidence gathered from intimate conversations with retired rebels and other stakeholders in the process of rebel retirement, this chapter establishes that personal safety and not economic prospects is the chief determining factor for rebels to disarm and demobilize. However, since there is no institutional mechanism in the surrender and rehabilitation process that guarantees rebels personal safety post-retirement, rebels may not be able to retire even when that is what they want. The fear of getting killed becomes particularly troublesome to rebels considering retirement because they believe that the state would not lose anything if they were killed. This chapter presented novel and granular evidence of how the harmonic exit network brings together MEs and RSs who, through trust and side payments, resolve this credible commitment problem impeding rebel retirement.

5

Rebel Retirement in the North through Discordant Exit Networks

There are three pockets of Maoist influence in Jharkhand: (a) northern Jharkhand districts of Chhatra, Palamu, Latehar, and Gumla, contiguous with the traditional Maoist strongholds in the Gaya, Aurangabad, and Jehanabad districts of Bihar; (b) eastern industrial districts of Bokaro, Dhandad, Jamtara, Dumka, Deoghar, and Giridih, contiguous with the Maoist-dominated Jangalmahal area of West Bengal; and (c) southwestern districts of West Singhbhum and Simdega, contiguous with the Maoist-affected districts of neighboring Odisha (Bandyopadhyay 2006; Misra 1987; Jaoul 2011; Frankel 1989; Sahay 2008). The Maoist Communist Center (MCC) dominated northern and southern Jharkhand, and Party Unity (PU) dominated eastern Jharkhand. Since 2007, 10 out of the 24 districts in Jharkhand have been among the 33 districts across India worst affected by the Maoist insurgency. Yet rebel retirement in Jharkhand is not evenly distributed among these three pockets of Maoist influence. Instead, it is concentrated mostly around the state capital of Ranchi and the neighboring Khunti district. Moreover, the total number of rebel surrender cases in Jharkhand between 2005 and 2014 is less than one-tenth that in the southern state of Andhra Pradesh.

In addition, the predominant post-retirement career choice of rebels in the North is electoral politics. Former Maoist area commanders in the North, with substantial control over a particular territory, become candidates for various political parties in the same electoral constituency. They hop from one party to another to secure nominations for national, state, or local elections from the same constituency. This is because their influence on voters, based on their fearsome guerrilla past or their reputation as generous outlaws, can only be leveraged locally. Other former combatants below the rank of area commanders, without enough independent clout to influence electoral outcomes, often find post-retirement employment as illegal enforcers in organized crime. Still others run tea stalls or grocery shops on the side, often

Farewell to Arms. Rumela Sen, Oxford University Press (2021). © Oxford University Press.
DOI: 10.1093/oso/9780197529867.003.0005

as façade hiding their illegal sources of income through extortion and rack-eteering. Despite some variation in what former rebels do in the North, most of them live off their ability to invoke fear in the minds of people, while they also live in fear themselves. Post-retirement career trajectory in the North is thus steeped in lawlessness, which is in sharp contrast to that in the South, where former rebels reintegrate, in both rural and urban areas, into variety of lawful roles from farmers, bus drivers, and homemakers to journalists, insur-ance agents, and professors. The Maoist Party in the North has often circu-lated death warrants against deserters. There are also at least five breakaway Maoist factions that function as deadly gangs hunting down former Maoists in the name of turf wars, personal vendettas, or at the bidding of others, while the state turns a blind eye to their extortion and kidnapping activities.[1] Many retired rebels have been brutally killed by their former comrades, police, or by the coal, timber, and mining mafia (Roy 2000a).[2] As a result retired rebels in the North have raised their own bodyguard armies to protect themselves from potential attackers.

Given the battles of area domination among these splinter groups in var-ious parts of Jharkhand, rebels cannot risk going back to their villages post-retirement. The local warlords of various splinter groups run their areas fiefdoms, prohibiting the return of retired rebels that might disrupt the local balance of power. The exit networks in the North, although steeped in crimi-nality and violence, are locally embedded and have no influence on multiple rogue gangs. It is because of the constantly shifting landscape of warlordism that the exit networks in the North have no local reintegration stewards (RSs) who can locally negotiate the safe return of former rebels to their own villages. Moreover, every surrender incident in Jharkhand since 2005 happened after the rebels were already apprehended and out in jail. While in the jail, they were subsequently persuaded to take a surrender package (money and other incentives) in return for their public disavowal of the Maoist party and sur-render of arms.

The history of competing mobilization of caste and class identities in Jharkhand shaped state-insurgency linkages in this conflict zone, which eventually influenced the type of informal exit network and post-retirement career choices of rebels as well. This chapter presents a brief context of the various political movements that shaped the trajectory of Maoist mobili-zation in the region. It shows how a popular tribal identity movement, an urban trade union movement, and the rural Maoist movement appealed to the same demography and alternately competed and collaborated with each other. The "silent revolution" in North India, heralded by an unprecedented mobilization of lower caste groups and their subsequent rise to power in 're- gional political parties, also impeded Maoist recruitment. The Dalits and backward castes, who once made up the rank and file of the Maoist party in the North, were now attracted to the democratic political space that opened up for them.[3] Multiple axes of polarization activated crosscutting caste and class cleavages, which disrupted Maoist organizational cohesion and limited their ability to form strong horizontal ties in the region. In the backdrop of these contextual factors, this chapter also presents the rebels' perspective on the challenges and opportunities they experienced in the process of retire- ment in the North of India. It highlights how the emaciated discordant exit network in the North, concentrated mostly in the capital city of Ranchi, was inadequate to alleviate retiring rebels' fear of being killed. These networks re- strict retired rebels to the same mafia-police-politician-bureaucrat network that they assisted during their insurgent days, which severely restricts the scope of their reintegration.

Setting the Context

In November 2000, the southern part of the state of Bihar was carved out to create the 28th state of India, named Jharkhand, with its capital in Ranchi (Figure 5.1).[4]

Jharkhand shares a boundary with West Bengal (to the east), Chhattisgarh (to the west), Bihar (to the north), Uttar Pradesh (to the northwest), and Odisha (to the south). Even before formal recognition of the south of Bihar as a separate tribal state (Figure 5.2), the region was recognized as distinct from North Bihar and Central Bihar.

Jharkhand, like its parent state of Bihar, is one of the poorest states in India (Ahluwalia 2002, 2013). The economy of Jharkhand is concentrated in its eastern districts, in the key urban areas of Jamshedpur (Tata Steel and Tata Motor plants), Bokaro (thermal and steel plants), Dhanbad (coal mining), and Ghatsila (copper mining). The state is known for its rich min- eral deposits of coal (32% of national deposits), iron-ore (30% of national deposits), copper (25% of national deposits), uranium, mica, and bauxite, among others. Yet Bihar was the only state in India to see per capita income decline in the 1990s. Even in the 1990s, agriculture remained stagnant in the undivided Bihar. Seventy-five percent of the population in Jharkhand

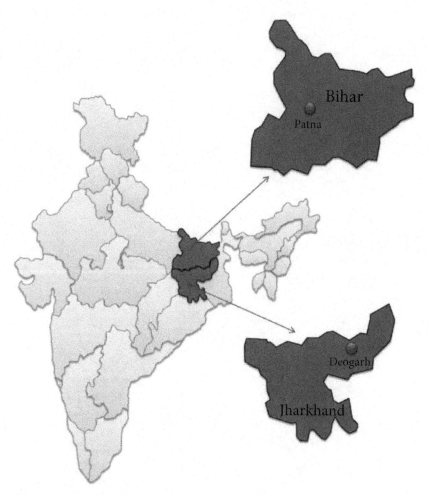

Figure 5.1 Jharkhand Was Created from South Bihar

depended on agriculture as its primary means of livelihood, although agriculture contributed only about 20% of the state's GDP (Datt and Ravallion 1998; Ravallion and Datt 2002). In spite of the rich soil, abundance of easily accessible water, and a rich peasant tradition, this stagnation has been ascribed to several factors, including the state's colonial legacy (Banerjee 2004; Banerjee and Iyer 2005; Bharadwaj 1991, 1993; Mearns and Sinha 1999), ecological conditions (Ballabh and Pandey 1999), demographic pressure,[5] and, most importantly, the land tenure system and the agrarian structure it supports (Ballabh and Pandey 1999; Henningham 1979; Kishore 2004;

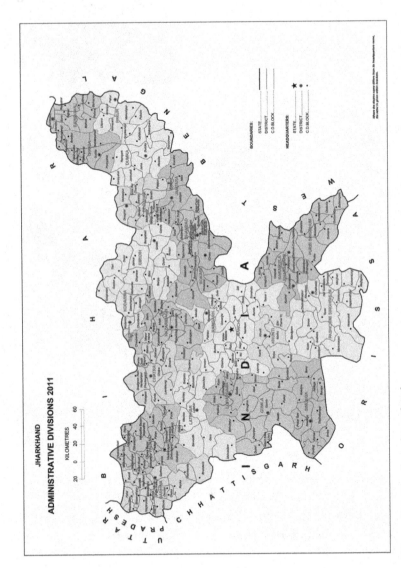

Figure 5.2 North and South Bihar

Richards, Hagen, and Haynes 1985; Sharma 2005). These factors are believed to have impeded the transition of Bihar's agriculture from a semi-feudal to a capitalist production system—an essential condition for agricultural growth (Patnaik 1987; Wilson 1999). At the time of the bifurcation of Bihar in 2000, the state's per capita agricultural income was about half of India's national average and about one-fifth that of the state of Punjab. By 1990, Bihar had the highest population share below the poverty line of any state (Sachs, Varshney, and Bajpai 2000; Thakur 2002). Bihar also had India's lowest state literacy rate, with only 47% of its population able to read and write in 2001 (Bandyopadhyay 2009). Thus Jharkhand started its career as a state on a very weak macroeconomic foundation.

Inequitable land distribution and perverse land tenure system were the primary reasons for the backwardness of Bihar, characterized as "semi-feudal" in Maoist literature. Comprehensive land reform not only requires abolition of landlords (locally known as *zamindari*) but also necessitates redistribution of surplus land, tenancy reforms, and land consolidation, all of which failed in Bihar. In fact, among all Indian states, land reforms have failed to the greatest extent in Bihar, even though it was the first state to formally abolish the *zamindari* system in 1953. While neighboring states like West Bengal (tenancy reforms) and Uttar Pradesh (land consolidation) pushed land reform forward, both of these projects were abysmally unsuccessful in Bihar (Haque and Parthasarathy 1992; Ojha 1976; Rogaly, Harriss-White, and Bose 1999).

The big landlords of Bihar derailed land reform via delaying tactics and by refusing to comply with paperwork. They refused to submit documents for their estates despite government orders and filed thousands of court cases halting the landholding ceiling and redistribution of over 9,000 acres of land across the state of Bihar. Since administrators and politicians came mostly from the same landed gentry upper castes as the landlords, the landlords exploited their kinship ties to have government field surveys halted, amended, and ultimately aborted. When the Abolition Act of 1952 was amended to permit the landlords to keep their homestead land and some additional land for trade, handicrafts, and storage purposes, the landed gentry of Bihar quickly divided the land among family members to keep their individual landholding under the ceiling in government records (Blair 1980; Dhar 1990).[6] The Bandopadhyaya Commission of Land Reform admitted that the "iniquitous, inegalitarian and exploitative agrarian asset" has been at the heart of rural violence in Bihar.[7] Changing the structure of landownership proved difficult in the North because the *zamindari* system was highly in-stitutionalized and the dominant groups were strongly entrenched in the state machinery. The land consolidation department, politically and admin-istratively deadlocked, was finally abolished in Bihar, keeping land reform unfinished.

Poor performance of rural credit schemes, de-electrification, unremu-nerative prices of agricultural products, an unreliable power supply, caste atrocities, hunger and persistent land inequality produced the deadly circle of miseries that made various parts of Bihar particularly responsive to Maoist mobilization. Faced with similar problems of inequality and infrastructure, peasant movements in western Uttar Pradesh, Punjab, Haryana, Gujarat, and Maharashtra have rallied for free electricity. They have organized within the democracy to demand that the state government write off farm loans. Through peaceful mobilization, these peasants in other Indian states have historically extracted concessions from the state. But such cross-class peasant mobilization has been absent in Bihar.

Retired Maoist Kameshwar Baitha (MN1), who represented the Palamu constituency of Jharkhand in the Indian parliament between 2009 and 2014, shared his personal experience that corroborated this analysis. Baitha rose to the position of an area commander of the Koel-Shakh zone (Palamu, Latehar, Garhwa, Gumla, Lohardaga, and Simdega districts) dominated by the PU faction of northern Maoists. He reminisced how a few club-wielding private enforcers of the local landlord flogged a close family member in the early 1970s. The man was nearly beaten to death simply because he was absent-mindedly lying down while a member of an upper-caste landlord family was passing by. Baitha poignantly pointed out that this man, then in his 30s, did not stay plopped on his handmade rope bed (called *khatiya*) as a deliberate act of silent protest against the caste system or feudalism. A bonded labor (locally known as *begar mazoorf*) on the same landlord's farm, he was merely exhausted and asleep. Baitha also shared stories of Dalit women in his neigh-borhood, who were not only forced to work without any remuneration in the name of ancient caste obligations but also subjected to routine sexual vi-olence. His motivation to join the Maoists were simple: He saw his parents work hard from dawn till dusk every day, rain or shine. Yet they never had enough to feed their children. There was nothing for him in the system. The only choice available to him as an young adult, in his words, was between dying while trying to dismantle the system or dying of starvation, disease, and humiliation.

But while the Maoist mobilization in the deeply feudal setting of the North gained popularity through the 1970s and the 1980s, it had to constantly negotiate and renegotiate its relationship with two other popular movements in region: an ongoing tribal agitation and a trade union movement in the industrial areas of southeast Bihar. The Maoists appealed primarily to the lower caste rural agrarian workers against the upper caste landed aristocracy. The trade union appealed to the urban working class against the factory and mine owners. The tribal identity movement was a separatist movement that demanded protection of the indigenous population from the migrating non-tribal outsiders in a separate tribal state. This three-way competition for popular support among the Maoists, the tribal separatists and the trade unions activated multiple cross cutting cleavages, which sometimes undercut and at other times reinforced each other. For example, the communist trade union movement collaborated actively with the tribal separatist movement for a long time despite conflicting mobilization strategy and common target audience. The trade unions wanted to unite both tribal and migrant workers, while the tribal separatist movement cast the migrant workers as corrupt agents of exploitation living off natural resources that rightfully belonged to the tribal population. However, both the trade unions and the tribal movement had a common enemy in the migrant capitalists who owned and managed the factories and mines in the region.

The Jharkhand separatist movement descended from a long line of popular tribal revolts against non-tribal migrants (referred to as *diku*) that goes back to the nineteenth century (Roy 2000b; Munda and Mullick 2003).[8] Originally *diku* referred to the non-tribal landed upper castes and their employees. In post-independence India, *diku* was used to refer to "the people of North Bihar," "those who came from the other side of the river," and "those who earn their living here and send their earnings to their own homes in Bihar" (Sengupta 1980). A central claim of the tribal movement, going back to the Chotanagpur Adivasi Mahasabha,[9] and continuing today, is that the indigenous tribal inhabitants continued to live in extreme destitution despite having rich forest resources and mineral reserves because they were robbed and deceived by non-tribal migrants. The newly independent Indian state, committed to modernism and heavy industrialization, worsened the situation by facilitating a heavy influx of skilled and low-skilled labor to work in government offices and new factories founded in the region (Corbridge and Harriss 2000). Moreover, massive construction projects of dams and roads also displaced a large number of tribal people. Through its long history of tribal mobilization, the Jharkhand movement blamed the Indian state for converting tribal land to an "internal colony" (Jones 1978, p. 9) caught between the prevailing feudal agrarian system in villages and an exploitative industrialization in urban areas (Rothermund, Kropp, and Dienemann 1980; Rothermund and Wadhwa 1978). The Jharkhand Party, formed out of the Mahasabha, swept all tribal constituencies (32 in total) in Bihar in the 1952 elections, establishing tribal agitation as a prime player in democratic politics of the region.

By the 1970s, as the communists identified the Jharkhand region as a fertile ground for organizing workers in mines and factories , they wanted to craft a new brand of radical ethno-regionalism that would not fracture the proletariat along ethnic (tribal vs. non-tribal) lines. Instead, they wanted to unite both tribal and migrant workers against rich factory and mine owners, while also recognizing that these rich capitalists were also non-tribal outsiders. Jharkhand was reconceptualized as *Laal khand* (meaning red land), which stood for a socialist society aligned with the inherently just and egalitarian values of a tribal society. The communists highlighted that both the tribal and non-tribal poor suffered due to poor working conditions and exploitative wages inflicted on them by landlords and factory owners. They raised new slogans of "*Maro Mahajan, Maro Daroga*" (meaning, attack the moneylenders and the police) and "*Fasal Zapt,ZzaminZzapt*" (seize the crop, seize your land), which reframed rich outsiders as the enemy and recast tribal politics in communist terms.

However, the urban trade union leaders did not see eye to eye with the Maoists primarily due to longstanding disagreements on the role of violent methods in the blueprint for socialist revolution.[10] The Jharkhand movement, however, collaborated with both communist traditions. On the one hand, Shibu Shoren, the charismatic leader of Jharkhand Mukti Morcha (JMM, or Morcha) since the 1970s, was handpicked and trained by A. K. Roy, the leader of the Dhanbad trade union movement. On the other hand, Vinod Mahato, another leader of the Jharkhand movement (also known as Morcha locally), who represented the inclusion of Mahatos (non-tribal lower castes called *Moolvasis*) into the movement, was close to the MCC faction of the Maoists as well as to Roy (Banerjee 2003). As for their support base, many rural youth freely swapped the green Jharkhand flag for the red MCC flag depending on context and convenience, giving rise to the local saying mentioned to me in jest by the police during my fieldwork in the North: "Morcha by day, MCC by night." In this environment where three different political platforms targeted the same demographic, the competing mobilization of caste and class identities activated crosscutting cleavages that eventually fractured Maoist organizational cohesion and hindered their project of area domination. As a result the Maoist organization in the North, discussed in Chapters 2 and 3, could not develop strong horizontal ties with Movement Entrepreneurs, which, in turn, constrained the exit network in the region to a criminalized nexus of state and nonstate agents without local popular anchoring.

The Rebel's Perspective

The story of Ranjan Yadav (MN2), a former Maoist commander turned politician in the North, is instructive in highlighting how crosscutting cleavages affect the Maoist organization as well as the retirement process in the region. I met him for the first time in October 2013 in the premises of the Jharkhand Legislative Assembly in Ranchi.[11] I shadowed him as he met politicians, primarily from the Rashtriya Janata Dal (RJD), to try to clinch a nomination in the 2014 election. I spoke to him for a total of 15–30 minutes a day. In addition, I had two long, open-ended follow-up conversations with him, each of which lasted for over three hours. I learned later that he was not able to secure an RJD nomination; instead he ran in 2014 election on Samajwadi Party ticket. In In his 5 years career in electoral politics, he had switched his allegiance between four political parties across the left–right ideological spectrum. Among all the former rebels I met in Jharkhand, Yadav was the most articulate and willing to talk. He described how he was arrested in Ranchi in 2006 when he was sneaking into the city to visit his family. However, a few local journalists and activists suggested that he got himself arrested deliberately because he was ready to quit the Maoist Party. Yadav did not confirm or deny that, but he shared that in pursuing a career in electoral politics that he was following the example of former Maoist zonal commanders Kameshwar Baitha and Yugal Pal (MN3), both of whom ran for office while they were still in jail.

I met Baitha earlier in the summer of 2013. Baitha was arrested in 2005. He was still in prison when he contested the Palamu by-election in 2007 on the Bahujan Samaj Party (BSP) ticket. Although he had finished second, hundreds of thousands of people had voted for him despite the fact that the Maoist Party had called for an election boycott and warned people not to vote for Baitha. Two years later Baitha left BSP, joined Jharkhand Mukti Morcha (JMM) and won from the Palamu constituency in 2009 parliamentary elections. Baitha lost in 2014 after he was refused a nomination by all major parties in the region and had to run on Trinamool Congress ticket, which did not have much hold in Jharkhand. Another former Maoist zonal commander, Yugal Pal, also got arrested before he went on to surrender. Pal joined JMM and ran for office in 2009 while he was still in prison. Baitha's brother was his campaign manager. The Maoists torched his election office in the Vishrampur Assembly Constituency, and they distributed pamphlets to warn other cadres not to join electoral politics. Encouraged by these example, Yadav also ran for office from the Chhatra constituency on CPI(ML) Liberation ticket during the 2009 parliamentary elections. Both Yadav and Pal lost the 2009 elections.[12] Pal, who had switched allegiance to the All Jharkhand Students Union (AJSU) for the 2014 election, also lost. Although Maoists did not call for a boycott of the 2014 elections, the party had issued six pages of condemnation and death warrants against Yadav and Pal, characterizing their participation in electoral politics as a betrayal that the Maoist party would avenge. I asked Baitha, Yadav and Pal how they picked their preferred political parties post retirement. All three of them replied that they based their decisions on personal networks of trust that they had developed with specific politicians during their insurgent careers. Various political parties sent emissaries to prison to meet retired rebels and make their offers. Yadav, Baitha and Pal were all deeply cynical about political parties; they picked political parties based on what they knew and what they offered, which made programmatic commitment of these parties irrelevant.

Yadav gave me names and contact information of other Maoists who retired after him in the North. I cross checked the names he shared with the list of surrendered rebels I had prepared from newspaper report of Maoist surrender, which I further amended based on meetings with local journalists and activists as well.[13] Later I got a list of 33 surrendered and surviving Maoists from the Jharkhand police headquarters in Ranchi. I was able to track down, meet or talk to of them, mostly in and around Ranchi and in the neighboring Khunti district. The most interesting informant (RN7) that Yadav introduced me to was a Maoist commander (last name Ghanju) from Chapra district who had not yet surrendered arms. He was still in the Maoist party but he admitted that he wanted to quit and he was weighing his options.[14] In his own words, he was in Ranchi scouting for opportunities to surrender. I met him twice, and asked him about the various factors he considered important in his decision to quit: the first meeting was a brief conversation of about half an hour in a nondescript tea shop in the Khunti district in November 2013. Shy and soft-spoken, he spoke in a low voice as he sipped his tea and kept his eyes down during the entire conversation. In January 2014 he met me again in a shady dance bar outside Ranchi that he identified as a safe spot. The meeting took place in a private room in the dance bar and lasted for over three hours.[15] Mr. Ghanju seemed shy and harmless as he shared his story, which helped me understand how he planned to navigate various potential threats to his personal safety. However, the very next day after I met him, two intelligence officers, one of them from Delhi, knocked on my door at 5 a.m. and demanded to see all transcripts of the meeting.[16]

All the former Maoist combatants that I met eloquently articulated their personal journey of becoming a rebel, which invariably touched on their experiences of interaction with the Indian state. Yadav, for example, revealed his experience of dealing with corrupt mainstream politicians, who he thought "sucked the country dry and went scot-free." He complained that it was unfair that there were two-dozen criminal cases pending against him; he insisted that I would find him an innocent patriot compared to the politicians and bureaucrats (*netas* and *amlas*, in Hindi), who used their office to run protection markets and plunder state coffers with impunity. It was, however, clear to me that Yadav was more critical and fearful of his former comrades, who, he knew, wanted to kill him for betraying them, than he was of the police and politicians. He shared his experiences with corruption within the Maoist party, particularly the self-aggrandizing behavior of some rebel leaders who struck deals with elected politicians, to help them siphon off stolen public funds to multiple fake accounts. In addition, corrupt rebel leaders in the North were also making money in protection rackets and various kidnapping and extortion schemes. The fratricidal wars among Maoist factions through the 1990s were as much about area domination as they were over control of lucrative protection rackets. These blood feuds killed many ordinary cadres, while the corrupt commanders amassed huge personal wealth and lived comfortably in their palatial houses; they sent their children to study abroad; often laundered money through their wives and family members; and, in the process, ruined the credibility of Maoist rebels in the North. Yadav admitted that his family and neighbors, who had once respected him as a Maoist commander, now despised and dreaded him and avoided contact with his wife and children. These accounts of corruption and lack of accountability within the Maoist party was confirmed by local vernacular journalists and other activists I met in the region.

Yadav, and several other former Maoists (RN12, RN13, RN16) also shared their experiences with competing factions within the party. A recurrent theme in these accounts was that these factions, organized along caste lines, perpetuated many corrupt practices within the organization, which gradually eroded their faith in the Maoist ideology, goals and leadership. The proverbial last straw that broke the camel's back for Yadav was the decision of the Maoist party to transfer him out of Jharkhand to Chhattisgarh. Yadav said half-jokingly that if he had to navigate factionalism and backstabbing, he would rather be a corrupt politician than a corrupt revolutionary. Having watched elected politicians from close quarters for many years, he yearned for the social respect and legitimacy that electoral victory bestows even on the most corrupt politician in North India. At the same time, Yadav insisted that he did not regret joining the Maoist Party because it was, according to him, the only party in the 1980s that drew attention to the extreme poverty and backwardness in the villages of the Palamu-Latehar region of South Bihar.

When he joined PU in the 1980s, social activists like Dr. Vinayan led PU recruitment drives in villages in Palamu-Chatra-Latehar districts with popular frontal organizations like Mazdoor Kranti Sangram Samiti (referred to as MKSS or Samiti).[17] The earliest Samiti causes Yadav joined opposed child marriage, dowry, and domestic violence. Eventually, he fled his village and joined the local Maoist army (known as *dasta*, or squad). In his two-decade insurgent career, he rose to the rank of area commander. He was most proud of installing a school outside his village, where college-educated revolutionaries mostly from the neighboring state of West Bengal (referred to as *dada*, meaning big brother) educated rural children free of cost. Successive district magistrates applauded his efforts privately and attended annual handicraft fairs that he organized in his area as an area commander. It was hardly considered exceptional that an area commander of a banned insurgent group maintained regular contact with the top echelons of law enforcement and civil administration. In the 1980s, the northern Maoists also had these horizontal ties to a broad array of state and civil society actors. Yadav admitted that these ties with scholars, lawyers, activists, college students were increasingly undermined through the 1990s and practically nonexistent thereafter.

As an area commander, Yadav had first-hand knowledge of how the Maoist party unleashed increasingly violent campaigns against landlords, and how that alienated the leaders of various popular Maoist mass organizations. As highlighted in Chapter 2, increasing militarization of landlord versus Maoist battles made the mass organizations working on popular causes vulnerable to state retaliation. On the one hand, the police hounded and harassed the activists who worked peacefully on various socially relevant issues. On the other hand, these popular mass leaders found themselves sidelined and their priorities and goals repeatedly sacrificed within the Maoist organization for military and strategic goals. Yadav, an area commander himself, reiterated that the militarization of the Maoist movement including the brutal suppression of landlords through public spectacles of merciless violence was necessary for consolidating Maoist gains in the North in the late 1980s and 1990s. He cited Mao in asserting that revolutions never happen at dinner tables, at academic debates, and in polite conversations; without copious bloodshed, entrenched power structures cannot be overthrown.

On the subject of northern Maoists meddling with election processes and outcomes, Yadav admitted that although the Maoist party formally rejected elections and warned people against voting, it would frequently meddle with electoral process to manipulate outcomes. For example, the commanders would persuade ordinary people in their areas of control to either boycott elections or vote for a certain political party and not others. Yadav insisted that he did not coerce voters at gunpoint during his insurgent career; the locals merely valued his advice when it came to making important decisions like voting. In return for their services in voter manipulation, political parties offered Maoist commanders cash and other non-monetary rewards, including contracts in government highway and construction projects. Yadav worked as a contractor himself before he became a Maoist leader. He explained unapologetically how he leveraged his political and prior professional connections and his status as a rebel commander to procure more employment-generating projects for his area and secure resources and respectability for his school. Although he did not admit to taking kickbacks from various mining and construction projects in his area, local journalists and civil society activists I spoke to were convinced that he almost certainly did.

Like everyone else in the North, Yadav did not surrender; he was arrested. Yadav admitted that he was afraid of being killed as soon as he stepped out of the jail unarmed. He suspected that his former comrades, as well as many others whom he had attacked during his insurgent career, would be baying for his blood. In his own words, when he was illegal, armed, and "dangerous," he was a much sought-after political operative whom everyone feared and revered. Retirement left him disarmed, defenseless, isolated, and vulnerable. Yadav admitted that he knew he could only rely on the police for his personal safety. It seems counterintuitive that a former Maoist found the police trustworthy, but Yadav clarified that the police stood to gain more from his surrender than from his death because there were significantly more career rewards (such as promotions and honorable mentions) and social recognition in supervising Maoists' surrenders than in having them killed. Besides, the police did not work alone. He knew that he needed to recruit other prominent actors in the region, particularly politicians and bureaucrats, who would band together their social networks and financial resources to eliminate, persuade, or buy off all potential threats to his life. Yadav was convinced that his family, except his wife, neither had the desire nor the capability to mobilize resources or networks to facilitate his return and reintegration, primarily because they could not risk retaliation from the community or the Maoist party. The prison kept him safe until he was ready to find his place in electoral politics, the only post-retirement career option he had considered.

As an insurgent, Yadav had spent years watching others run for office. Intimately aware of party fundraising and the nomination process, Yadav was confident that since he had delivered big chunks of votes from his area to candidates, enabling their victories, he could do the same for himself. To stay alive in the face of violent threats from his former comrades, Yadav considered politics his only safe haven. Political clout, he argued, was the only countervailing force against Maoist death warrants. However, the protection he had been afforded through electoral politics, he knew, worked through the same mechanisms of violence and corruption that plagued his insurgent career. Protection rackets are mostly associated with organized crime and insurgency, but electoral participation by former rebels, based on Yadav's account, runs very much like traditional protection with the advantage of legitimacy—in return for their open denouncement of Maoists, former rebels are recruited to perform the same functions of fearmongering and money laundering that they did as rebels. These relationships work in ways that put insurgency and electoral politics on the same continuum of illegality (Shah 2006).

As a result, it was very hard to broach the subject of Maoist movement or rebel retirement in the villages in the North. Ordinary people in the rural areas of Khunti, where many former rebels now live, and in the Palamu or Saranda regions where most of them originally hail from, shut their doors to me and abruptly ended conversations at the very mention of Maoists. The politicians I spoke to, who have been known to recruit notorious former Maoists in their electoral campaigns, were not very keen to talk about the process either. As I proceeded to contact the retired rebels listed in the database that the Jharkhand police shared, I found that almost all of them were relatively recent recruits, joining the Maoist party in the late 1990s or after. They were between 30 and 40 years old, and unlike their southern counterparts, showed little understanding of the Maoist ideology. Most of them admitted that joining the Maoists was a youthful mistake. A couple of them were newly married, but most of them did not have any close family in the Ranchi and Khunti districts where they lived. These former rebels confirmed that they received cash, ranging from one lakh Indian rupees to about seven lakh, which they claimed to be investing in building small businesses. I wanted to find out how they perceived this payment. I was baffled to discover that they compared these payments to the pensions that former freedom fighters and retired police and military personnel receive for serving their country. In their minds, their war against inequality and injustice was also ultimately a service to the country and its people.

Thus there were two major trends in rebel retirement in the North that emerged from my interviews: First, every one of the surrendered rebels I spoke with in the North decided to surrender after they had already been arrested. In contrast to our general understanding of the retirement process in the South or elsewhere in the world, the northern Maoists did not approach the police to express their desire to quit. This might strike as logically untenable to an external observer. I pointed it out to the police, administrators, and to the rebels that it seemed odd that the state would offer additional incentives like money for rebels to surrender when it could just keep them in custody forever. Interestingly enough, the police and bureaucrats thought it made total sense to permanently lure rebels away from an extremist group in return for some cash. The rebels also, as discussed above, they deserved a pension commensurate with their rank and length of service in the insurgent organization.

Secondly, retired Maoists in the North joined electoral politics in two capacities: The first group, made of area commanders and zonal commanders like Baitha and Yadav, ran for office post-retirement. They spoke proudly of their rebel career and attributed their decision to quit to disillusionment with the direction and leadership of the insurgent organization. Their names were not in the list of surrendered Maoists shared by the state police. The second group, the 33 surrendered Maoists in the list provided by the police head-quarters, were located mainly in Ranchi and Khunti districts. They had a deep sense of regret for wasting their youth in an insurgency that was doomed to fail. They were extremely critical of the Maoist leadership and showed no interest in or understanding of the Maoist ideology. There was little clarity in how they earned their post-retirement livelihood . Some said that they lived off their retirement money, which is bound to run out sooner or later. The local journalists I met confirmed that some of them were real estate goons and others worked as henchmen of some politician or the other. Some of them were allegedly never Maoists but just hardened criminals who may or may not have worked in the protection rackets of Maoist commanders. Both groups of retired Maoists, despite differences in their rebel careers and retirement outcomes, shared similar retirement process through an informal exit network that could not completely address the fear and insecurities that they faced in the process.

Discordant Exit Network

The informal exit network in the North is discordant because movement entrepreneurs (MEs) in the North, unlike their southern counterparts, were not tied by prosocial commitment to a non-excludable public good like peace. The northern MEs mobilized their resources and networks toward construction of collective preferences around rebel retirement only if they expected to individually profit from it. Moreover, the exit networks in the North were devoid of reintegration stewards who mediated consultations and consensus around rebel retirement locally. Given the double movement of discord both within the exit network and between the MEs and civilians who are the local stakeholders in the retirement process, I call the informal exit networks in the North 'discordant'.

Much like the South, my conversations with the rebels, bureaucrats, police, politicians, civil society activists, and ordinary people in the northern conflict zone pointed to a sprawling overlap between the state and insurgent camps. The retired rebels knew that once they stepped out of prison disarmed and defenseless, they could be killed. Most of them identified their former comrades in the Maoist party as the predominant threat to their personal safety. In order to mitigate this threat that is not addressed by the existing institutions and policies, the northern rebels set out to build their informal exit network that could compensate for the institutional deficit locally. However the northern exit network originates and works very differently than the southern one. Unlike the South, this gray zone was steeped in anti-social criminal networks, where the limits of legality are continuously pushed.

The distinctiveness of the northern gray zone stems from the secret and semi-secret ties that northern rebels build with state agents like police, politicians, and bureaucracy on the one hand and various nonstate agents like mafias and businesses on the other hand. These ties, steeped in violence, fraud, fear, and exploitation, constitute the vicious gray zone of state-insurgency interface in the North where the exit networks grow. As discussed in Chapter 3, the distinctive caste/class dynamics and land relations in the North, which spew intense militancy and limits horizontal ties of insurgent organization, contribute to the dominance of perverse criminality in the northern gray zone. As a result, northern rebels are limited in their options. For example, when Yadav wanted to surrender, he met with politicians, police, and bureaucrats who assured him that they would offer him protection (*suraksha*, in Hindi) to make sure that he would not be killed when he was released from jail. However, he did not reach out to any human rights activists or civil liberty lawyers who could alleviate his apprehensions and insecurities. It is not as if there are no civil liberty activists in the North. Yadav knows who they are. But the ties he made with the state and nonstate agents to run for office either precluded broad networks with various societal actors or made them vestigial. The former combatants in the North, who do not run for office but sell their services (as thugs) to the highest bidders, usually a politician or organized crime, in and around the capital city of Ranchi, also mentioned meeting with at least two agents of the state (police, politicians, or bureaucrats) in prison. These meetings offered assurance to the rebels that they would not be hunted and killed by their former comrades post-retirement. The northern exit networks are also relatively opaque; I could not precisely match incentives and side payments offered to identifiable outcomes. For example, although all retired rebels were loyal to some locally prominent political party, it was impossible to identify what the incentive structure of MEs were in specific cases. I found that for retired rebels who use threats, extortion, assault and assassination as private enforcers the informal exit network provided a façade of legitimate livelihood as a mechanic, driver, shop keeper or tailor, which the rebels valued a lot.

In sharp contrast to their southern comrades, northern rebels did not reach out to their family and friends who could mobilize local public opinion in favor of rebel return to their family homes. Thus the discordant exit network was completely devoid of reintegration stewards (RSs). Yadav could not conceive how ordinary people, that he did not know or incentivize in some way (through threats or payments), could become his RSs working toward his safety by reaching out to their personal social networks and staking their personal reputation in the process. Other northern rebels also dismissed such grassroots safety networks for returning rebels as completely impracticable and unnecessary in the North. However, some (RN11 and 13, for example) also admitted that the protection offered through their exit network is hardly full proof.[18] The retired rebels in the North knew that coming out of an insurgency through an exit network of violent entrepreneurs limits the prospects of reintegration of former combatants into their pre-insurgent lives.[19] 80% of the northern rebels shared how much they yearned to get back their pre-insurgent lives in their ancestral villages. However, they were also deeply resentful that the people in the North attach stigma and disrespect to their insurgent past. Unlike the South, I did not meet poets, politicians, musicians, academics, and journalists in the North who would talk eloquently about the valor and sacrifice of Maoists. Instead they mostly ridiculed the rebels as greedy bandits uneducated in the intricacies of revolutionary ideology.

Summing up, there were two levels of discord working in the northern exit networks—the first dissonance, captured in the absence of RSs in the architecture of northern exit network, arises from the fear and resentment that ordinary people in the North have against former rebels. Nobody wanted retired rebels to come back and live in their neighborhoods. In addition, discord in the retirement network also originated in the conflict of interest among various state and nonstate agents like politicians, police, mafia, and bureaucrats who banded together in the North to secure safe passage of retired rebels.

Given many differences in interests and motivations among them, how do MEs come together in the first place? It is necessary to account for their incentives in facilitating rebel retirement. What is the private good/selective incentive that only participants in this exit work accrue that glues them together? What provides the northern MEs a unity of interests and purpose? I argue that the northern MEs have experience of successful collaboration in organized crime and protection rackets they ran across the state. It is this track record of reciprocity and intertwined interests that convince retiring rebels that their MEs would not abruptly walk out of the exit network leaving them in a lurch. The high financial stakes in the protection rackets propel the police, politicians, bureaucrats, and mafia to construct a single, collective preference schedule on rebel retirement. That each individual participant in the exit network may have somewhat divergent interests on the issue of retirement does not necessarily tear them apart as long they have overarching unity necessary for maintaining the profitability of their criminal networks. As long as retired rebels leverage their new roles within the political establishment and criminal enforcement system in the North to increase the size of this pie, the MEs band together in the exit network despite disparities and discord.

In a place where protection has always been a commodity sold to the highest bidder, the diverse MEs do not offer protection to former combatants for free. In other words, when MEs expend their resources and networks to offer protection to retired rebels, they must always receive something in return. Yadav argued that he was a winning political candidate for any political party, and many wanted to recruit him. A large number of voters in the areas he controlled during his insurgent career would readily vote for him. However, Yadav never won a single election, which raises questions about alternative values that he must be contributing to the network that endorsed and sponsored his retirement.

Much like the South, the police and bureaucrats in the North also highlighted that they must protect retired rebels from harm so that other rebels would know that and would feel confident enough to quit. The media attention and the professional rewards for all state agents involved in rebel surrender are added incentives. But these incentives do not explain why the mafia in Jharkhand would be motivated to allow rebels to retire safely and reintegrate into the mainstream. Based on intimate conversations with multiple stakeholders in the northern epicenter of Maoist conflict, I argue that the retired Maoist rebels increase the size of the pie for their MEs in two ways: First, those who join politics mobilize their access to state power and resources to shield the MEs in their exit networks from law enforcement; Second, they also mobilize financial incentives for MEs in the form of lucrative government contracts; Third, those who become criminal enforcers risk their lives to entrench protection rackets in their turfs.

Protection, as Charles Tilly famously argued, is an ambiguous commodity. It invokes an image of shelter against danger provided by a powerful friend. Protection rackets, like those run by Latin American gangs, and the Sicilian or Russian mafia, are powerful and deeply entrenched locally (Gambetta 2000; Nardin et al. 2016; Varese 2001). There are various protection rackets in North India that predate the Maoist insurgency. In their most common form, local henchmen sometimes force various merchants to pay a fixed amount of cash periodically to run their businesses smoothly. Sometimes protection rackets provided genuine protection to their buyers, deterring thieves and other criminals from exploiting businesses. Historically, the boundaries between criminal protection rackets and the state are porous in the North. Mafia dons become politicians; ministers marry into mafia families; the police turn a blind eye to mafia businesses; different mafia groups finance election campaigns of competing candidates; politicians protect mafia from law enforcement. Public and private sector businesses also collude with racketeers, which imposes negative externalities on other businesses, initiating a cascade that forces all business owners to associate with them in order to keep up with the competition, which imposes a cost on all. They also extract resources from the ordinary citizens, providing little in return and inflicting physical or economic violence upon those who refuse to pay them. In addition, illegal transactions in protection rackets breed crime and murder and allow markets for harmful goods and services and exact a heavy toll on the economy. In this criminalized state and market, the MEs are all entrepreneurs selling protection (Vaishnav 2017).

The caste antagonism in northern villages, intensified by the Maoist insurgency, added a new dimension to the existing protection markets since the 1980s. As discussed in the Chapter 3, an intersection of land ownership, caste dominance, and political power bred rural caste hostility, which was by no means unique to Bihar. But landlords raising caste armies to mercilessly slaughter Dalit women and children with impunity made the entanglement between caste/class disparities and land ownership particularly potent there. The state was hardly a neutral bystander in these clashes. An upper-caste chief minister of Bihar, for instance, was instrumental in the decision to arm the upper-caste militias against the Maoists in 1986. Elected MPs and MLAs, politicians of opposition parties, state and federal ministers, and even a former prime minister were among the well-known patrons of the upper-caste militia of Ranvir Sena (Sinha and Sinha 2001; Chandran and Gupta 2002).[20] In response, the Maoists also unleashed unprecedented brutalities on the upper-caste landlords, slaughtering their families, burning their houses, and destroying their crops and properties.

Terrified and panicked, landlords offered huge payments to Maoist commanders so that they would not attack them. Some commanders took payments to protect landlords from other Maoist commanders. The landlords knew that law enforcement was inadequate. The security forces were ineffective not only because they were weak but also because they became active stakeholders in the Maoist protection market. In return for hefty payments, they overlooked it when the rebels broke the law and even used police forces to hunt down citizens branded by rebels as "wanted." In this environment, each landlord understood that protection is more valuable if he is one of the few to receive it, which implies that each landlord is willing to pay more if only a few receive protection.

As protection became a lucrative business, the Maoists recruited more criminals and mafia to instill fright in the local community. The Maoists unleashed spectacular violence against civilians, preempting noncompliance or punishing it severely. The Maoists increasingly adopted the same intimidation techniques that the agents of the state had used before them. The rebels also hijacked existing protection rackets and recruited their own supporters. Every large government contract passed through these rackets. As their criminal infrastructure expanded, these rackets ran many side businesses like kidnapping and extortion affecting all sections of population. During their insurgent careers, many rebels developed clandestine ties with state agents often collaborating with some while exchanging fire with others.

Alongside the perverse dynamics of simultaneous conflict and collaboration between state agents and insurgents, the mafia also maintained ties to both. This created a vicious gray zone of state-insurgency interface in the North steeped in violence, danger, and fear. The protection rackets occupying these gray zones replaced legal venues of politics and business in the North. Thus the institutions of democracy, capitalism, law enforcement, criminal enterprises, and insurgency routinely intersected in the North, so frequently and incessantly, that it is unremarkable and hardly spotted; it is a way of life, no longer an obstacle to the market or the state. As the Maoist organization in the North imitated and took over protection rackets they merely became an extension of it. The organization was a dreaded refuge of bandits and delinquents, which made it unattractive to ordinary villagers, the urban working class, the intelligentsia, and activists. The northern epicenter of conflict is thus India's Wild West, locally known as Jungle Raj (or Mafia Raj).[21]

In this atmosphere, violent entrepreneurs, both state and nonstate, could underwrite rules of the market through threats of grave physical or economic harm (Varese 2001; Volkov 2002). They facilitate tax evasion, depriving the state of revenues and its citizens of public goods. In this environment where rapidly expanding opportunity in mining, industrialization created lucrative business opportunities, the corporations and local businesses also embraced the Jungle Raj and invested in a long-term enforcement partnership (Volkov 2000) with the violent state and nonstate actors, further intensifying the extralegal networks in the gray zone. In their all-encompassing reach, the protection rackets undermined people's trust in political institutions, law enforcement, and in lawful economic transactions. The swift, brutal exemplary retaliations against anyone who challenged the rackets further tightened their grip on ordinary people.[22] That requires flouting the law and not getting caught, which called for recruiting more police, politicians, and bureaucrats into these rackets. Thus protection rackets grew out of weak state institutions. As it proliferated, it further slackened the rule of law and tainted the business climate, creating a vicious cycle of a criminalized nexus between police, mafia, politician, bureaucrats, and businesses.[23] The mafia raj also creates silence and subjugation among ordinary people, either via intimidation or by employing many of them in a lucrative parallel economy. For example, a section of trade union leaders in Dhanbad coal mines became indistinguishable from the upper echelon of the coal mafia via vested interests as well as kinship ties (Goyal 2018; Roy 2000a). Even those who are not plugged into the mafia raj cannot dodge the all-encompassing control of the racket where it exists. Whether it is buying land, applying for a government job, securing a contract, applying for a trade license, or securing a death certificate, the corrupt racket has set a price on everything.

In this reigning anarchy, ordinary people often seek stability in the comfort of their networks of kinship ties, which traditionally compensated for almost nonexistent social safety nets in the rural North. These networks helped people coping with an unforgiving environment of severe poverty, physical harm, governmental neglect, inadequate formal credit, and insurance markets, as well as a thinly stretched welfare state. Whenever a lower-caste person suffered some gruesome injustice or an everyday indignity, there was no other redress except griping and grumbling about shared grievances within caste networks of individuals who do manual labor for subsistence. A group of women in the Giridih district, for example, shared deeply humiliating experiences of how upper-caste contractors would stalk and badger them. Women in the Manoharpur block of the West Singhbhum district shared similar frustration with the seeming impunity of upper-caste men. Unable to hold their tormentors accountable, these women would seek comfort in their caste networks where the whisper campaigns warned women of whom to avoid and how to protect themselves. There is a large literature (e.g., Rosenzweig 1988; Rosenzweig and Stark 1989; Fafchamps and Lund 2003; Munshi and Rosenzweig 2006) documenting the exchange of services and the provision of public goods between households of same castes through informal, nonmarket, and nonpolitical ways. In the low income rural North, kinship networks also work as risk-sharing mechanisms. If a farmer is ill, for example, and cannot complete a critical harvest on time, labor pooling within caste networks is the norm. Yet kinship networks did not evolve into informal exit networks to facilitate rebel retirement and reintegration. The overpowering criminality and violence undermined the autonomy of caste networks in carving out an independent space for deliberation. In addition, caste emerged as the primary axis of divide among the northern Maoists. For example, the Third Preparatory Committee (TPC) was formed by Maoist cadres of primarily Ghanju castes who complained about the domination of the Yadav caste in the decision-making process of (CPI)Maoist. There are at least five major splinter groups in Jharkhand, who are more warlords than revolutionaries, running their own protection rackets and killing each other and attacking CPI(Maoist), with the police acting as both protector and provocateur.[24] They recruit along caste lines, which precludes the possibility of villagers sheltering retired rebels of their own castes independent of these rackets. For example, in a village near the Jharkhand–Orissa border, I heard how a Maoist leader drove a pregnant woman to the nearest healthcare center, which saved her life. The woman was full of gratitude. Although the rebel belonged to the same caste as her, no one in the community wanted him back in the area. They argued it would expose many old wounds and cause more bloodshed in the village. However, the single most important objection came from the fact that a returning Maoist would be dangerous destabilizer in the villages. They could upset the balance of power among the existing violent entrepreneurs in the region, breeding more danger and uncertainty, which the people wanted to avoid at any cost. Devoid of RSs tied to violent MEs, the exit network in the North cannot trigger broad consensus on rebel retirement, which explains why few rebels retire in the North.

Conclusion

This chapter sheds light on the retirement networks in the North and explains why they are discordant, which in turn explains why retirement in the region is low. Based on their personal stories, I argue that retired rebels in the North can be grouped into two kinds: First, the high-ranking rebels in the Maoist organization, area commanders and zonal commanders, who run for office post-retirement. Second, the ordinary squad members who become henchmen for local politicians and mafias. Despite differences in insurgent career and retirement outcomes, both groups surrender after they are arrested and put in jail. They retire through the discordant exit network that grew out of the sprawling protection markets in the vicious gray zone state-insurgency interface in the North. These protection markets, that predate the Maoist insurgency, are made up of state actors like police, bureaucrats, and politicians, as well as nonstate actors like mafias, corporations, and small businesses. With their growing military clout in the region, the Maoists joined some protection rackets and created some new.

When rebels retire, they reach out to the police, politicians, bureaucrats, or mafias they knew during their insurgent career. Once the rebels got themselves arrested, these state and nonstate agents banded together to co-opt them in their political and criminal networks. In return, the rebels are expected to increase the size of their pie, either as elected politicians or as strongarms and operatives aiding elected politicians . Thus the retired Maoists continue to operate as violent entrepreneurs albeit within the realm of electoral politics. Thus retirement builds a façade of legality, which lets retired rebels to live outside jungles and jails. However, this coverup is not enough to persuade ordinary people in the conflict zone to invite them back into society. The retired rebels in the North are acutely aware of the dread and distress they bring to their families and neighbors. Their inability to reintegrate into their pre-insurgent social lives, in turn, discourages other rebels from quitting the insurgency in the North.

Unable to return to their villages, most retired rebels in the North settled around Ranchi and Khunti districts, close to the police headquarters in the capital city. This is because the MEs in the discordant exit network do not have weak ties with locally entrenched RS, which limits their capacity to expand their web of influence beyond urban pockets. This chapter explains how pre-war caste relations and criminalization of business and political activities lead to intense militarization of the Maoist movement in the North, which deters growth of weak ties between MEs and RSs in the North. The protection offered by MEs in discordant exit network does not extend to far-flung districts, which are dominated by various warlords from different Maoist splinter groups. These splinter groups run their own extortion and kidnapping rackets, where returning rebels are viewed as potential challengers who could upset the fragile local balance of power. In addition, the incentives for MEs to participate in the exit networks is tied to their ability to recruit former Maoists in their political and criminal enterprise, which is more likely when retired rebels are isolated from social support and dependent on MEs for their life, livelihood and legitimacy.

6

Conclusion

In search for an explanation of varying retirement rates in the two epicenters of Maoist insurgency in North and South India, this book reveals the role of informal exit networks. Divergence in the type of exit network, resulting from difference in prewar social bases of insurgency and insurgent organizational ties to state and societal actors, has powerful implications on the process and outcome of rebel retirement. In the North, a discordant exit network exacerbates the fear and insecurities of retiring rebels, deterring retirement significantly. In the South, the harmonic exit network weaves together multiple stakeholders in an amalgam of roles and alliances to build momentum for exit.

The theory of this book is quite simple: Rebels cannot quit even if they want to because they are afraid that they would be killed as soon as they disarmed, either by the landlords they had targeted during their insurgent career (as is generally the case in the South) or by their former comrades who condemn their retirement as an act of betrayal (as is generally the case in the North). Maoist rebels in India believe that while they might lose their lives to return to the democracy, the Indian state would not lose anything if it failed to keep its side of the bargain and protect them. This creates a problem of credible commitment, which deters retirement until informal exit networks resolve it locally, which they do more effectively in the South than in the North. The existing surrender and rehabilitation schemes, offered in India and elsewhere, do not address this credible commitment problem. Instead they assume that rebels can be lured away from extremism with a promise of economic rehabilitation.

In this chapter, I first consider the scope, conditions, and applicability of the theory of rebel retirement through informal exit networks beyond India. Second, I examine the scholarly implications of this book on areas of conflict and peace studies, as well as for democratic consolidation in developing countries. Third, I examine how the process of retirement of rebels in North and South India can suggest some actionable instruments for policymakers to influence militant disengagement, particularly in cases where a ceasefire

Farewell to Arms. Rumela Sen, Oxford University Press (2021). © Oxford University Press.
DOI: 10.1093/oso/9780197529867.003.0006

between the state and rebels does not produce large-scale demobilization of thousands of rebels laying down arms in an organized manner. Specifying this projects has implications for postconflict outcomes, consolidating peace, and state-building. Policymakers concerned with weaning rebels away from extremism might therefore find these conclusions useful.

Scope, Conditions, and Applicability of the Theory beyond India

The primary contribution of this book is that it presents the rebel's perspective on what holds them back even when they want to quit. Its central theoretical innovation is the idea of informal exit network, which was born in the field and distilled from intimate conversations with Maoist combatants in North and South India. In course of these conversations, it was clear to me that rebels contemplating retirement are more anxious about their lives than their livelihood. Rebels I interviewed in the field, in North and South India, and subsequently in Nepal, consistently reported that monetary incentives do not shape their experiences after retirement or their decisions before retirement. Yet the policy focus is overwhelmingly on economic reintegration. More crucially, former combatants are also keenly aware that while they risk their lives to disarm, the state would lose nothing if it failed to protect disarmed rebels. This creates a problem of credible commitment afflicting rebel retirement, which is likely to resonate in other conflict locations as well. For example, Sinhalese armed forces have been accused of killing many surrendered Tamil rebels, deterring further reconciliation. This happens despite assurances to protect retired rebels from the United Nations and the highest offices of the country, including the president and defense secretary.[1] Kashmiri rebel groups have executed their former comrades if they suspected they would surrender.[2] There are organized protests in Kashmir against the Indian government's rehabilitation policy of 2010 that allegedly lured former rebels back with false promises and later had them killed.[3] The Burundi police and National Defense Force killed 47 surrendered rebels in one month (January 2015). Surrendered rebels were beaten to death, shot at point-blank range, and thrown off cliffs. [4] After the Syrian President Bashar Assad offered a general amnesty to militants who surrender to the government authorities, surrendered rebels attending reconciliation camps were butchered.[5] There is no dearth of examples from around the world to illustrate that retired rebels face myriad threats to their personal safety. This book contends that these threats, overlooked by institutional mechanisms in rebel surrender and rehabilitation programs, propel retired rebels to seek out informal exit networks that ensure their post-retirement safety and social reintegration.

The retired Maoist leaders and cadres I interviewed in Nepal during the summer of 2018 shared how informal exit networks played a crucial role in determining their post-retirement experience, particularly in terms of prospects of community assimilation. After a decade-long civil war in Nepal (1996–2006), the Communist Party of Nepal (Maoist) signed the Comprehensive Peace Agreement (CPA) in 2006, which officially initiated Disarmament, Demobilization and Reintegration (DDR). The United Nations Mission in Nepal (UNMIN) set up a verification process for former combatants, and approximately twenty thousand eligible rebels were sent to seven main cantonments. In 2008, the Maoist party emerged as the largest party in the first Constituent Assembly.

I picked Nepal as a test case because Nepal is an unlikely candidate to illustrate the importance of informal exit network. The Maoists in Nepal morphed from lawless rebels to elected politicians, who supervised the process of retirement and reintegration of the rank and file Maoist soldiers. Therefore, it is unlikely that Maoist combatants in Nepal would face potent threats to their personal safety. I also expected the UN-backed DDR process in Nepal to be effective enough to make informal networks unnecessary in rebel retirement and reintegration. Yet I found that rebels who formally surrendered arms and received cash compensation for it found it difficult to reintegrate back into society and politics, in spite of the fact that the Maoist party came power in Nepal.

To illustrate the role of informal networks in rebel retirement, I propose an analytical division of the retired Maoists in Nepal into two main groups: first, those who formally surrendered arms under UNMIN supervision and second, those who bypassed the UNMIN surrender program in their disarmament and reintegration. This distinction, drawn from self-identification of interviewed retired rebels I met in Nepal in 2018, also resonates with the local experience and the empirical literature on peace process in Nepal (Bleie et al.2012; Robins et al. 2016). Group I of former combatants of the Maoist army (Peoples Liberation Army, PLA) were sent to cantonments in 2006. They were asked to wait until the state and international agencies finalized terms and conditions of their surrender. But they ended up staying in cantonments for six years until 2012, when PLA was finally dissolved.

The second group is made up of former combatants who joined the Youth Communist League (YCL), which was an unarmed grassroots youth organization of the Nepal Maoists. Group II, unlike Group I, did not remain confined to the cantonments helplessly watching the political elites, media and international actors quarrelling over their contribution, compensation and future, while the general public became impatient and cynical about them (Subedi 2014; Robins et al. 2016). Many YCL members found political platforms for themselves, often critiquing the policies of the Maoist party in electoral politics. Group II also includes former combatants who were declared 'unqualified' by UNMIN for being child soldiers and late recruits, The defining characteristic of Group II is that, unlike Group I, they never went to any of the seven cantonments. These former PLA members also did not receive any monetary compensation package or the vocational training and they 'reintegrated' themselves back into their communities outside DDR framework.

There is no systematic documentation of where and how these Group II ex-PLAs reside in post conflict Nepal. However, their local communities know who they are and I was able to locate and meet Group II commanders and foot soldiers. During interviews, these retired Maoists shared that they found their ways back to their pre-insurgent communities by mobilizing their personal networks, which inevitably began with family members and included neighbors and community leaders who agreed to welcome these rebels back. In former Maoist strongholds in mountainous Nepal (West of Kathmandu), ordinary citizens, aided by grassroots civic associations, acted like Reintegration Stewards, removing roadblocks to return of rebel: First, they assured rebels that local hostilities against returning rebels would not escalate into violent retaliation against returning rebels. Second, they assured that their communities that inviting rebels back would not jeopardize local tranquility and balance of power. The informal exit network in Nepal is more bottom heavy, with Reintegration Stewards playing a bigger role locally than Movement Entrepreneurs. This is because the upper echelons of Nepal Maoists were mostly drawn into the peace process and postconflict state-building in Nepal.

Group I ex-PLAs followed a very different trajectory out of extremism. First, they spent six years in cantonments (2006–2012), exasperated, desolate and with little agency to shape their own destiny. These rebels also confirmed that they received cash payment as part of their surrender package, as well as some vocational training, which was mostly characterized as unsubstantial.

High ranking Maoist leaders and international observers acted as Movement Entrepreneurs for them, ensuring that they were compensated before they left cantonments. They brought attention to various drawbacks of state and international organizations in DDR process, gaining media attention and social recognition in the process. Second, these rebels confirmed that they face great obstacles in returning to their communities. As a result they huddle together outside Kathmandu (capital of Nepal), where they run their small businesses and 'hide' in urban anonymity. This is very similar to the experience of northern Maoists in India. However, the Maoist Party in Nepal, unlike its Indian counterpart, is not a banned insurgent organization. Their national and international legitimacy showered on Nepal Maoists still did not create enough positive spillover for their former rank and file combatants to return to their communities, which demonstrates that community assimilation of former rebels needs to be treated as a distinct process by policymakers, independent of concerns around demobilization and compensation

Third, Group I rebels insisted that they did not choose to abandon their communities and families to avoid poverty and inconvenience of rural Nepal, as some commentators have claimed. An ex-PLA commander from Group I admitted that the surrender money helped him start his own small business near Kathmandu. Despite living a relatively comfortable life in the city, his one abiding dream is to return to his village. He admitted that his own community ridicules and rejects him for abandoning them in 1990s for a revolution that left them empty handed, beaten and vanquished. Thus DDR of ex-PLAs leaving cantonments did not go beyond cash payments.

During a three-hour long interview in Kathmandu in June 2018, a former Maoist commander who joined the YCL and avoided formal surrender under UNMIN, pointed out that the disarmament-demobilization-reintegration (DDR) program humiliated and isolated ex-PLAs, robbing them not only of agency but also of their political legacy. The highly contested public confrontation among the multiple domestic and international stakeholders over compensations due to rebels negatively impacted the social acceptability of former combatants held in cantonments under DDR. In contrast, those who were not confined to cantonments for five years were more successfully reintegrated via their informal exit.

Yet DDR and security sector reform (SSR) reduces the challenge of rebel exit to one of economic anxiety and poor institutions respectively. The surrender and rehabilitation policies for Maoists in India do not look past the DDR/SSR framework. The policy prescriptions following from DDR are lucrative incentives (land, cash, or vocational training) to entice rebels away from extremism, while simultaneously increasing the accountability and effectiveness of security institutions (via human rights and rule of law). The key elements of the Integrated Action Plan (IAP) of the surrender-cum-rehabilitation scheme (SCR) of the government of India for Maoists are three: security (law and order); development; and public perception management.[6] IAP in India assumes that Maoist rebels are just misguided youth who can be weaned from extremism by a blanket policy of offering gainful employment and entrepreneurial opportunities. These prescriptions have generally been derived from large-scale demobilization, implying formal controlled discharge of hundreds of thousands of militants laying down arms in an organized manner. This happens only with a formal ceasefire agreement, often mediated by international actors and supported by security forces of their respective governments who guarantee the personal safety of retiring rebels. Under those circumstances, the second-order problems of livelihood may have taken precedence over the more pressing concerns about staying alive. However, as is evident in Nepal, even in those cases where international organizations support rebel retirement, surrendered rebels are unable to assimilate into civilian communities. In Nepal, both Group I and II rebels want their contribution to abolition of monarchy and establishment of a democratic system to be recognized and acknowledged, internationally, nationally and within their communities. But DDR cannot do that because its thrust is on defanging rebel groups, destroying their chain of command and treating rebels as unencumbered rational utility maximizing individuals who can be lured away by incentives. It is important that policymakers look beyond top-down policies of DDR, SSR and democracy promotion and instead adopt a more bottom-up approach of incorporating the rebel's perspective and priorities into policies.

This book shows that exit processes and outcomes are locally embedded. The pre-war social bases of insurgency determines the strength of vertical and horizontal ties of insurgent organization, which, in turn, determine the dynamics of state-society-insurgency interaction in the gray zone of their interface. The grassroots civic associations in these gray zones host informal exit networks facilitates rebel return.

The non-consultative, opaque incentive-based approach to lure rebels away from extremism fails to harness the grassroots processes that impact rebel retirement. In addition, such an approach creates mistrust among civilians and civil society, who are major stakeholders in rebel retirement,

Alongside economic incentives, often sponsored by generous donors, surrender and rehabilitation program must create opportunities for social reintegration and political rehabilitation of former rebels.

Historical Specificities versus Generalizability

This books shows how pre-existing land relations and local socioeconomic cleavages (caste and class structure) affect the insurgent organization, its ties to local community, its military capabilities, staying power, effectiveness, and group cohesion. Crossnational quantitative research on civil conflict has often been too aggregated to capture these local conditions. Micro level studies of civil war, on the other hand, can sometimes become too focused on preferences and strategies of various actors to consider the historically determined structural limitations to those choices. The challenge is to "historicize war without abandoning generalization" (Staniland 2014, 219), which requires showing (a) the mechanisms of how the historically and locally contingent processes circumscribe individual choices, and (b) how those specific mechanisms can be generalized into abstract conceptual categories that travel across contexts.

The theory advanced in this book attempts to achieve the balance of historical specificity and generalizability in a two-step causal structure: The first step is the structural component and it focuses on pre-war social bases (land relations and the type of crosscutting cleavages), which determine the militancy and the level of social polarization in an insurgency. Social polarization and militancy, in turn, influences the strength of ties an insurgent organization forges with the local population. I show how pre-war caste and land relations in the North led to high militancy and ambiguous social polarization, which weakened horizontal social ties of the Maoist organization there. In contrast, the southern Maoists, shaped by local caste and land relations, achieved sharp social polarization with much less militancy, which allowed them to forge strong horizontal ties. As the state, society and insurgency co-evolve, a gray zone of state-insurgency-society interaction grow in conflict zones. It is in these gray zones that the second step in the causal process transpires.

The second step in the process of retirement depicted in this book focuses on the dynamics of strategic interaction among various stakeholders in rebel retirement. I show how the North-South differences in individual preferences and strategies, stemming from differences in underlying structural factors depicted in Step 1 (structural component), lead to different exit networks and retirement outcomes in the two regions. In the South, on the one hand, Movement Entrepreneurs and Reintegration Stewards use trust and side payments to operationalize a harmonic exit network to ensure safe return and reintegration of rebels. In the North, on the other hand, MEs are plugged into the corrupt criminal nexus dominating the North, which makes the exit network discordant and incompetent to secure safe return and reintegration of rebels.

The causal mechanisms in Step I (structural component) are as follows: If the dependence of the rural elite on land is high, as in the North, the feudal landowners have incentives to fight unrelenting pitched battles against insurgents to protect their assets, thereby raising the level of militancy. However, if rural elites have non-land sources of income in cities, they choose to migrate to cities rather than engage in deadly confrontation with rebel groups, which produces lower level of militancy (as in the South). They might still offer information support, shelter, ration and supplies to the state counterinsurgency forces to protect their wealth and property, but they will not enter a battle of life and death with rebels, which will reduce militancy of local struggle. Landholding patterns can result from factors predating and exogenous to the insurgency, like martial traditions of the ruling class, penetration of the colonial state and rural political economy, specifically agrarian capitalism or lack of it. Another crucial element in Step I(structural component) of the theory is whether or not pre-existing social cleavages create favorable conditions for an insurgent group to sharply polarize local population into two antagonistic sides (e.g., upper caste/landowners v lower caste/landless) with clearly juxtaposed interests and identities, as the Maoists did in the South. When social and economic fault lines (caste and class, for example) do not overlap neatly, rebel groups cannot sharply polarize local population into two antagonistic camps. When low militancy of local struggle coincide with high social polarization, 'virtuous' (pro-social) grey zone with secret and semi-secret links among state-society-insurgency emerge. The counter intuitive element in this analysis is how high social polarization breeds a cohesive insurgent organization, which, develops ties and civic associations that allow MEs and RSs to emerge, particularly when local militancy is low. In contrast, low social polarization and high militancy weakens internal cohesiveness and confidence of insurgent organization to collaborate with state and societal actors in gray zone, ultimately producing low retirement through discordant exit networks.

The causal mechanisms in Step II (Incentive Component) stems from how MEs and RSs mobilize trust and side payments. If a conflict zone resembles the South, the MEs and RSs networks are likely to be strong, producing a harmonic exit network that effectively alleviates the fear of retiring rebels through both trust and side payments. If the underlying conditions in a conflict zone, on the other hand, resembles the North, the overcast of fear and insecurity in the grey zone will generate discordant exit networks. These feeble exit networks do not have far reaching RS networks to neutralize the stigma and rejection that returning rebels often face.

Given the complexity of every case of civil war, the intent of the 2x2 table (Figure 6.1) is modest. II seek to show that India is not unique and the conditions present in North and South India can exist elsewhere as well. Although the values of variables, their relative importance, the nature of their interactions might be different in other contexts, and the units of analysis might diverge from those that I have used in Indian case, there is reason to believe that looking into the underlying socioeconomic factors and the resulting ties among state, insurgent and societal actors will shed light on conflict processes as well as post conflict outcomes.

Figure 6.1 shows that in some conflict zones horizontal ties of insurgent organization are strong, while their vertical ties to local population is weak. In those cases, the MEs will emerge strong and the RS will be weak. As

Movement Entrepreneurs	Reintegration Stewards	
	Strong	Week
Strong	Both Trust and side payment strong High Retirement; High Reintegration. Harmonic Exit Network	Trust mechanism weak Outcome: Limited Retirement and much lower Reintegration
Weak	Side payments weak Outcome: Limited retirement, High Reintegration	Both Trust and Side Payments are weak Low Retirement; Low Reintegration; Discordant Exit Network

Figure 6.1 Various Retirement and Reintegration Outcomes in Conflict Zones

illustrated in the case of Group I ex-PLAs in Nepal, this will facilitate demobilization and disarmament through various government surrender schemes negotiated between MEs and the state, without commensurate reintegration of rebels into their local societies. The fourth quadrant in Figure 6.1 depicts a condition where the exit network does not have an overarching ME network mobilizing side payments. However, it has strong vertical ties that allows emergence of RS allowing some rebels to return discretely to their families without much oversight of a surrender policy. The experience Group II ex-PLAs in Nepal illustrates this combination of factors.

It is very likely that various other permutations and combinations of interests and alliances will arise in other conflict zones, which would cumulatively lead to retirement-enhancing dynamics or not. I have reasons to believe that if researchers were to ask the same questions as I did in the book, it would yield insights into the process of rebel retirement in conflict locations beyond India. For example, what is the geographical pattern of rebel retirement? How do rebels earn their livelihood post-retirement? Do they settle in their family homes where they lived before their insurgent career? What are the biggest fears and the biggest succours of retired rebels? Who did the rebels reach out to first when they decided to quit? However, the trajectory of rebel retirement through informal exit networks will not hold up in environments of state failure because the dynamics of interaction with state agents is crucial in defining the gray zones where retirement transpires.

Implications for Scholarship and Policy

This book presents a path-dependent, locally embedded study of civil conflict that does not accept the zero-sum relationship between states and insurgency. It shows how the local state shares sovereignty with insurgent actors, not only in areas where insurgents establish territorial domination but also in places where there is a constant tug of war, shifting the balance one way or another. In fact, despite the overarching confrontation among state and insurgent agents, the local state maintains multiple secret and semi-secret ties with the insurgents at the same time and place they fight each other in pitched battles. The biggest policy implication of this argument is that it questions the effectiveness of a counterinsurgent Leviathan. The societal actors, primarily civilians and civic associations, also actively forge ties with both sides. These ties vary across conflict zones, robust and prosocial in some places (like the

South) and antisocial and corrupt in others (like in the North). This variation is largely independent of whether state or rebel groups achieve territorial control and endures even when rebel rule gives way to state control and vice versa. The ties among state, insurgent, and societal actors also give rise to grassroots civic associations, which are fairly stable characteristics of local politics.

This book also shows how structural factors like land relations and social cleavages constrain insurgent organizations and their vertical and horizontal ties. A few questions remain unanswered in this inquiry that might offer opportunities for future research: How do these ties among state, insurgent, and societal actors in conflict zones facilitate or inhibit state building? Is it likely that rebel groups that have prosocial ties with state actors produce different postwar outcomes than those that have antisocial ties? For example, what kinds of network connections among actors in conflict zones are more amenable to postconflict rebel electoral participation? In answering these questions, field evidence that researchers encounter might defy expectations of rational bargaining. For example, between vendetta and a license to a gas station, I was not able to explain fully why the MEs in the South preferred the latter. Future researchers can discuss these and other anomalies in such decisions to create new theories of bargaining among multiple actors under conditions of uncertainty prevailing in conflict zones.

This book presents cases of individual disengagement of Maoist rebels in India that is distinct from demobilization of large group of rebels under international supervision. However, the findings on the role of informal exit networks also resonated in Nepal, where a formal ceasefire was followed by a peace process mediated by the UN. Research on processes of militant disengagement has long been considered immensely difficult due to scarcity of data, security concerns, and ethical considerations about sensitive information on controversial subjects. This project was not designed to collect individual stories of disengagement, which is also a useful and challenging research endeavor. Many former rebels shared their personal journeys of hope and despair, divulging many exceptional and mundane stories of their lives. But in this book former combatants are not treated as autonomous agents. Over time the stories and experiences they shared revealed that actors in conflict zones are locally embedded, which implies that they are restricted in their choices, preferences, strategies and outcomes by a web of relationships as well as underlying structural factors. The policy implication of this finding is that surrender and rehabilitation programs need to go deeper than an apolitical, ahistorical approach of incentive-based individual targeting of rebels. As the Nepal case illustrates, imposition of transitional justice without local adaptation is unlikely to produce desired outcomes even under most favorable conditions imaginable in post-conflict settings.

This book presents research on clandestine and semi-secret networks among civilians and insurgents, integrating insights on how these ties, both prosocial and antisocial, pull in state actors, influencing outcomes in other areas such as governance, rule of law, and public service provision. Extending this research on state-society-insurgent ties beyond the environment of civil war, to study criminal violence, campaign finance, gangs, or other kinds of conflict (religious or ethnic) can contribute to our understanding of state-building and democratic performance. The Maoist grassroots organizations gave voice and visibility to the most marginalized population of India, created a vibrant civil society made up of not only ascriptive associations but also modern, voluntaristic ones. These associations created opportunities for the disenfranchised poor to grow into meaningful democratic actors who participated in rallies; filed public interest litigations; and made persistent demands for social justice, representation, and service provision from the judiciary and bureaucracy. Future research can highlight the mechanisms of democratic deepening through which these insurgent-driven activities increased the transparency and accountability of the democratic institutions. Methodologically these might raise concerns of endogeneity, which future researchers should not take as an excuse to gloss over the messy endogenous processes at the heart of conflict and state-building.

Coming back to the literature on democracy promotion, it assumes that rebel electoral participation under international oversight creates a path to durable peace. This is an untested assumption much like the DDR assumption that retired rebels are beset either by economic insecurities. The democracy promotion literature makes an argument about including provisions for rebel participation in postconflict elections as a conflict resolution mechanism. Democratic participation is taken as an evidence of peace. However, retired rebels in the North confessed that they run for office not because they want to, but because it is taken as evidence of their deradicalization. This book shows that, contrary to popular expectations, when rebels run for office, as in the North, it is more of a continuation of their rebel career than a clean break from it. This is because violence is integral to electoral strategy in many postconflict settings, and retired rebels are inducted into it as violent entrepreneurs who can wield the gun and other intimidation tactics to deliver votes for political party. Enticing rebels to quit is not as easy as implementing lucrative surrender packages and electoral participation provisions. Surely, economic rehabilitation is not detrimental to the well-being of retired rebels, and perhaps certain kinds of insurgencies are more amenable to such enticements than others. However, these incentives become relevant during reintegration, after the rebels have already disarmed. Surrender and Rehabilitation policies worldwide need to focus on what rebels consider important in leaving extremism, and this book seeks to make a contribution in that direction.

The evidence presented in this book also makes an argument against treating conflict studies as a distinct field, simply on the basis of having armed actors in politics. This because civil conflicts do not begin with a shot fired. Nor does it end when rebels silence their guns and run for office. Policies need to move beyond counting the number of surrendered guns or the proportion of rebels running for office. Policies have also preached about institution building while overlooking remilitarization of former combatants until casualty figures are above a threshold. This book shows that new inputs for policymaking can be drawn from acknowledging and exploring the gray areas of continuities between peace and conflict. Researchers can also look into the institutions, networks, and exchanges that precede conflicts, evolve during wars, and inevitably shape postconflict outcomes.

Conclusion

Throughout history ordinary men and women have taken up arms hoping to radically improve their social, political, and economic circumstances. Equally often, rebels have given up arms to return to the mainstream. But while a lot has been written on why men rebel, we know very little about how rebels quit. This book presented the rebel's perspective on the barriers they had to overcome to quit an armed group and return to the mainstream. It presents novel, fine-grained field evidence to show that it is personal safety that becomes the primary concern of retiring rebels. Since nothing in the surrender and rehabilitation policies address this fear, rebels retire through informal exit networks that resolve the problem locally. The book marries micro-level accounts of rebel retirement with an understanding of meso-level strategic interactions among various stakeholders in the exit networks, which is then traced back to macro-level structural factors shaping the interactions. In doing so it builds on insights from classic and recent works on civil conflict. This is a new, empirically validated theory of rebel retirement that has policy implications for practitioners trying to wean rebels from extremist groups. In this account of multiple actors in conflict zones banding together for facilitating rebel return, I have presented a glimmer of hope that we can magnify and harness collective capacities of ordinary people for building peace and a more just, equitable society.

Preliminary Statistical Analyses

The statistical analysis presented here shows that controlling for area and population of the district as well as the percentage of the scheduled-caste (SC) population, the variable organizational density, measuring district-level density of grassroots civic associations, has a positive, statistically significant relationship with rebel retirement across 318 districts of 10 Maoist-affected states in India. It also tests alternative explanations of the effects of development (access to household assets, access to education, access to healthcare), industrialization, mining, and repression on rebel retirement. Most of the effects are insignificant, and effect sizes are small. The effect of organizational density on retirement is stable and significant in all the models.

Dependent Variable (Retirement, RTRMT)

The retirement (RTRMT) of Maoist rebels varies across various states in the Red Corridor and across districts within a state. I created a district-level data set on Maoist surrender over a period of 10 years (2005–2014) in 318 districts of 10 Maoist-affected states of Andhra Pradesh, Bihar, Chhattisgarh, Jharkhand, Maharashtra, Madhya Pradesh, Odisha Uttar Pradesh, and West Bengal. The data set is built from information on rebel surrender available on the South Asia Terrorism Portal (SATP), which, based on newspaper reports, lists all surrender events by date.[1]

Of these 318 districts in 10 Maoist-affected states, a total of 77 districts have been reported as the worst affected by Maoist insurgency. Of these 77 districts, retirement of Maoist rebels has occurred at least once in 48 districts over 10 years (2005–2014). Over 75% of these retirement events are, however, concentrated in 14 districts in six states. The SATP data roughly matches roughly the Ministry of Home Affairs (MHA) data on surrender of Maoists between 2005 and 2012.[2] In 2013 and 2014, however, SATP data on surrender is disproportionately higher than MHA data. In 2013, while the MHA reports a total of 671 surrender events, SATP reports 1,950, of which 1,765 were in one district (Koraput) in Odisha between April 6 and 17. Further investigation of the underlying media reports show that SATP wrongly counted return of tribals belonging to a landless labor organization (Chashi Mulia Adivashi Sangh, CMAS) to their villages as Maoist surrender.[3] In 2014, SATP records 651 surrenders in Chhattisgarh compared to MHA data of 157. SATP overestimates surrender in Chhattisgarh because of exaggerated media reports that the state hit the jackpot in securing rebel surrender by advertising generous offers in its new surrender policy in BBC radio, which the Maoists regularly tune into.[4]

Independent Variable: Organizational Density (ORGDENS)

The primary hypothesis tested is that higher district-level organizational density (ORGDENS) encourages retirement of rebels within the given district.

Table A1.1 India's Red Corridor

State	# of Districts in State	# of Districts Affected	Districts Affected
Andhra Pradesh	13	8	Guntur, Prakasam, Anantapur, Kurnool, Vizianagaram, East Godavari, Srikakulam, Visakhapatnam
Bihar	38	11	Aurangabad, Gaya, Rohtas, Bhojpur, Kaimur, East Champaran, West Champaran, Sitamarhi, Munger, Nawada, Jamui
Jharkhand	24	18	Hazaribagh, Lohardaga, Palamu, Chatra, Garhwa, Ranchi, Gumla, Simdega, Latehar, Giridih, Koderma, Bokaro, Dhanbad, East Singhbhum, West Singhbhum, Saraikela Kharsawan, Khunti, Ramgarh
Chhattisgarh	27	9	Bastar, Bijapur, Dantewada, Kanker, Rajnandgaon, Sarguja, Jashpur, Koriya, Narayanpur, Sukma
Maharashtra	35	3	Gadchiroli, Chandrapur, Gondia
Odisha	30	9	Malkangiri, Ganjam, Koraput, Gajapati, Rayagada, Mayurbhanj, Sundargarh, Deogarh, Kandhamal
Telangana	10	8	Warangal, Karimnagar, Adilabad, Khammam, Medak, Nalgonda, Mahbubnagar, Nizamabad
Uttar Pradesh	75	3	Sonbhadra, Mirzapur, Chandauli
West Bengal	19	3	Bankura, West Midnapore, Purulia
Madhya Pradesh	50	1	Balaghat
Total	318	77	

H1 *A high rebel retirement is expected in those districts where organizational density is high.*

The variable organizational density (ORGDENS) is constructed from the ME1 to ME10 variables of the India Human Development Survey (IHDS) 1 data set and from the ME1 to the ME14 of the IHDS 2 data set by computing the sum of positive values and assigning a density level accordingly. In particular, the sum corresponds to the level unless the sum is larger than 3. In that case, the density level is set to 3.[5] The IHDS includes questions on membership in various organizations (some sample questions are in Table A1.2) based on responses from 44,000 randomly selected individuals in about 320 districts collected in two phases (2005 and 2011–2012).

I collapsed the individual responses to obtain the district-level mean response on membership of various associations (caste groups, religious groups, women's groups, *panchayat* office, professional groups, agricultural co-ops), as well as trust and participation in various government institutions.

Table A1.2 Organizational Membership in IHDS

Variable	Survey Question
ME1	Does anybody in the household belong to a *Mahila mandal* (women's organization)?
ME2	Does anybody in the household belong to a youth club, sports group, or reading room?
ME3	Does anybody in the household belong to a trade union, business, or professional group?
ME4	Does anybody in the household belong to a self-help group?
ME5	Does anybody in the household belong to a credit or savings group?
ME6	Does anybody in the household belong to a religious or social group or festival society?
ME7	Does anybody in the household belong to a caste association?
ME8	Does anybody in the household belong to a development group or NGO?
ME9	Does anybody in the household belong to an agricultural, milk, or other co-operative?
ME10	In the most recent national elections, did you vote?
ME11	Have you or anyone in the household attended a public meeting called by the village *panchayat/ nagarpalika/*ward committee in the last year?
ME12	Is anyone in the household an official of the village *panchayat/nagarpalika/*ward committee? Is there someone close to the household who is a member?

I construct a district-level variable called ORGDENS, which is then ordered as high, moderate, or low to measure grassroots civic participation and act as proxy of grassroots-level lure of democracy in a district. A high ORGDENS would imply higher civic participation in a district than a moderate or low ORGDENS. When ordinary people are members of multiple organizations, the high contact is more likely to foster informal networking to facilitate local peace by safeguarding the life and livelihood of rebels who wish to return. Thus I expect that rebel retirement is higher where *orgdens* is higher.

My analysis also reveals that ORGDENS within a district has an effect on the number of retired rebels. When controlling for area and population of the district as well as the percentage of SC population, an organizational density level of 3 affects the incident rate by a factor of 1.9. Thus in districts with the highest organizational density we expect almost twice as many rebels to retire compared to a district with the lowest level. Therefore, we conclude that organizational density is an important influence on the motivation to retire from the rebel movement. This effect is also stable when we control for the other influences as well as under the IHDS 1 and IHDS 2 data sets.

ORGDENS is treated as a factor because it cannot be considered a continuous variable. An initial box plot suggests that only an ORGDENS level of 3 has an effect on *RTRMT*. An ORGDENS level of 3 increases the incident rate by a factor of 1.9. Thus in a district with the highest organizational density we expect almost twice as many rebels to retire compared to a district with the lowest level of organizational density. This effect is also stable when we control for the other influences as well as under the IHDS 1 and IHDS 2 data sets, confirmed by the regression analysis.

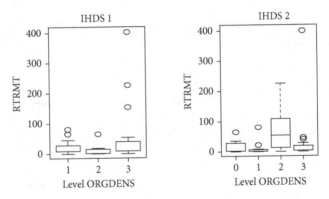

Figure A1.1 How ORGDENS Impact Retirement

The policy literature often expects rebel surrender to be higher in those districts where standard of living, indicated by access to household assets (transistor radio, television, bicycles, two-wheelers, cars, etc.), access to healthcare, access to education (Literacy), is better and where investment in industrialization and mining is higher. In order to test these alternative explanations, the following hypotheses (H2–H7) are derived.

Access to Household Assets

H2 *A high rebel retirement is expected in districts with improved access to household assets.*

Development, it is hypothesized, can lure rebels back into the mainstream by increasing access to specific household assets that give a sense of improved standard of living to the lowest strata (scheduled caste and scheduled tribe, SC/ST) of rural society in conflict areas. Based on census of India data (2001 and 2011), I measure this formulation of development by a variable (DIFFHHASSETS) that captures difference in aggregate rural SC/ST household access to radio/transistor sets, televisions, bicycles, two-wheelers, and cars at the district level. In this argument, development is expected to positively impact our variable of interest. The household assets increased in almost all districts, besides two. However, the analysis shows that there appears to be no strong correlation between retirement and the difference in household assets.

Access to Healthcare

H3 *A high rebel retirement is expected in districts with improved healthcare access.*

In policy circles, better public service provision, measured in terms of access to health and education services, is the second understanding of development that is expected to increase rebel retirement. The IHDS questionnaires in both phases ask whether a respondent saw a doctor, a nurse, a pharmacist, or none in case of minor illness to measure healthcare access. Healthcare service is a good proxy for public goods provision that requires cooperation across multiple levels of government. In addition, there is enough evidence that citizens themselves consider access to healthcare as critically important public goods and indicator of progress and modernization (Banerjee and Duflo 2007, 2009). As shown in Figure A1.2, the correlation between rebel retirement and access to healthcare is very weak in phase I and slightly negative in phase 2.

Access to Education

H4 *A high rebel retirement is expected in districts with improved access to education.*

The variable measuring access to education is constructed from IHDS by taking into account the highest education level of both male and female members, not merely presence of schools in the vicinity of a household. Access to education is a primary public service of importance in rural India (Barakat and Urdal 2009; Datt and Ravallion 1998). I collapse household data to district level to construct an index measuring literacy on a scale of 0–3. In the Maoist-affected districts there are several districts with a low literacy rate and a few with a high value of literacy. Literacy has slightly improved from survey 1 to survey 2. Preliminary analysis, however, shows that correlation between rebel retirement and access to education (variable name literacy) is slightly negative (Figure A1.3).

Industrialization and Mining

Often industrialization and mining are considered important predictors of rebel retirement. I obtained data on investment in six industry types: construction, energy (electric), public, private-foreign, private-domestic, and mining from the Center for Monitoring the Indian Economy's (CMIE) Capital Expenditure Database (CapEx).[6] During preliminary analysis, scatter plots show that there is a slight negative correlation between the dependent variable of rebel retirement and investments in the electric industry and

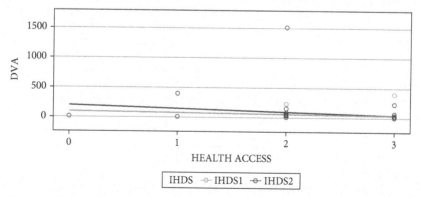

Figure A1.2 Correlation between Rebel Retirement and Access to Healthcare

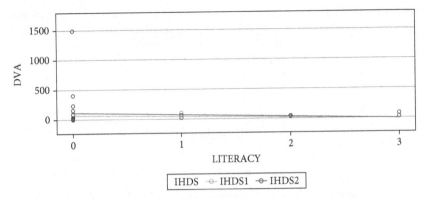

Figure A1.3 Correlation between Rebel Retirement and Literacy

a positive correlation between the dependent variable and investments in construction. Other investments do not appear to be correlated with dependent variable.

I obtained the data on the volume of bauxite, iron-ore, and coal extraction for the period 2001–2005 from Indiastat.com. All mining data is given in levels, with 0 representing no mining and 11 representing high levels of mining. The data on crude petrol exhibits a low level of variance and is excluded from analysis. Preliminary scatter plots suggests a slightly negative correlation between coal mining and retirement.

The following two hypotheses test if mining and repression matter for rebel retirement.

H6 *A high rebel retirement is expected in districts with high mining activity.*
H7 *A high rebel retirement is expected in districts with high Maoist casualties.*

Repression

The evidence in the literature on repression and political violence is at best indeterminate. Policymakers seem more convinced than academics that inflicting high casualties on rebels suppresses insurgency and will likely increase desertion and the return of remaining rebels. Some have argued in favor of a linear function whereby repression dampens recruitment by raising the costs to individuals of joining insurgent organizations (Tullock 1971). Others have specified a concave function whereby participation peaks at intermediate levels of repression but declines thereafter (Gurr 1970). Still others have claimed that the relationship between repression and rebellion is convex: Higher levels of repression increase resentment, and, therefore, repression feeds protest and rebellion, reducing retirement. In this argument, repression against its own citizens reduces the government's legitimacy, politicizes the apathetic, and radicalizes free riders into revolutionaries, thereby spreading conflict (Lichbach 1987). Wood also argues along similar lines that rebels successfully incorporate the government's indiscriminate violence into their appeals to recruit more supporters (Wood 2003).

In order to test if repression affects retirement, I measured repression in terms of Maoist casualties, obtained from the National Counterterrorism Center's World Incident

Tracking System (WITS) until 2009 and from SATP between 2010 and 2014. Since development and repression work in tandem, it is difficult to isolate their impact on the extent of rebel retirement.

Control Variables: Geography, Ethnicity, Land Inequality, Crime

I included controls for the population and the size of a given district because the state is typically thought to have a harder time rooting out the Maoists in larger districts. Since Maoists are generally thought to control more remote areas and to use the forest for cover, I included controls for the percentage of a district's area covered by forest.[7] I included controls for the percentage of the population that is made up of SC/ST, as these are the main aggrieved groups who have taken up arms against the state (Urdal 2008). The IHDS also provides data on how people felt about crime in their vicinity, asking respondents if they heard about theft (variable LC1), break-ins (LC2), threat at knife point (LC3), and street harassment of women in their area (LC4) over the last 12 months.[8]

Descriptive Statistics

Table A1.3 shows the descriptive statistics of all explanatory and control variables.

Negative Binomial Regression and Robustness Checks

To investigate the relationship between the dependent variable, RTRMT, and the independent variables, I used a negative binomial regression.[9] ORGDENS at level 3 is statistically significant and this effect is stable when we control for the other influences, as well as under the IHDS 1 and IHDS 2.

The increase in household assets has a negative impact on RTRMT, however, it is not significant, influencing retirement by a factor of 0.62. Access to healthcare, on the other hand, shows a positive effect, impacting incident rate by a factor of 11.6. The effect of education access on retirement is positive but small. Confidence in institutions has a negative impact on the number of retired rebels. On average it impacts the retirement rate by a factor of 0.43 (Table A1.5). The results are robust using values of explanatory and control variables from IHDS 2 data set, except access to education has a small negative effect on retirement.

As shown in Table A1.5, I find that all forms of investments in industry, contrary to the policy prescription, have a negative impact on rebel retirement. Most effects are, however, insignificant. Only domestic investments seem to have a significant impact. With mining variables the regression results show a positive effect for mining activities, with the exception of coal mining, which shows a negative effect. None of the effects is, however, significant. None of them exhibit large effect sizes. The effect of organizational density on retirement is stable and significant in all models.

Table A1.3 Descriptive Statistics

Variable	N	Mean	SD	Min.	Max.
Investments Electric (INV_ELECTRIC)	237	0.2353	0.257	0.0004735	1
Investments Construction (INV_CONSTRUCTION)	219	0.1624	0.2669	0	1
Investments Foreign (INV_FOREIGN)	154	0.08216	0.2436	0	1
Investments Domestic (INV_DOMESTIC)	310	0.1174	0.1849	0	1
Investments Public (INV_PUBLIC)	197	0.1071	0.2172	0	1
Investments Mining (INV_MINING)	228	0.07216	0.2007	0	1
Mining Crude Petrol (CRUDE_PETROL)	310	0.4	1.163	0	6
Mining Coal Lignite (COAL_LIGNITE)	310	2.8	4.715	0	17
Mining Metal Ores (Metal_Ores)	310	2.033	4.098	0	16
Mining NonFerrous Metal Ores (Non_Ferrous_Metal_Ores)	310	0.1333	0.5713	0	3
Difference Household Assets (DIFFHHASSETS)	318	3.496	2.169	−1.417	11.43
Health Access (HEALTH_ACCESS)	318	2.447	0.928	0	3
Literacy (Literacy)	318	0.5957	0.9007	0	3
Percentage of Argricultural Labor (r_pct_maglb)	310	0.2297	0.09891	0.0803	0.4649
Confidence in Institutions (CONFINST)	318	2.021	0.9205	1	3
Crime (CRIME)	318	1	0	1	1
Natural Logarithm of Area (ln_area)	318	8.778	0.9361	5.22	9.859
Natural Logarithm of Population (ln_population)	318	14.51	0.6125	13.13	15.58
Area Covered with Forest (forest_cover)	315	26.56	17.85	0	67.2
Percentage of SC Population (r_pct_sc)	318	0.1609	0.0726	0.02499	0.3248
Percentage of ST Population (r_pct_st)	318	0.2481	0.2341	0.000751	0.7021

Table A1.4 Organizational Density and Rebel Retirement

	RETRMT (IHDS 1)	RETRMT w/Controls (IHDS 1)	RETRMT (IHDS 2)	RETRMT w/Controls (IHDS 2)
(Intercept)	2.875*** (0.269)	1.001 (3.180)	2.880*** (0.374)	1.956 (3.407)
ORGDENS: 2/1	−0.148 (0.548)	−0.015 (0.574)	1.445* (0.594)	0.945 (0.635)
ORGDENS: 3/1	1.138** (0.398)	0.652* (0.413)	0.686* (0.473)	0.096* (0.584)
r_pct_sc		−5.843* (2.733)		−6.932* (2.860)
ln_area		0.331 (0.351)		0.250 (0.385)
AIC	407.177	376.118	409.802	371.400
N	318	316	318	317

Notes: Negative binomial regressions. Dependent variables are number of Maoist surrender events. Standard errors in parentheses. *** $p<0.01$, ** $p<0.05$, * $p<0.1$

Table A1.5 Impact of Investment on Industrialization

	RTRMT (1)	RTRMT (2)	RTRMT (3)	RTRMT (4)	RTRMT (5)	RTRMT (6)
(Intercept)	1.464 (3.781)	0.401 (3.973)	−17.570** (5.983)	1.121 (3.349)	1.896 (3.636)	−1.524 (4.157)
ORGDENS: 2/1	0.065 (0.658)	0.185 (0.668)	−0.524 (1.324)	−0.195 (0.649)	−0.050 (0.633)	−1.390 (0.805)
ORGDENS: 3/1	0.677* (0.492)	0.001* (0.499)	0.418 (0.720)	0.505* (0.437)	0.835* (0.469)	1.250* (0.555)
r_pct_sc	−8.100* (3.449)	−11.042*** (3.208)	−2.618 (4.523)	−6.152* (2.991)	−6.873* (3.011)	−0.569 (3.663)
ln_area	0.358 (0.406)	0.531 (0.457)	2.438*** (0.692)	0.363 (0.372)	0.262 (0.399)	0.534 (0.465)
INV_ELECTRIC	−1.640 (0.873)					
INV_CONSTRUCTION		−0.282 (0.977)				
INV_FOREIGN			−0.869 (1.095)			
INV_DOMESTIC				−2.492* (1.136)		
INV_PUBLIC					−0.305 (0.966)	
INV_MINING						−0.481 (1.239)
AIC	278.041	244.017	126.771	353.668	315.125	255.815
N	231	218	150	306	190	228

Notes: Negative binomial regressions. Dependent variables are number of Maoist surrender events. Standard errors in parentheses. *** $p<0.01$, ** $p<0.05$, * $p<0.1$

Table A1.6 Impact of Mining on Retirement

	RETRMT (1)	RETRMT (2)	RETRMT (3)	RETRMT (4)
(Intercept)	−0.151 (4.221)	−3.984 (4.112)	−1.444 (4.083)	−1.314 (4.044)
ORGDENS: 2/1	−1.302 (0.788)	−1.657* (0.775)	−1.452 (0.780)	−1.493 (0.772)
ORGDENS: 3/1	1.313* (0.556)	1.304* (0.543)	1.327* (0.557)	1.284* (0.548)
r_pct_sc	−1.563 (3.705)	0.502 (3.542)	1.443 (3.703)	1.232 (3.674)
ln_area	0.385 (0.472)	0.808 (0.464)	0.466 (0.458)	0.462 (0.455)
Crude Petrol	0.117 (0.191)			
Coal Lignite		−0.087 (0.049)		
Metal Ores			0.066 (0.054)	
NonFerrous Metal Ores				0.579 (0.374)
AIC	255.434	253.540	254.846	254.020
N	301	301	301	301

Notes: Negative binomial regressions. Dependent variables are number of Maoist surrender events. Standard errors in parentheses. *** $p<0.01$, ** $p<0.05$, * $p<0.1$

Table A1.7 Access to Assets and Public Service

	RETRMT (1)	RETRMT (2)	RETRMT (3)	RETRMT (4)	RETRMT (5)
(Intercept)	0.536 (3.172)	−2.311 (2.950)	1.117 (3.556)	2.553 (3.230)	3.769 (3.538)
ORGDENS: 2/1	0.112 (0.590)	0.238 (0.524)	−0.369 (0.581)	−0.321 (0.587)	−0.663 (0.590)
ORGDENS: 3/1	0.909* (0.409)	0.495* (0.395)	0.280** (0.444)	0.526* (0.422)	0.218* (0.431)
r_pct_sc	−6.379* (2.802)	−7.132** (2.509)	−4.535 (2.931)	−7.086* (2.869)	−6.767* (2.953)
ln_area	0.431 (0.347)	0.535 (0.326)	0.319 (0.388)	0.138 (0.365)	0.121 (0.369)
DIFFHHASSETS	−0.138 (0.087)				
HEALTH_ ACCESS: 1/0		0.088 (1.060)			
HEALTH_ ACCESS: 2/0		2.449*** (0.724)			
HEALTH_ ACCESS: 3/0		1.583* (0.641)			
LITERACY: 1/0			−0.030 (0.449)		
LITERACY: 2/0			−1.108 (1.350)		
LITERACY: 3/0			0.249 (0.811)		
REPRESSION				1.946 (2.188)	
CONFINST: 2/1					−0.841 (0.597)
CONFINST: 3/1					−0.831 (0.477)
AIC	369.969	370.620	382.741	377.123	377.279
N	312	301	310	310	310

Notes: Negative binomial regressions. Dependent variables are number of Maoist surrender events. Standard errors in parentheses. *** p<0.01, ** p<0.05, * p<0.1

Table A1.8 Robustness Tests (IHDS II)

	RETRMT (1)	RETRMT (2)	RETRMT (3)	RETRMT (4)
(Intercept)	2.573 (3.445)	−4.041 (3.408)	2.772 (3.283)	0.583 (3.699)
ORGDENS: 1/0	−0.176 (0.573)	−0.633 (0.491)	0.027 (0.545)	−1.402** (0.524)
ORGDENS: 2/0	1.174 (0.626)	0.449 (0.622)	1.320* (0.609)	0.729 (0.571)
ORGDENS: 3/0	0.401* (0.601)	−1.320* (0.573)	0.401* (0.617)	−0.547* (0.533)
r_pct_sc	−7.700** (2.899)	2.064 (2.714)	−6.214* (2.752)	−5.147 (2.770)
ln_area	0.226 (0.382)	0.580 (0.346)	0.162 (0.371)	0.400 (0.393)
DIFFHHASSETS	−0.123 (0.093)			
HEALTH_ ACCESS: 1/0		5.808*** (1.396)		
HEALTH_ ACCESS: 2/0		2.533* (1.014)		
HEALTH_ ACCESS: 3/0		1.963* (0.854)		
LITERACY: 1/0			−1.258* (0.505)	
LITERACY: 2/0			−0.730 (0.536)	
LITERACY: 3/0			−1.195 (0.633)	
CONFINST: 2/1				1.473** (0.536)
CONFINST: 3/1				−0.374 (0.455)
AIC	371.826	356.366	369.592	363.254
N	312	310	312	312

Notes: Negative binomial regressions. Dependent variables are number of Maoist surrender events. Standard errors in parentheses. *** $p<0.01$, ** $p<0.05$, * $p<0.1$

Methods Appendix

The evidence on the process of rebel retirement presented in this book is gathered primarily through interviews with current and former Maoist rebels, as well as politicians, law enforcement agents, bureaucrats, activists, journalists, academics, and ordinary people in the two conflict zones in India. Most of this fieldwork was carried out over a period of 18 months during 2013–2014, with some preliminary groundwork, archival research, and statistical analysis between 2009 and 2012. The purpose of this Methods Appendix is to provide readers a summary of the interview method used in this project, and it includes discussions on sample frame construction, response rate and type, format and length of interviews, recording method, accuracy of reporting, and confidence level in the information acquired through interviews.

I used both semi-structured and life history format interviews for this project. Of the 103 interviews with retired rebels in North and South India, 35 were long, open-ended conversations in life history format where respondents decided what they were comfortable sharing,[1] which not only complied with standards of ethically responsible research in postwar settings but also seemed intuitively respectful (do no harm) particularly given my higher status in the research sites (Büthe et al. 2015; Dauphinée 2016; Pachirat 2011; Wood 2006). I was able to organize focus groups, surveys, and iterative conversational interactions (ranging from 20 minutes to 4.5 hours) with civilians in conflict zones, particularly those who were directly involved in or shared intimate knowledge of many wartime clandestine networks and grassroots civic associations, examples of which are discussed throughout the book. Most interviews and focus group discussions involved written concurrent notes, and supplementary follow up notes written within an hour or on the same day. Some interviews with academics, journalists, and politicians included audio recording alongside handwritten notes. These notes identified respondents by category and number rather than names, identifiers like name and location being saved in different virtual documents. Some respondents, including Maoist leaders, former rebels, politicians, and police, requested or required full or partial confidentiality. Some of the comments made off the record were not used to form any of the conclusions in this book.

Choice of Interviews as Primary Method of Data Collection

Broadly speaking, the methodological landscape in social science offered three choices for this project in terms of methodology: experimental methods, survey methods, or ethnographic methods. Although experiments have been used effectively for testing hypotheses in some conflict zones and they have the definite advantage of high internal validity, the random allocation of research subjects to those affected or unaffected by the explanatory variable was not practically, politically, and ethically possible in this case of exploratory, theory-building research. There is also an overwhelming preference for surveys in social research, their primary value being the scale and representation of the populations that allows for more generalizable conclusions. Although surveys could allow for a larger sample size, in a more cost-effective and timely manner, particularly because researchers generally do not administer their surveys themselves but contract it out to some local agency, it became apparent during two 100-respondents pilot surveys in Andhra Pradesh (South) and in Jharkhand (North) that survey penetration is shallow, easier done in some areas than others, and has to be concentrated on what was measurable, side-stepping the less tangible and more qualitative or descriptive aspects of the information obtained.[2]

I also conducted a few focus groups with civilians in both the conflict zones, three in the South (Karimnagar, Warrangal, Nalgonda) and two in the North (Ranchi, Khunti) to discuss questions centered on the process and impact of democratic transition of former rebels. The primary reason behind organizing these focus groups was to generate data at three levels of analysis: individual, group, and their interaction. Although focus groups have their own utilities in increasing transparency and replicability of qualitative data (Cyr 2016), gathering 8–10 people for focus groups eventually drew the attention of local police and politicians, which, in turn, had a negative impact on the prospects of active engagement by participants. The underlying purpose of focus groups for this project was to generate multiple individual data points simultaneously. I was also interested to see if there could be ways to assess the level of agreement or strain within the groups on the prospect of and impact on return of rebels into their communities, which, was, however, an issue that most participants deferred to each other and did not tackle openly.

In contrast, I found one-on-one conversations better suited in reducing the social desirability bias (Mosley 2013; Tansey 2007) that creeps in both in surveys and focus groups, particularly when respondents are expected to address sensitive issues, painful memories, or intimate personal experiences of loss, violence, and trauma. For a researcher interested in understanding social outcomes in terms of the beliefs, incentives, and strategic choices of individuals, the life history format interviews were very effective in generating many data points to assess the roots of individual actions alongside additional metadata about their attitudes. Relative to an individual survey response, a single interview generated more points of inferential leverage—I had information not only on what a respondent said but also on how the respondents behaved during the interview, whether they hesitated in discussing some issues but not others, which generate useful metadata that facilitates more accurate use and interpretation of interview data, in a way that often is not possible for survey responses. But the depth of understanding comes at the cost of reliability and generalizability. In addition to a much deeper set of responses, interviews provided opportunities for me to ask follow-up questions. My field notes also recorded participant observation, which include thousands of informal conversations with various stakeholders, which shed light on their interests and incentives of other stakeholders in this conflict, as they understood it in their social context. These notes along with the metadata about respondents provide a strong foundation for conclusions presented in this book.

Semi-structured interviews were more readily administered to the police, bureaucrats, and politicians that I spoke to, which were particularly valuable in triangulating evidence on their interests and incentives around surrender of Maoists and on the clandestine and semi-secret networks between insurgency and civil society organizations. The rich data I gathered is particularly suited in fleshing out causal mechanisms via process tracing (George et al. 2005; Mahoney 2000; Mahoney and Schensul 2006). In the light of the recent focus on increasing rigor and transparency in collection and reporting of interview data (Elman, Kapiszewski, and Vinuela 2010; Lupia and Elman 2014; Moravcsik 2010). The rest of this Appendix discusses how this book tackled the strengths and weakness of the interview method under three headings: representativeness of sample, type and quality of information obtained, and accuracy of reporting.

Representativeness of Sample

Interviews and surveys, both based on responses gained from human informants, fall on a continuum, with trade-offs between small- and large-N studies. Surveys often report response rate because higher the response rate the more valid the survey results are generally perceived to be. However, authors who conducted numerous interviews typically report some information about the interviewees, names and job tiles, place and date, and cite the information from interviews in quotations as evidence of an argument. The biggest challenge in this format of reporting interview data is that in the absence of any reference to a theoretically motivated "ideal" sample frame of target interviewees generated before going into the field, which could then allow researchers to assess response rates or potential nonresponse bias in interviews (Bleich and Pekkanen 2013; Mosley 2013). The problem of biased results is further exacerbated by the snowball-sampling technique of seeking additional interview leads from existing interviews (Cohen and Arieli 2011). Although there is much to recommend snowballing, particularly in a postconflict environment where interviews are hard to come by without referrals, the biggest drawback of this method is that researchers can become confined to a set a respondents who are all interconnected and see the world through the same lens.[3]

To avoid these pitfalls to some extent, I constructed a sample frame for this research, which included 8 Categories of respondents based on my knowledge of the topic: current Maoists (Category 1), elected politicians (Category 2), police (Category 3), bureaucrats (Category 4), retired Maoists (Category 5), experts including academics and journalists (Category 6), activists (Category 7), and civilians in conflict zones (Category 8). The purpose of constructing this sample frame was to identify and include all classes of actors that could be potentially relevant to the process of rebel retirement and to collect balanced information from multiple sources. This was taken as a step toward creating a representative sample and also allowed me to be mindful of the systematic error that could be introduced by the degree to which those who cannot be contacted or refuse to be interviewed in a category could differ in traits or attitudes from those who are successfully contacted and interviewed. I also tracked whether I achieved saturation (reached the targeted threshold of interviews) in some categories over others, so that my interview data did not overrepresent viewpoints of those who were more accessible and willing to be interviewed than others, introducing systematic errors that jeopardize the generalizability of conclusions based on such a biased sample.

I was cognizant of the fact that it would be hardest to procure interviews from current Maoist rebels engaged in an ongoing insurgency for personal safety reasons and given travel restrictions, and included 10 target respondents in the sample frame, five from each region and from across the organizational hierarchy.[4] I was able to interview six respondents (labeled L1–6) in this category, two in Hyderabad, two in Delhi, and two in Ranchi, of which all except one were urban upper-caste men with college educations, representative of the Maoist leadership but not of the entire movement. These were semi-structured interviews, lasting between 2–3.5 hours, confidentiality was required for all except two. Although these interviews gave me valuable insights, particularly an ability to triangulate responses of retired rebels on internal organizational procedure of retirement,

I was aware of missing the specific challenges that women and Dalit rebels might face in the Maoist movement. It was entirely expected that I was not able to interview rebels who were currently in the insurgency and were contemplating retirement soon, but I did not expect their takes on the process of retirement to be systematically different from those of the recently retired rebels that I was able to interview.

This brings us to the special challenges of research in conflict zones, of which there are many (Lehmann and Romano 2006; Kapiszewski, MacLean, and Read 2015). Understanding an armed conflict requires access to all the groups involved in or affected by it. However, for protagonists on two sides of a conflict, who, by definition, do not accept the legitimacy of their adversary, any association with "the other side," which includes meeting and speaking to them, can be interpreted as a hostile act. I found this the biggest challenge: My respondents, both in rebel and state camps, wanted to assess my personal belief systems and socioeconomic position and sometimes asked for samples of written work that would allow them to assess where I stood personally with respect to the insurgency before granting interviews. Thus, in the end, scheduling and completing interviews with current and former rebels in an ongoing conflict takes a fair bit of luck, and access to interviewees and their willingness to speak trumps everything. I constructed the sample frame with the realistic expectation that a representative sample is of little use if the researcher cannot access the sampled units. Knowing that, having a fairly clear idea of the sample frame before starting the interviews was particularly helpful in keeping track of when I achieved saturation in some categories over others.

In Category 2, I targeted respondents from the political parties in power in New Delhi, Jharkhand, and undivided Andhra Pradesh, which included Indian National Congress (INC) in New Delhi, Jharkhand Mukti Morcha (JMM) and Bharatiya Janata Party (BJP) in the North and Telugu Desam Party (TDP), INC, and Telangana Rashrtriya Samiti (TRS) in the South. Since there is lot of publicly available information on the positions of these various political parties on questions of surrender and rehabilitation of Maoists, I focused more on meeting local politicians, mostly current or former members of legislative assembly (MLA) with direct experience in dealing with surrendering Maoists. I was able to meet one central minister (the minister of Rural Development, Mr. Jairam Ramesh), and five politicians from across the TRS, TDP, and INC ideological spectrum in the South (PS2–6), and four from Trinamool Congress, BJP, JMM, and CPI(ML) Liberation from the North (PN7–10).[5] These were semi-structured interviews, lasting between 20 minutes to 1.5 hours, all were face to face except one (PN8 via phone for 45 minutes). I decided that I had achieved saturation in this category when (a) recommendations for further interviews mirrored the list of politicians already interviewed, and (b) respondents were reporting the same processes and challenges in rebel surrender and rehabilitation as previous interviewees, with some predictable disagreements.

My sample frame for police (Category 3) originally targeted Gray Hound commandos, who were known to have been important in counterinsurgency. It turned out that police officers in the South were reluctant to be identified as Gray Hounds or to be interviewed, and I was not able to reach saturation in Category 3 in the South. I was, however, able to interview the officers in the anti-Naxalite cell in the police headquarters in Ranchi. Any experienced field researcher knows that the sample frame can dramatically change in the field, but knowing that I did not attain saturation (defined as reaching the target interview number and variation) in Category 3 in the South, allowed me to compensate for it by incorporating secondary evidence as well as interviews with scholars and retired police officers specializing in anti-Maoist policing. The average length of interviews in Category

3 was 30 minutes, and the interviewees were selected through snowball sampling. There are also reasonable doubts that some of my interviewees in this category were very cautious of what they can or cannot say. But there were others who were quite surprising in their frankness, which often seemed against their own interests, and were very credible.

I achieved saturation in my sample frame in Category 6 (academics and journalist), including scholars from both the North and South, and journalists from vernacular and English-language newspapers. I went beyond my sample frame in Category 7 (activists), both in the North and South, because my expectations of their roles as movement entrepreneurs (MEs) and reintegration stewards (RSs) evolved in the field. Snowball sampling proved particularly useful in this category, as my interviewees pointed me to networks and people who played active roles as MEs and RSs. I had originally planned surveys in the North and the South, which I decided to not do after administering 100-respondent surveys both in the North and South. In the course of the survey, I was able to conduct in-depth semi-structured interviews with 23 civilians (Category 8), 17 in the South and six in the North, which was not included in the initial pre-field sample frame.

In the North, I was able to contact all the retired rebels (Category 5) based on the list and contact information of retired rebels in the police headquarters in Ranchi. With the exception of those who were killed or were still in prison as a protection against death threats from Maoists, I spoke to 33 rebels, of which 18 were life history format interviews. To carve out a representative sample of retired rebels in the South, I interviewed retired rebels at various levels in the Maoist organization hierarchy, including both men and women rebels, covering high- and low-retirement districts in both northern and southern conflict zones.[6] I met retired rebels through snowball sampling in the South. But my sample frame, representing the trend in the population of retired rebels, included proportionately more low- and mid-level cadres, and more men than women.[7] I met many of these former rebels more than once, after a period of four to six months, for follow-up interviews. I achieved saturation in this category when I realized that new interviewees reiterated what previous interviewees had already mentioned.

I wanted to achieve variation in movement intensity and retirement in my fieldwork sites, where I could interview ordinary people who populated the quotidian and formal civic associations that nurtured the exit networks. In the South, based on local knowledge, as well as relevant historical texts (such as official documents and party publications), various memoirs, surveys, vernacular newspapers, secondary cases, and Maoist theoretical literature, I picked five out of 10 districts in Telangana, of which Warangal and Khammam had the highest incidence of retirement events between 2005 and 2015, Karimnagar had a moderate incidence, and Adilabad and Nalgonda had the lowest incidence of retirement events, thereby maximizing variance on the dimension of interest.[8] In each of these districts, I picked one *mandal* that was highly affected by the insurgency, one that was moderately affected, and one that was sparsely affected.[9] Subsequently in each highly affected mandal, I randomly chose two villages, and in each moderately affected and sparsely affected village I picked one village each, allowing me to cover four villages in each of the five districts. In the North, however, the two districts with highest surrender events in Jharkhand (Ranchi and Khunti) were not among the 12 Maoist-affected districts in the state. Therefore, I distributed my fieldwork in the three Maoist pockets in North (Palamu district), east (Giridih district), and South (West Singhbhum district) Jharkhand.[10]

Accuracy of Reporting

One ideal standard for improving accuracy of reporting in case interview research is qualitative data archiving, which allows sharing full interview transcripts, which, however, was neither possible nor ethical in this particular project. Since the Northern Ireland/Boston College fiasco,[11] the problems and pitfalls of transparency in the context of conflict research is well recognized. In my kind of research, the priority has to be on protecting informants' personal safety over research transparency. I have not quoted interviewees because researchers are particularly open to the charge of simply cherry-picking the most eye-catching statements, without regard to representativeness. It is important to represent that the quotation is representative of the average intensity and direction of response. Although providing quotes is not the same as providing transcripts, thick description of life in certain districts and villages of India, even without proper nouns, will allow people to connect the dots, turning them into intelligence assets. In this book de-identification of my interlocutors goes beyond merely removing the name, title, or institutional affiliation of my research participants (Parkinson and Wood 2015). I have changed names and attributes of informants, along with the names of neighborhoods and villages, because these details presented as evidence can be enough for a local to identify key players and/or informants. For example, in my conversations with former rebels and activists, I would begin with one question: How did they become Maoist rebels or grassroots rights activists? Their answers inevitably consisted of detailed accounts of the violence that they and their families have observed or experienced in very specific ways that would be identifiable even if I removed the research participant's name, location, or title. With that in mind, I have avoided using these direct quotes from rebels even if it would serve my interests in proving my case.[12]

If these fears sound exaggerated, there is often no way to know whether a civil liberty activist or an academic, for example, who judges herself to be safe one day will be criminalized tomorrow, next month, or in five years. For example, many activists I spoke to during my fieldwork in 2013–2014 were identified as "urban Naxals" in India recently. Many of these well-known rights activists and journalists branded as "invisible enemies of the state" fear for their lives, and some have in fact been killed and others jailed indefinitely. A lot of area studies expert knowledge can be re-purposed in the interest of the national security state. In my experience, the representatives of an IRB, as easy as it is to caricature them, are actually sympathetic to the idea that total transparency is, when it comes to war zones, neither feasible nor desirable. This does not mean that we cannot improve transparency in qualitative research that aims to make causal claims but rather that the criteria be flexible. For example, in this book, instead of cherry-picking quotes and sharing them as evidence, I have reported what percentage of interviewees under Category 5 (retired rebels) recounted, without being prompted, that physical safety was the more pressing concern for them compared to post-retirement economic security.

Notes

Chapter 1

1. Of the total 6,760 casualties, 715 were in Andhra Pradesh, 2,262 were in Chhattisgarh, 1,364 were in Jharkhand, and 699 were in West Bengal. Data is sourced from the South Asia Terrorism Portal (SATP), http://www.satp.org/satporgtp/countries/india/maoist/data_sheets/fatalitiesnaxal05-11.htm (accessed on June 18, 2015).
2. Strategic documents describing the methods and goals of CPI (Maoist) are available at http://www.bannedthought.net/India/CPI-Maoist-Docs/ (accessed February 6, 2019).
3. In 2004, PW merged with the Maoist Communist Center (MCC) and CPI (Party Unity) (PU) based in the eastern states of Jharkhand, Bihar, and West Bengal to form an all-India united front CPI (Maoist). Post-unification, the Maoists leapt to national prominence, proclaiming control over continuous territory across six states dubbed the "Red Corridor." This name given to the Maoist-affected states invokes the reference of the Maoist red flag planted in firm declaration of territorial control.
4. Man Mohan Singh, "Focus on Good Governance, Reducing Deprivation and Alienation," Concluding Remarks at the Second Meeting of the Standing Committee of Chief Ministers on Naxalism, April 13, 2006, available at http://pib.nic.in/release/rel_print_page.asp?relid=17128 (Link no longer available).
5. This data is sourced from the South Asian Terrorism Portal (SATP), a website maintained by the Institute of Conflict Management in New Delhi. SATP is a non-governmental organization that provides consultancy services to governments on insurgency-related activities. Their website collates and summarizes data based on news articles, highlighting the date and location of the incident and the number of casualties; injuries, and abductions. Surrender data, based on media reports, is listed by the year along with district and state information. Between 2005 and 2012, 142 rebels surrendered in Bihar, 140 in Odisha, 115 in Chhattisgarh, and 39 in West Bengal. Data on surrender of Maoists in India is also recorded by the Naxal Management Division of the Ministry of Home Affairs (MHA) of the government of India. The MHA data is based on reports submitted by police stations in various Maoist-affected states. In general, both data sources show similar yearly trends; MHA data are slightly higher than SATP data on surrender, except in Odisha in 2013. On examination of the underlying media reports that SATP used to compile this data, I found that they coded en masse "surrender" of activists of a popular tribal organization (Chasi Muliya Adivasi Sangh, CMAS) as Maoist surrender, while MHA did not recognize them as Maoist.
6. The Maoists draw their recruitment primarily from the SC, formerly untouchables and ST, indigenous groups populations. The SC/ST population is comparable in

the two states, and yet retirement is disproportionately high in the South. The SC/ST population of Jharkhand, for example, is over 70% of the SC/ST population of Andhra Pradesh according to census 2011 data, while retirement in Jharkhand is less than 7% than in Andhra Pradesh. Between 2006 and 2012, aggregate rebel casualties were higher in the North compared to the South. In absolute numbers 245 Maoist rebels were killed in the state of Andhra Pradesh in the South compared to 323 in the state of Jharkhand in the North. However, both the Telangana region of AP and Jharkhand (which was South Bihar) are historically considered two pockets of Maoist strongholds with a high concentration of worst affected districts, comparable number of Maoist incidents and comparable Maoist casualty in proportion to total casualties.

7. Many flaws of SATP data have been known to researchers. The compilers of the SATP data rely primarily on English-language newspapers and do not provide a codebook. They are not entirely transparent in their data-extraction methodology. Even beyond SATP, conflict data is inherently problematic, but there is no evidence that any systematic error distorts the surrender data of one region versus the other. The concerns about reporting bias and deliberate suppression of exit news or their deliberate exaggeration are not very relevant to the central arguments made in this book because the focus here is on the huge North-South variation, which is too large, obvious and stark to be undercut by random errors in the sample or even by systematic bias, if any.

8. In Ranchi, the capital of Jharkhand, I have spent time idling around the Secretariat and talking to mid- and high-level bureaucrats. It became apparent that they were under pressure from the Home Ministry in New Delhi to match the high surrender rates in Andhra Pradesh. The police officers in charge of anti-Naxal operations in Ranchi expressed frustration over the constant belittling by state and central bureaucrats and ministers for the officers' inability to secure more Maoist surrender on a par with their counterparts in Andhra Pradesh. During annual meetings among chief ministers of Maoist-affected states, the prime minister of India routinely sings the praise of Andhra Pradesh for its remarkable success in luring rebels away. The example of Andhra Pradesh was repeatedly invoked during my meetings in policy circles in Delhi and in the state capitals of Jharkhand and West Bengal.

9. The CPI(Maoist), the largest umbrella organization uniting the largest Maoist factions, was formed in 2004. It is often referred to as Maoist Party in this book as is the norm in the media and in policy literature. The term Naxal or Naxalite is also used as a blanket term to refer to the Maoist in India. Anti-Maoist counterinsurgency measures across states has historically been coordinated from center, through an Integrated Action Plan (IAP). Prime Minister Manmohan Singh, in his address in the meeting of chief ministers of Naxal-affected States in New Delhi on July 14, 2010, said, "Though law and order is primarily a state subject, the ramifications of the problem of Left Wing Extremism call for sustained coordination between the Centre and the States not only regarding the overall strategy but even on the regular operational issues. In particular, we need greater coordination and cooperation in crucial matters like intelligence gathering and intelligence sharing." In addition, the police and administration in Jharkhand acknowledged the pressure to follow Andhra Model of counterinsurgency, which they tried to do without much success. For more details on centralization of

counterinsurgency, please see https://satp.org/document/paper-acts-and-oridinances/pm-s-opening-remarks-at-the-meeting-of-chief-ministers-of-naxal-affected-states.

10. A little more than 50% of former rebels, both in the North and the South, volunteered this description of themselves as retired rebels or retired soldiers while discussing their perception of their career and their most important contribution. For example, one of the earliest and most eloquent articulations of this parallel was made by a respondent (MS3) in Nalgonda, Telangana, who pointed out that since he quit voluntarily and not under any kind of duress the term "surrender" is inappropriate. Another respondent (MS7) in Karimnagar, Telangana, mentioned that he and his former comrades joked about hosting a retirement party for recently disarmed Maoists. Later another former Maoist (MS15) argued that when it came to patriotism and sacrifice for their country and people, there is not much difference between former Maoists like him and retired freedom fighters in India, who are referred to as "retired" and awarded pensions by the government of India. See, e.g., https://pensionersportal.gov.in/Briefsssp.asp. Over 85% of respondents who were specifically asked about it agreed that they were retired rather than had surrendered because they made the decision to leave their career and did not necessarily do it under duress.

11. The Appendix on interview research methods discusses the various categories of respondents included in the pre-field sample frame for this study. During this time, these rebels were mostly out of touch with their families and did not visit their ancestral villages in daylight. Although five years of absence from the mainstream was used as a cut off, 85% of the former rebels I met were in the guerrilla army or in other branches of the organization, including district and state committees or in the Central Committee and Politburo, for over a decade. The five-year cut off was used to exclude those who might dabble with the insurgency for short-term gains in local prestige or access to firearms. It also excludes many Maoist sympathizers who were part of various Maoist frontal organizations who cannot be categorized as former combatants.

12. The Surrender and Rehabilitation Program of the Government of India is available at https://www.mha.gov.in/sites/default/files/surrrenderPolAendments070909_0.pdf.

13. I use the term "retire" to highlight the protracted process of leaving an insurgency in which surrender of arms and reintegration come as the very last steps. By retired rebels, I refer to former guerrillas who have been away from their families and ancestral villages for at least five years. In many cases they have been away for over a decade.

14. Since the total number of rebels in each state is not known for certain, it is impossible to compute retirement in proportion to total rebel population.

15. *Mandal* is the second level in the three-tier local body/*panchayati* raj system. Many *gram panchayats*/villages make a mandal, and many mandals make a district, and many districts make a state.

16. Srinivasa Rao A, "Why the Maoists are Desperate to Regain Grounds in Andhra, Telangana," *Hinudstan Times*, October 25, 2016. http://www.hindustantimes.com/india-news/why-maoists-are-desperate-to-regain-andhra-telangana-strongholds/story-LUZAg3Hr9jT5PyUYlrP9zL.html.

17. It was customary to refer to the Maoist leaders from the state of West Bengal as "dada," meaning elder brother in the local language (Bangla). But no one in Jharkhand or Bihar referred to the ordinary Maoist members as "dada."

18. The Greyhounds were a special force introduced in the South (Andhra Pradesh) in 1989 to hunt down Maoist rebels. The first version of the Surrender and Rehabilitation package, which was pithy and did not contain many lucrative offers, was introduced in 1994.

19. Data on district-level surrender of Maoist rebels is taken from SATP available at http://www.satp.org/satporgtp/countries/india/maoist/data_sheets/maoist_datasheet.html.

20. Since 2009, I have spent four years in the Telangana region of Andhra Pradesh (Nalgonda, Karimnagar, Warrangal, Adilabad, and Khammam districts), Jharkhand (Ranchi, Khunti, Palamau, Giridih, and West Singhbhum districts), West Bengal (primarily West Midnapore district), and New Delhi exploring these questions. In addition to retiring rebels, I also spoke to many Maoist sympathizers, who were active in their various frontal organizations, like writers' associations, cultural fronts, and anti-caste organizations. But these individuals never took up arms against the state and did not need to go underground, and hence were not "rebels" that needed to disarm or reintegrate. The fieldwork in 2013–2014 was supported by the junior research fellowship by AIIS, Cornell University, and Center for Economic and Social Sciences (Hyderabad, Andhra Pradesh) Jadavpur University (Calcutta, West Bengal).

21. For example, see http://indianexpress.com/article/india/big-gain-in-jharkhand-top-maoist-surrenders-4656072/ (accessed July 24, 2017).

22. I was questioned by central and state intelligence agencies about my interlocutors and their activities in Ranchi in October 2013, which convinced me even more that there should be nothing in my writing, outside of illustrating an understudied and underreported process of rebel retirement, that could become bases for any harm, including arrests, career backlash, or violence. It is not unheard of that area studies expert knowledge can be repurposed in the interest of the national security state.

23. Among some notable politicians located in Delhi who had knowledge of Maoist areas, organization, and ideology, I met Jairam Ramesh when he was in office as the minister of rural development in 2013, as well as R. Vineel Krishna IAS, who was abducted by the Maoists in Orissa in 2011. I also spoke to Derek O'Brien of Trinamool Congress and Dipankar Bhattacharya and Kavita Krishnan of CPI (ML) Liberation in New Delhi.

24. I met professors at various universities and colleges in the fields of political science, economics, sociology, history, and anthropology. I spoke with the local journalists of vernacular newspapers in West Bengal, Jharkhand, Chhattisgarh, and Telangana who have experience interviewing local Maoist organizers and had firsthand insights on their recruitment and mobilization techniques.

25. The government of India has identified 128 organizations across the country as so-called front organizations operating on behalf of the CPI-Maoist. According to an internal report prepared by the Intelligence Bureau, there were 17 such organizations operating in Jharkhand; 13 in Andhra Pradesh; 12 in Karnataka; 10 each in Bihar

and Odisha; nine each in Delhi, Maharashtra, and Bengal; eight in Haryana; six in Chhattisgarh; four each in Kerala and Tamil Nadu; and three in Gujarat. The home ministry official quoted earlier said these bodies had been linked to CPI-Maoist by verifiable associations of their cadres with known Naxal operatives. For more information on these see https://www.livemint.com/ (accessed April 19, 2019).

26. I also met with activists in other civil liberty organizations, including Association for Protection of Democratic Rights (APDR) and Peoples' Union for Democratic Rights (PUDR) that litigate the rights of political prisoners and unlawful detention; Peoples' Union for Civil Liberties (PUCL); Andhra Pradesh Civil Liberty Committee (APCLC); and many other grassroots and well-known activists including Varavara Rao, Gautam Navlakha, G. N. Saibaba, and Anand Teltumbde, among others. This was more successful in the South than in the North. My attempts to talk to people in the North about the former Maoists met significant resistance. In the small towns and villages, people hastily shut doors or abruptly ended conversations the moment I mentioned "*maovadi*" (Maoist), which was also an important difference in public response to the rebels between the North and the South.

27. Surveys were not of much use in these settings, where (a) every time I randomly selected a household at a convenient time when they took break from agricultural work, the neighbors and passersby came in uninvited and unhindered, and (b) respondents did not have definitive answers to questions like whether they were open to former rebels returning to their neighborhood or whether they were comfortable voting for them if they ran for office. The more well off and younger respondents sometimes advised the crowd that they should quickly pick an answer from the multiple choices I gave them, just like in exams. When I expressed my desire to hear long-winded responses as well, the opinions converged to a more ambivalent response on their attitude toward the state, elected representatives, and other institutions. In course of the conversations, it became clear that people often assembled in local libraries, sports clubs, union offices, and temple premises to discuss and often collectively decide various issues affecting the community, including how to vote, where to invest their money, and whether to build a toilet.

28. I felt the need to edit parts of the quotes from former rebels and various local and more well-known activists that I included in earlier drafts of my dissertation to protect their identities and to more closely follow the institutional review board requirements.

29. Examples in the northern epicenter include the derailment of an express train, see https://timesofindia.indiatimes.com/india/Maoist-attack-derails-13-coaches-of-Express-train-68-dead/articleshow/5983218.cms. In the South, the ambush on 76 members of the Central Reserve Police Force (CRPF) drew international attention see https://www.thehindu.com/news/national/Maoists-massacre-74-CRPF-men/article16364513.ece.

30. Most notable among them was Santosh Rana who led the Debra-Gopiballabhpur uprising in 1960s, under the direction of Charu Mazumdar, which was a successful peasant uprising outside Naxalbari. Rana led hundreds of landless peasants harvesting standing crops that they grew without the landlord's consent. He later

denounced armed struggle and was the first to contest and win an assembly election from prison.

31. I had offers from two competing activist networks and from the police to visit rural areas of Jharkhand. It is impossible to work in rural Jharkhand without an adequate network of protection. I picked an activist network affiliated with the Indian Institute of Management (IIM), Ranchi. This choice was deliberate and, in hindsight, might have restricted access to certain areas and persons. In Palamau, I had personal connections with retired Maoists, which helped me step out of this network.

32. The central government, specifically the Rural Development Ministry of India launched Saranda Action Program in 56 villages of Saranda in January 2012, and it comprised a concerted use of security forces and civil administration in tandem in a Maoist zone..

33. These areas saw the Lalgarh uprising in 2008–2009. Since 2011, the dominant regional party (Trinamool Congress, roughly translated as Grassroots Congress) came to power ending over three decades of left rule in the state. Journalists and activists, as well as eventually villagers, often quoted a local saying about people in region: *Din e Trinamooli, raat e maovadi* (TMC by day, Maoist by night).

34. I talk more on the difficulties I experienced during the pilots trying to administer surveys in Chapter 4 and 5.

35. Central intelligence officers (from New Delhi) woke me up at 5 AM in Ranchi in October 2014, inquiring about my visits in sensitive areas, meetings with "dangerous" men, and demanding to see my research notes. I had a carefully coded system for concealing the identities and locations of my informants, and interviewees were only identified by their gender and role (former rebel, woman-commander, family member-mother and so on) in my field notes. During my trips to the villages in the South, I had my phone taken from me or my signals jammed, leaving me with no way to contact my family and my barely one-year-old daughter. During focus groups, or even while hanging around villages for participant observation, I was stopped multiple times by local policemen. Despite trying to blend in with the locals, I was asked to show my "papers" (Cornell ID, letter from my adviser on university letterhead, my local institutional affiliation, my voters ID proving my Indian citizenship) and state why I was inquisitive about Maoist issues.

Chapter 2

1. The archival research had three main parts: First, at the Taraknath Das Research Center, Calcutta, I was able to access vernacular newspaper reports from the first phase of the Naxalbari uprising in 1967 to the most recent Maoist incidents in West Bengal, Bihar, and Jharkhand. Second, I was able to access the debates in the Communist Party of India (Marxist Leninist), a.k.a. CPI(ML), camp that eventually led to fragmentation of the radical left as published in Naxal journals: *Deshabrati* (*The Patriot*), *Liberation*, and the *Peoples' March*. In addition, the *Frontier Weekly* edited by Samar Sen and started in 1968 was the important platform for debate among various

ML factions. It is now digitalized and available at http://www.frontierweekly.com/. Third, I was able to interview surviving Naxalbari activists in Calcutta (not everyone wants to be identified), most notably Santosh Rana.

2. Kanu Sanyal wrote, "The struggle of the *Terai* [outer foothills of the Himalayas, where Naxalbari is situated] peasants is an armed struggle—not for land but for state power." The limitations of an "economistic struggle" for land without an understanding of the state character and structural violence was highlighted by Charu Mazumdar in his writings, including the historic Eight Documents available at Marxists.org, https://www.marxists.org/reference/archive/mazumdar/index.htm.

3. The central grievance that motivated the movement was that sharecroppers, known as *adhiar* (from *adha* meaning half) in North Bengal, *bhagchasi* in other parts of the province, and as *bargadars* in the legal contracts, had to hand over 50% of the crop to the *jotedar* (landlord) as land rents while the entire cost of cultivation was borne by the sharecropper himself. Historically exploited in the feudal regime, the modern-day peasants joined the Bengal provincial branch of the All-India Kisan Sabha and the Bengal Provincial Committee of the Communist Party of India (CPI).

4. The movement was led by Godavari Parulekar and her husband, Shamrao Parulekar, both urban, educated members of the CPI. The movement was the strongest in the Dahanu and Umbergaon *taluks* (blocks) of the Thane district of Maharashtra, where Warlis formed 55% of the total population.

5. In 1946, Sir C. P. Ramaswami Iyer, the Diwan of Travancore, proposed constitutional reforms that the communists opposed as too similar to the "American model" of administration. The communists opposed this move with the slogan "American Model Arabi Kadalil," meaning chuck the American model into the Arabian Sea. The Punnapra-Vayalar uprising was named after the two places in Kerala where it was most intense. It emerged as a continuation of the Coir factory workers strike in 1938 and the Mopala rebellion (by Muslim tenants in the Malabar region of Kerala) of 1921.

6. Under the patronage of the Nizam, an organization called Majlis-e-Ittehad sent their militant arm known as *razakkars* (paramilitary forces) to plunder, kill, rape, and generally terrorize members of peasant resistance groups.

7. The CPI upheld Khrushchev's thesis of "peaceful coexistence" presented at the Twentieth Congress of the Communist Party of the Soviet Union held in 1956, which repudiated the need for revolutionary war against class enemies and proclaimed that transition to socialism was possible through parliamentary means. Following Khrushchev's thesis, the Palghat Program (April 19–29, 1956) of CPI paved the way for the party's participation in the second general elections in 1957. Subsequently, the CPI government was formed in Kerala. Further, during the Khrushchev-Nehru entente, CPI leadership advocated cooperation with the Congress, which they recognized as a party of "national bourgeoisie" fighting against the principal enemies of imperialism and feudalism on the side of the Indian poor.

8. At the second congress of CPI in Calcutta on February 28, 1948, B. T Ranadive upheld the Zhdanov line of insurrection against P. C Joshi's line of collaboration with the Congress. Ranadive's open call for taking up arms is known as the "Calcutta thesis."

9. Part VII of the 1964 CPI(M) Party Program held that the party would "not hesitate to lend its unstinted support to the Government on all issues of world peace and anti-colonialism . . . on all economic and political issues of conflict with imperialism, and on all issues that involve the questions of strengthening our sovereignty and independent foreign policy" (Paragraph 7.13) The Party program is available at https://www.cpim.org/party-programme

10. Dakshin Desh worked primarily in West Bengal (Kolkata, Howrah, Hooghly, Medinipur, Burdwan, Birbhum, and 24 Parganas) and in parts of Assam and Tripura and Bihar. The Dakshin Desh group, critical of Charu Mazumdar's assassination line, considered extensive politicization of the peasantry as a precondition of armed action and censured the formation of CPI(ML) as hasty, untimely, and motivated by impatient personal ambitions of its leaders. Led by Kanai Chatterjee and Amulya Sen, this faction evolved into what became known as the Maoist Communist Centre in 1969. They trace their origin to the Chinta group, which ran a secret journal within the CPI(M) called *Chinta*. Later they published an open journal *Dakshin Desh*.

11. The CPI(ML) Second Central Committee formed in 1972, under the leadership of Azizul Haq, Nishith Bhattacharya, and Mahadeb Mukherjee, and represented this pro–CM trend. They supported the Gang of Four line (Mao's wife and her followers) in China, upheld the goal of revolutionary armed struggle in India, and rejected mass mobilization and electoral participation. Soon after formation, however, this faction was further divided when the pro–Lin Biao members led by Mukherjee were expelled from the party. Another important pro-CM, anti-Lin Biao faction (Lin Biao, was Mao's chosen successor later condemned as traitor) was known as the Bhojpur Committee. Led by Subroto Dutta (Jauhar), the faction opposed the Gang of Four and supported the leadership of Hua Guofeng in post-Mao China. Rigid in opposition to mass mobilization during its initial period of armed insurgency in Bhojpur (Bihar), this pro-CM group, now known as CPI(ML) Liberation, subsequently plunged into electoral politics. Under the leadership of Vinod Mishra, it emerged as the most successful ML electoral party with representatives in the state assemblies of Bihar, Jharkhand, and Assam.

12. Prominent groups in this trend included the CPI(ML) Provisional Central Committee (PCC), CPI(ML) Kanu Sanyal, and the CPI(ML) New Democracy. CPI(ML) PCC descends from the Bihar State Committee of CPI(ML) led by Satyanarayan Singh, who was expelled from CPI(ML) in November 1971 for accusing CM of left sectarianism. This group, opposed to the Gang of Four and supportive of the leadership of Hua Guofeng and the Three Worlds Theory, was the first among ML groups to contest elections. Kanu Sanyal, the second in command of the Naxalbari uprising after CM, also denounced the left adventurist deviation of CM and formed the Communist Organization of India (Marxist Leninist). His group maintained its own identity and sphere of influence in North Bengal among the farmers and tea plantation workers. In the early 2000s, he formed an alternate CPI(ML) by merging with a faction of the Central Reorganizing Committee CPI(ML) that worked in Kerala and conceptualized the Indian state as a neo-colony, rather than a semi-feudal, semi-colony. Other prominent groups in this second trend were the CPI(ML) Janashakti, which has flip-flopped

between periods of electoral participation and armed insurgency, and CPI(ML) New Democracy, which participates in elections and has had some success in the states of Bihar and Andhra Pradesh.

13. The CPI(ML) People's War Group (PWG), long-dreaded in Andhra Pradesh, and the CPI(ML) Party Unity (PU), equally feared in Bihar and Jharkhand, were proponents of this trend. The CPI(ML) PWG was founded on April 22, 1980, in Andhra Pradesh by Kondapalli Seetharamaiah from a faction of CPI(ML) Central Organizing Committee (COC), which descended from the undivided CPI(ML). Another faction of CPI(ML) COC led by M. Appalasuri and operating in the Palamau-Jehanabad area of Bihar formed the CPI(ML) Party Unity.

14. The Dakshin Desh/MCC leader Kanai Chatterjee stated categorically that political power grows out of the barrel of a gun. But that would not rule out creating a mass organizations with cadres organizing in the open, building schools, cultural movements, professional associations. The task of building up of the people's army and red base areas through an underground party and a guerrilla army was, however, considered the first, primary, principal and the central task. Open mass organizations were secondary and would automatically follow once base areas were consolidated. MCC also accepted the secondary role of mass struggle when the time and condition was right, which allowed it to merge with PWG and PU eventually.

15. The AICCR met on February 7–8, 1969, and abruptly disaffiliated from the APCCCR, alleging that the latter were not loyal to the Chinese Communist Party, that they were not supportive enough of the Srikakulam struggle, and that Nagi Reddy, APCCR leader, did not resign from the Andhra Pradesh State Assembly (Ghosh 2009). APRCC later split into CPI(ML) New Democracy operating primarily in Andhra Pradesh and the Unity Center of Communist Revolutionaries of India (Marxist Leninist), or UCCRI(ML), active in parts of Andhra Pradesh, Bihar, and Punjab. One major faction emerging from the UCCRI(ML) merged with six other communist groups to form CPI(ML) Janashakti. The new faction retained a fraternal relationship with the Maoists but never merged. It carried open mass activities for some time, but later became re-immersed in armed struggle. Currently, it maintains its independent existence in parts of Andhra Pradesh but has been severely weakened by desertions, state repression, and clashes with CPI(Maoist).

16. Landless peasants were required to cultivate the landlords' land for a stipulated number of days without remuneration. In addition, if poor peasants had already lost all their land and their belongings (e.g., pots and pans) to repay loans, they were obligated to work as bonded labor on the landlords' farms and household at his beck and call 24/7 for 365 days a year as long as they lived.

17. Other non-Maoist left parties of India critique this somewhat outdated characterization of the Indian state. For example, the parliamentary left recognizes that capitalism, though "slow and uneven," is the dominant mode of production. Even some ML factions, like CPI(ML) Red Flag, active in Kerala, argue that "neocolonial" is a more apt description of the character of the Indian state than "semi-feudal, semi-colonial." Other factions like CPI(ML) Liberation and CPI(ML) New Democracy, emerging from the Naxalbari tradition, while subscribing to the "semi-feudal, semi-colonial"

thesis, still participate in state and national legislatures as means of political change. The Maoists consider all these critiques "revisionist"; the other left groups, in turn, dub the Maoists as "left sectarian" and "anarcho-militarist."

18. This is based on an interview with comrade Katakam Sudarshan, aka Anand, Polit Bureau member and the secretary of the Central Regional Bureau, CPI(Maoist), and published in the Maoist Information Bulletin, dated December 7, 2009. Available at http://www.bannedthought.net/India/CPIMIB/MIB-13.pdf.

19. About 40% of retired Maoist rebels I interviewed in the North acknowledged, without being asked or prompted, that the Lohia line helped them in two ways: On the one hand, they agreed with Lohia when he underscored the overlap of caste and class interests. On the other hand, Lohia's politics of preferential treatment for lower castes did not have any meaning or practical utility in the lives of the rural lower-caste population. Armed struggle emerged as the only match to the prevalent feudal caste atrocities they faced. Theoretically, the Lohia line was part of his vision of seven revolutions. It was a departure from the Marxist line of a class-centric program for a socialist revolution. It also went beyond the Gandhian emphasis on a constructive program of ending untouchability and casteism. For more discussions on Lohia line please see http://www.mainstreamweekly.net/article1242.html.

20. Retired Maoists belonging to the Ganju caste I met in the North recounted two-decades-old stories of their Yadav comrades' high-handedness with great animation and details.

21. In the Chatra-Palamu districts of South Bihar, the dominant Rajput-Pathhan land-owning castes formed the Sunlight Sena to counter MCC, the most dominant Maoist faction in the region. Closer to Patna, the capital of Bihar, the Kurmi landowners set up the Bhoomi (meaning, land) Sena. Yadav landowners set up the Lorik Sena. Rajputs in Bhojpur set up the Kunwar Sena, and the Brahmins set up the Ganga Sena. Mere 40 kilometers from the state capital city of Patna, Kisan Sangh set up its armed wing, the Kisan Security Tigers, patronized by Janata Dal.

22. It had the blessings of "King" Mahendra, former MP and MLA, like Abhiram Sharma, Sardar Krishna Singh of Arwal, Jagdish Sharma, and others, with the present Congress Legislative Party leader, Ramashraya Prasad Singh, then a powerful minster, backing them in Patna.

23. CPI leader and MP, Ramashraya Singh Yadav, had, in the meanwhile, set up the Lorik Sena, exploiting the linkages between the Yadav landowners and the contractor-caste criminal combine to take on the leftist squads.

24. Prominent political personalities in support of the Sunlight Sena included Ram Naresh Singh, MLA and later MP, who was close to Satyendra Narain Sinha, former two-term chief minister of Bihar, and belonged to the princely Deo family of Aurangabad. Ram Naresh Singh was looked upon as a savior of the Rajput land-owners of the erstwhile Palamau Paragana and Chatra regions. Ram Naresh Singh's alias was Lootan Singh: *Lootan* means one who loots or grabs. He started his career as a criminal and later went on to become a contractor. Among other well-known patrons of Sunlight Sena was Bhisma Narain Singh, of the Manatu family of Palamu, who was former governor of Tamil Nadu and Tripura.

25. In 2015, evidence came to light that many BJP leaders, including Murli Manohar Joshi, C. P. Thakur, and former Prime Minister Chandra Shekhar, were complicit in the Bihar Dalit massacres committed by the Ranvir Sena, while the backward-caste governments of Nitish Kumar, as well as his arch rivals, Lalu Prasad Yadav and Rabri Devi, declined to order investigations into the massacres despite knowledge of them.   (https://www.thehindu.com/news/national/cobrapost-film-on-bihar-dalit-massacres-exposes-bjp-links/article7551350.ece)

26. The Kammas made up about 4–5% of the state's population, but they were mostly concentrated on the coasts, which is outside the purview of this study. The Velamas constituted another 1–2% of the population. They were as wealthy as the Reddys and the Kammas and were concentrated mainly in the two Telangana districts of Karimnagar and Khammam and in the northern coastal district of Visakhapatnam. The Kapu caste constituted 10–12% of the population and currently forms the caste base of one of the largest regional parties in the South (Telugu Desam Party).

27. These castes have been given reservation under the Other Backward Castes (OBCs) category since 1961. Out of the 50-odd backward castes listed by the Indian government, the major ones are the Yadava, Gowda, Padmasali, Rajaka, Mangali (who call themselves Nai Brahman), Kamsali (Viswa Brahman), Mudiraju, Boya, Waddera, Uppara, Kummari, Kammari, Medara, Pallekari (Agnikula Kshtriya), Perika, Gandla, Bhatraju, and Kalavanthavulu.

28. The government claimed that the backwardness of education in Telangana made filling posts with well-qualified non-Mulkis inevitable, and when steps were taken to expand education, it was also inevitable that a large number of non-Mulki teachers had to be imported early on. But discontent over the situation became so rife that in 1959 the central government felt it necessary to promulgate the Andhra Pradesh Public Employment (Requirement as to Residence) Rules, providing that 15 years continuous residence would be required for appointment to government jobs. The Rules, however, provided loopholes, and false "Mulki certificates" were not hard to obtain. This discontent was a major factor in sparking off the 1969 agitation.

29. Andhra Mahasabha was a cultural organization of Telugu-speaking people in the erstwhile Hyderabad state of India. Started as a subsidiary of the Indian National Congress, the major faction of it later joined hands with CIP.

30. In the 1980s, MKKS led many grassroots struggles against share cropping (*bataidari*), bonded labor (*begaar*), and untouchability. MKSS, popularly referred to as Sangathhan (meaning organization), was led by Dr. Vinayan, a medical doctor from the neighboring state of Uttar Pradesh.

31. MKSS split in 1987, and the pro-Vinayan followers were all forced to form a new organization, named Jana Mukti Andolan (Peoples' Liberation Movement), completely outside of the Maoist platform. The tension within MKSS became irreconcilable due to the differing positions taken by two of its founding members, Dr. Vinayan and Arvind Singh. Arvind Singh wanted the MKSS to work in close relation with the PU and its armed squads. In consultation with PU leaders, he expelled Vinayan from the MKSS. Singh then made a press statement in Patna: "Samiti [MKSS] has dismissed its

founding president Dr. Vinayan due to his anti-party and reformist activities" and for taking a "wrong class direction."

32. Investigations by India's National Commission for Scheduled Castes and Scheduled Tribes, the National Human Rights Commission, the National Police Commission, and numerous local nongovernmental organizations all concur that even in the few cases where police were not hostile to Dalits, they were generally not accessible: Most police camps were located in the upper-caste section of villages, and Dalits were simply unable to approach them when seeking protection. In many instances, police and district officials ignored repeated calls for protection by threatened Dalit communities.

33. Encounter killing refers to the extrajudicial execution of an arrested person by the police and security forces and staging it as the consequence of an armed confrontation. This is done to avoid lengthy trials in a court of law, where the accused may walk away free or with a lesser sentence than the state would like.

34. For example, S. R. Sankaran, an Indian Administrate Service (IAS) officer and former principal secretary of social welfare in Andhra Pradesh and secretary to Union Ministry of Rural Development, was known to be widely respected by Maoists. Sankaran was instrumental in abolishing bonded labor in Andhra Pradesh and was very close to the civil liberty activists in the state, " 'People's IAS Officer' S.R. Sankaran No More," 2010, http://www.thehindu.com/todays-paper/tp-national/tp-andhrapradesh/peoples-ias-officer-sr-sankaran-no-more/article818981.ece.

35. Allam Narayana, the editor of the largest vernacular newspaper, was a former PWG guerrilla.

36. In the insurgent horizontal ties to rights activists and academics were tested when the activists criticized the insurgents for their brutal violence against suspected informers and spies. However, the horizontal network in the South did not cut off ties with the insurgent organization as they did in the North.

Chapter 3

1. I saw the tea stall set up by a former Maoist outside the police headquarters in Ranchi, the state capital of Jharkhand. Some former Maoists were also interviewing for jobs in the state police department. However, these are the people more likely to be targeted by Maoists as suspected informers, and the rebels often assassinate them to send strong messages to potential "traitors."

2. For example, MN1, a retired Maoist turned politician, Kameshwar Baitha, began his story by saying that he had a change of heart and decided to quit the insurgency when he was in prison. But he also added that although the media interpreted his transition from insurgency to democracy as a paradigm shift of sorts, what he did before was not very different to him from what he did as a member of parliament (MP). He highlighted that both as an MP and as a Maoist leader, he was a politician who met people and addressed their needs and demands as efficiently as he could. Violence, lawlessness, and coercion, he pointed out, remain integral to electoral

politics as well, and neither he nor the ordinary people have any illusion about that. In separate interviews, MN2 and MN3, both Maoists turned politicians, agreed that being politicians running for office in a democracy brought them more media attention than ever, and made it easier for their families to gain social acceptance in some circles. However, all this was contingent on their rebel career, which generated a mix of both support and fear, necessary to pursue their career in electoral politics.

3. According to interviews with politicians (Category 2) PN7 (JMM) and PN8 (CPI(ML) Liberation) and activists (A1 and A2) in October 2014.

4. A Jharkhand legislator, booked on charges of ordering the killing of a 25-year-old man who had eloped with a woman belonging to another caste. See https://www. hindustantimes.com/india/jmm-s-bokaro-mla-accused-of-ordering-kill-in-kangaroo-court/story-MlRWzCqo6GNg4JTWrDHUGK.html.

5. This is based on interviews C18–23 conducted February 2014 and a 100-respondent survey in the North in October 2013. Interviews C18–21 were conducted in the Chhatra district, Jharkhand, and interviews C22–23 were conducted in the Khunti district, Jharkhand. Ordinary people in the North were not open to talking about former Maoists or other politicians in their area for fear of retaliation. But all six respondents said without being prompted that, former Maoists or not, the politicians were all the same.

6. This was pointed out to me by A33, a human rights activist in Ranchi, Jharkhand, and later confirmed by C19–20 and MN2–5.

7. The most recent example is the defeat of Kundan Pahan in the 2019 Jharkhand Assembly election for the Tamar Assembly seat in Ranchi district. Pahan was facing over 100 cases, including the murders of senior police officers that carried a reward of Rs 15 lakh on his head. He had surrendered before the police in 2017. In 2009, Kameshwar Baitha (MN1), a former Maoist commander and regional committee member, was the only former Maoist known to win the Lok Sabha elections from the Palamu constituency as a candidate of Jharkhand Mukti Morcha (JMM). After JMM denied him nomination in 2014, he joined BJP and then the Trinamool Congress and eventually lost in the 2014 elections. In neighboring Chhatra, constituency of Jharkhand, former Maoist commander and state committee member Ranjan Yadav (MN2 in interview sample) also lost in the 2009 Assembly elections on CPI(ML) nomination and lost again in the 2014 parliamentary elections in the Samajwadi Party (SP) nomination.

8. Yugal Pal (MN3) a founding member of Party Unity and a former central committee member of CPI(M), contested on a JMM ticket from Vishrampur in the Palamu district. But he lost to the Congress candidate. Satish Kumar, a former member of what is called 3U-SAC (Uttari Bihar-Uttaranchal-Uttar Pradesh Special Area Committee), was the JMM candidate from Daltonganj, the district headquarters of Palamu. He lost too. Polush Sarin and Masih Charan were the other two former Maoists contesting on JMM tickets—from Torpa and Khunti, respectively. Sarin won, but Charan lost. Besides JMM candidates, Keshwar Yadav, aka Ranjan Yadav, contested from Paki on a Rashtriya Janata Dal ticket, and lost. Kuldeep Ganju, a former zonal committee

member of the underground outfit, was the All Jharkhand Student Union (AJSU) candidate from Simeria. He lost too.

9. Based on interviews with PN7 (JMM), PN8 (CPI(ML)Liberation), and PN9 (BJP) in October 2014. This was confirmed by journalists J2 and J3 as well.

10. In long conversations, Kameshwar Baitha, the only former Maoist who became an MP, shared how the aura of legitimacy in electoral politics, being surrounded by ordinary people and other political leaders showing faith in him, made all the difference to his family. He argued that he was always a public servant even as a Maoist. The people voted for him, and he won the election from jail because he had worked on their behalf, getting road, water, and schools that they needed through his insurgent career.

11. In the 2014 Assembly elections in Jharkhand, for example, three senior political leaders were endorsed by Maoists. For more details, see https://indianexpress.com/article/india/politics/maoists-in-jharkhand-eye-new-future-through-electoral-democracy/.

12. The BJP awarded a ticket to Narayan Bhokta in 2014, once a deputy zonal commander of the Tritiya Sammelan Prastuti Committee, and took it back only because the TSPC itself let the party know Bhokta had outstanding warrants against him. The BJP also gave a ticket to Manoj Nagesiya, a former Maoist sub-zonal commander who had reportedly not yet surrendered or left his extremist tendencies. The Congress awarded a ticket to Nirmala Devi, wife of jailed former minister Yogendra Saw, who allegedly formed two criminal gangs that called themselves LWE outfits. In 2014, the Jharkhand Party became the de facto electoral wing of the Peoples' Liberation Front of India (PLFI) faction of Maoists, with PLFI offering support to its Torpa, Simedega, and Kolebira candidates.

13. Conversations with civilians C2 and C5 and interviews with activists A1, A2, A3, A7 October–November 2013. C2, for example, could not point to any phase in her 50-plus years when she lived in peace (*shanti*), defined as absence of danger (*khatra*) and violence (*hinsa*). The sources of threat and violence were sometimes the upper-caste men, sometimes the rebels, sometimes the local politician (MLA), and sometimes the police. She was not sure who killed her husband—police or rebels. Her son-in-law was summoned by both the police and the rebels and subsequently found dead as well.

14. For example, C9 in the South shared that he had thrice sheltered and arranged food for the Maoist squads, and he also had the phone number of the local police station on speed dial. He said jokingly that he, and everyone else, does what he needs to do to stay alive, to have a roof over his head, and food in his belly. He added that a lot of people feel guilty about their conduct during the conflict, and they have learned to remain silent about these experiences.

15. Activist respondent A1 in the North described how the CPI(ML) legislator Mahendra Singh, a popular politician in the Giridih district, was killed in January 2005. His son, former MLA Vinod Singh, during an interview with the author, stated that his family had lodged a First Information Report (FIR) against the then superintendent of police and minister (a BJP leader) Ravindra Rai for conspiring the killing of his father

Mahendra Singh. Singh had presented a detailed set of documents in the Jharkhand Assembly in December 2004, including a report of an inquiry conducted by the Vigilance Department, which exposed the murderous nexus between Superintendent of Police Deepak Varma, senior BJP leaders, and the state's notorious coal mafia.

16. A Janatana Sarkar is a parallel government set up by the Maoists in Chhattisgarh to raise taxes and provide education, healthcare, and security in return. For more information, see https://www.thehindu.com/sunday-anchor/view-from-the-maoist-side/article7117393.ece (accessed February 16, 2019).

17. By grounded theory I refer to the general methodology for developing theory that is grounded in data systematically gathered and analyzed. The theory evolves during actual research through an interplay of analysis and data collection. According to the guidelines of this method called "constant comparative method," one can generate theoretical insights from initial data analysis, and these insights can be elaborated or modified as incoming data are continuously played against them. Thus it is an inductive approach of theory building rather than a hypothetic-deductive approach.

18. *Anganwadi* is a type of rural childcare center in India. They were started by the Indian government in 1975 as part of the Integrated Child Development Services program to combat child hunger and malnutrition.

19. For more on the onslaught against the so-called urban Maoists see https://foreignpolicy.com/2018/09/06/indias-aging-guerrillas-still-believe-in-the-struggle/.

20. The urban, college-educated women members of PW organized the Dalit women locally.

21. These committees, run and led by mostly Dalit women, received political tutelage and moral support from state-level mass fronts like Jana Vigyan Vedika (aided by the CPI(M), the Progressive Organization of Women (aided by a CPI(ML) group), and Andhra Pradesh Dalit Mahasabha, which helped them frame the movement as caste, class, and gender issues, adopting mobilization techniques that were homegrown as well as spectacular.

22. The CPI(M), the chief among the parliamentary left, celebrated its involvement in the movement by conducting a national seminar at Hyderabad through its front organization Jana Vignana Vedika and all political parties, except BJP, attended.

23. As the excise became high, the substantial burden of the regressive excise duty was borne by the poor. The number of Arrack shops increased from 7,159 in 1969–1970 to reach the peak of 22,803 shops in 1987–1988 but declined to 16,436 in 1990–9091. This sharp decline did not mean a decline in consumption. This was due to an ingenuous innovation in 1986 of Arrack being packed in 90-ml and 45-ml polythene sachet. Arrack in sachets started flowing to doorsteps by peddlers on foot and by bicycle. This innovation afforded the convenience of Arrack being carried to any place.

24. Also noteworthy is that drinking was a social taboo among the forward castes and some groups of the backward classes, particularly among the middle classes and among women. Drinking Arrack or toddy by schedule castes did not carry any social stigma.

25. As the Congress government gained popularity due to its subsidized "Rupees 2 per kg" rice scheme in the villages of Andhra Pradesh, they saw in the anti-Arrack movement

an opportunity to further consolidate their local support among Dalit women. Older women brought up the subsidized rice scheme again and again as prime evidence of the benevolence of the state. They mentioned how they were grateful to Indira Amma (former prime minister of India, Mrs. Indira Gandhi) for understanding the pain of mothers who were not able to put food on the table. They also mentioned that the "Arrack demon" was their other enemy, which she understood as a woman.

26. The Anti-Arrack platform is so popular in Telangana that political parties still use it. See, e.g., https://timesofindia.indiatimes.com/city/hyderabad/hubby-changed-in-govt-ad-woman-cries-insult-to-family/articleshow/65466841.cms.

27. The idea of increasing Arrack consumption and demand among the rural poor by peddling Arrack in plastic bags door to door is attributed to N. T. Rama Rao, the charismatic TDP leader who understood its importance for state revenue. The same leader, realizing the importance of appearing on the right side of the issue, stopped the passenger train he was riding to address people on the issue of opposing Arrack.

28. In the Nellore district alone, the Anti-Arrack Coordination Committee was made up of 36 voluntary organizations. In the Chttoor district, there were 250 voluntary organizations comprising mostly women active in the village committees.

29. The ABMS activist was included in the sample frame under Category 7 and is identified as A25.

30. Some ABMS activists had personal ties or knew someone who had ties to various Maoist mass organizations, like the anti-caste organization Kula Nirmulana Poratha Samithi (KNPS) and their cultural front Jana Natya Mandali (JNM), which has wide membership in big cities and small towns, both inside college campuses and outside. Even though JNM is now banned, I was able to meet prominent members of the organization. Some of them are well-known public figures, and they live in and around the city of Hyderabad.

31. This does not mean that the state in the South did not use repressive measures against Maoists. Civil liberty organizations have meticulously documented how the police tortured rebels in custody and killed them in fake encounters. Fake encounters, or encounter killings, are used in South Asia to refer to the shooting of suspected terrorists and criminals by police, allegedly in self-defense but more likely to avoid the due process of law.

32. There are many other examples of networks of reciprocal assistance among state, societal, and insurgent agents. A police superintendent took in the daughter of two insurgents and raised her to be a doctor. An ordinary villager in Srikakulam raised the abandoned daughter of a well-known Maoist leader. For more details, please see https://www.dnaindia.com/india/report-andhra-police-adopt-maoist-s-daughter-1064051(accessed November 28, 2011).

33. When the state is one of the actors, the network is political. When the state is not one of the actors, the network is social.

34. Networks are clandestine (or secret or concealed) if no one knows anything about the exact nature of transactions except that they exist.

35. During my interviews with police and administrators in Ranchi, Jharkhand, it was readily admitted that such connections exist. Former Maoist area commanders

corroborated it. A number of bureaucrats were specifically named as being deeply involved in these payoffs. Given their secret nature, there is not much evidence of the transactions in print. However, their existence is common knowledge locally.

36. There are many anti-Maoist armed rogue gangs in Jharkhand with secret connections to the police, see https://www.hindustantimes.com/static/the-jungle-gangs-of-jharkhand/

37. More about this secret connection was published after the death of Nayeem, the gangster, who was almost an urban legend because no one had seen him in years and yet everyone still feared him. For more details see https://timesofindia.indiatimes.com/city/hyderabad/Nayeem-the-gangster-who-knew-too-much-shot-dead/articleshow/53609263.cms

38. It is widely known that the Maoists in the South alternately helped the TDP and Congress government to win chief ministership of the state. In West Bengal, the local Maoist leader claimed to have an instrumental role in the victory of the Trinamool Congress in 2011. In the North, an MP wrote a book mentioning how he and other top Trinamool Congress leaders (Partha Chaterjee and Shisir Adhikari) secretly met Maoist leaders (referred to as land rights activists) at the party headquarters. For more details, please see Kabir Suman, *Nishaner naam Tapasi Malik* (in Bengali).

39. Another IAS officer reportedly exclaimed, "They seem to know everything." It was widely acknowledged in the newspapers around that time that if a groups of very young men and women could engage and impress the best and the brightest of the Indian bureaucracy with socioeconomic analysis and encyclopedic knowledge of local history, it is enough proof of the caliber and strength of the Maoist PWG organization in Andhra Pradesh. However, the central security forces sent to free the kidnapped IAS officers complained that the officers were colluding with the kidnappers. See "Kidnapped!," *Sunday Magazine*, January 10–16, 1988.

40. Sankaran was hardly an exception. There were other bureaucrats and police officers who were known as "left leaning" and sympathetic to the Maoists. B. N. Yugandhar, also an IAS officer and the state government's industry secretary at the time of kidnap, who initiated talks with the rebels through layers in state civil liberties organization, was also known as a bureaucrat with left leanings. He has written many reports and headed many committees in addition to working as the secretary of the Ministry of Rural Development in New Delhi. Yugandhar, widely known as an upright bureaucrat, is also the father of Satya Nadella, the CEO of Microsoft. See, e.g., https://economictimes.indiatimes.com/news/company/corporate-trends/satya-nadellas-father-a-high-achiever-himself-has-strong-left-leanings/articleshow/29784783.cms.

41. By 1965 there were three important groups of poets that emerged from the Progressive Writers Association, who were to rock the Telugu literary world: the Hyderabad-based Digambara poets, the Warangal-based Thirugubatu (revolt) poets, and the Guntur-based Pygambara poets. After the Naxalbari uprising these poets and authors merged to form Virasam, the Viplava Rachayithala Sangam, or the Revolutionary Writers Association (RWA) in 1970. Vara Vara Rao has emerged as the most well-known face of Virasam in recent years.

42. Karamchedu, a prosperous village in the Prakasham district in coastal Andhra, rich from cotton and tobacco cultivation, witnessed a 3,000-strong mob of upper-caste Kamma landholders assault the scheduled caste Madigas (chamars), killing six men, raping three women, and seriously injuring many more. For the first time, terrified by the attack, the victimized Dalits in blood-splattered clothing, carrying their dead and injured, deserted the village and fled to the nearby town Chirala to seek sanctuary in a church. For details on events leading to this massacre of dalits, see APCLC report on the incident titled "The Karamchedu Massacre: A Report," available at https://www.google.com/search?q=karmachedu+APCLC+1985&ie=utf-8&oe=utf-8&aq=t&rls=org.mozilla:en-US:official&client=firefox-a&channel=sb# (accessed October 10, 2014).

43. Padma Rao, associated with Hetuvada Sangham, was a leading rationalist, orator, Sanskrit scholar, ML sympathizer, and lecturer in a Guntur college. Bojjatarakam was a government lawyer in the High Court, civil rights activist, a ML sympathizer, a conscious Ambedkarite who led Yuvajana Sanghams in 1970s, and son-in-law of Boyee Bheemana (an organic Dalit intellectual).

44. Court cases against Chenchu Ramaiah, the Kamma landlord and chief accused of Karamchedu, dragged on. The government-appointed judicial inquiry commission could not find a clear reason behind the massacre. The chief witness of Karamchedu, a woman named Alisamma, was murdered.

45. After Karamchedu, the impunity of the Kamma landlords demoralized Dalits. Kammas were protected by political connections to the ruling TDP, known statewide as a Kamma party. Assertive Dalits were threatened with Karamchedu-style massacres unless they backed down. With PW killing Chenchu Ramaiah, Dalits were able to predict dire consequences for assaults against them (based on author's interviews).

46. The DMS-formed Dalit Kalamandali, Jana Chaitanya Mandali, which were modeled after PWG's Jana Natya Mandali, bring together cultural activists and balladeers who wrote very popular poems and songs that conveyed the brutality of Karamchedu, the underlying grievances of the Dalits, the injustice of caste inequality, and the need for public uprising against it.

47. Nalupu was founded and edited by Bojja Tarakam, the DMS leader and lawyer. Edureetha was launched by the Dalit poet K. G. Satyamurthy, who was also the top leader of PWG.

48. The CPI(ML) Janashakti and CPI(ML) New Democracy factions of Maoists in the South combined armed struggle and electoral battles against democracy. Janashakti descends from the mass line tradition developed by Chandra Pulla Reddy and T. Nagi Reddy, legends of the Telangana rebellion of 1946–1951. In the 1994 assembly elections of Andhra Pradesh, Vidhan Sabha won a seat, in addition to other victories in local elections in the Karimnagar district. New Democracy also followed a combination of both armed underground and parliamentary methods of struggle. The party has open mass organizations like the Indian Federation of Trade Unions for industrial workers and the All India Kisan-Mazdoor Sabha for farmers and agricultural

workers. CPI(M-L) ND has two big student unions, it had one member in the Andhra Pradesh state assembly between 1983–1994 and 1999–2009.

49. Retired Osmania university professor and the leader of the Telangana Joint Action Committee, M. Kondaram, who was second in command after K Chandrasekhar Rao, the current chief minister of Telangana, is known to have had Maoist affiliations in college.

50. For further details, see http://democracyandclasstruggle.blogspot.com/2012/07/remembering-comrade-kanhai-chaterjee.html (accessed November 28, 2009).

51. The civil liberty activists, led by K. Balagopal, who were as critical of the insurgents' violation of human rights as much as they were critical of the state's treatment of political prisoners, formed the Human Rights Forum.

Chapter 4

1. For further details, see Shapiro et al., available at https://scholar.princeton.edu/sites/default/files/jns/files/svia_2017_india_state_coin_histories.pdf (accessed February 18, 2019).

2. In the Red Corridor, among 11 states variously affected by the Maoists, both Jharkhand and Andhra Pradesh have been consistently categorized as severely affected and comparable in terms of number of districts affected as well as total death per hundred thousand. For more on this, see SATP Maoist datasheets at http://www.satp.org/satporgtp/countries/india/maoist/data_sheets/maoist_datasheet.html.

3. At first the Telugu areas of the erstwhile Madras State were separated with Andhra and the South interior region of Rayalaseema forming the "Andhra State" and Telangana becoming part of the Nizam's princely state. Three years later, on November 1, 1956, Telangana merged with Coastal Andhra and Rayalaseema to form the state of Andhra Pradesh with Hyderabad as the capital.

4. The Coastal Andhra region consists of nine districts (Srikakulam, Vizianagaram, Visakhapatnam, East Godavari, West Godavari, Krishna, Guntur, Prakasam, and Nellore) and comprised 69.2% of the state population in 2011. *Rayalaseema* (meaning, the land of kings) consists of four districts (Chittoor, Cuddapah, Anantapur, and Kurnool) with 18% of the population. Telangana (the land of Telugus) consists of 10 districts (Mahbubnagar, Ranga Reddy, Hyderabad, Medak, Nizamabad, Adilabad, Karimnagar, Warangal, Khammam, and Nalgonda) with 40.5% of the population.

5. Real names of former rebels have been changed to protect their identities. Raju Anna is MS7 in the interview sample.

6. I encountered some other interesting signs on NH7 which read: "Are you in trable [*sic*]?" followed a kilometer later by "Are you in troble [*sic*]?" In case the answer was "yes," there were telephone numbers provided to call for help. Incidentally, none of the phone numbers worked when I called, just like many other phone numbers for ministers and bureaucrats on their websites that give an automated message that the line has been disconnected.

7. Telugu Desam Party (TDP), the major regional party, fought and lost the 2004 assembly elections on a platform of development called "India Shining," which highlighted roads, infrastructure, and information technology as development indicators.

8. From the author's interview with R. Vineel Krishna, principal secretary to the union rural development minister in Krishi Bhavan, New Delhi on July 14, 2013. Krishna, originally from Andhra Pradesh, was once abducted by the Maoists during his tenure as district collector in Malkangiri, Orissa.

9. Seelam Naresh aka Murali, Nalla Adi Reddy aka Shyam, and Yerramreddy Santosh Reddy, known by the nom de guerre Mahesh—were killed in the Koyyuru encounter on December 2, 1999. This incident was cited by 11 southern Maoists to illustrate how none of them contemplated quitting after this incident, which was acknowledged as one of the biggest shocks to their organization. One respondent, who personally knew these leaders, however, accepted, without being prompted, how valuable the Central Committee (CC) members were to the Maoists, particularly because CC members in Maoist parties rise through the ranks and cannot be easily replaced. He attributed his retirement to the loss of direction and leadership in the highest ranks caused by this incident.

10. In 1975 four young student activists of the Radical Students Union (RSU) were taken to the Giraipalli forests and shot dead by the police. They are remembered by Andhra Maoists as Giraipalli martyrs. Raju Anna joined the Maoists immediately afterward and moved to Dandakaranya in 1981. He shared many stories of Dandakaranya, including his meeting with Arundhati Roy, the Booker Prize–winning author who wrote her lyrical essay, "Walking with the Comrades," based on her stay with Maoists in the forests of Chhattisgarh.

11. When asked about the conditions of their retirement, all 67 former Maoist combatants in the South confirmed that they were expected to not share details about their former comrades. However, there is potential social desirability bias at work here because snitching is universally considered undesirable behavior.

12. The newspaper reports of his surrender state that Raju Anna had to quit due to illness, which made it difficult for him to live in inhospitable conditions in the forests of Chhattisgarh. It took me several meetings with a few retired rebels to realize that "illness" was the party-approved reason for surrender that rebels inevitably cited when they had to elaborate on the reasons for quitting.

13. By retired rebels, I refer to former Maoists who have experience in a Maoist guerrilla army, with active deployment of at least five years outside their home village and/or district. Most retired rebels I met in the South had spent the last 15–20 years of their lives in a guerrilla army, cut off from their families and friends. They were keen students of local politics and had strong bonds with their underground comrades. They all felt a sense of guilt asking for help from friends and families they had abandoned many years ago, particularly given that their return might jeopardize the routine and stability in their own lives as well in their friends' and families' lives, practically turning it upside down. Raju Anna was also worried that the revolution remained a distant dream. Despite his years of struggle in Chhattisgarh, his rich life

experiences, he was worried that his village might not forgive his failure to bring them the revolution they hoped for. "Nothing's changed," he said. "People have a little bit more to eat and wear. But the injustice and inequality . . . as it is. The market has now engulfed our lives, and it is all about money now. Earlier the rich and the poor all had bad education, bad healthcare. Now some of us can afford private schools and expensive nursing homes. Others are dying without doctor—no one wants to come to the villages. It is worse than before."

14. The respondents in the South used the words "prasiddha" (well-known), "manager," "risk," "sammanita" (respected), "nayakudu" (leader), and "sahnubhuti"(sympathizer) along with Svartha (self-interest), and "samajika network" (social network) to describe these prominent personalities. I use the term "movement entrepreneur" to combine the sense of a "risk-taking, well-respected leader" with someone "sympathetic to the movement" who also has a self-interest in supporting retiring rebels. The retired rebels identified "kriti" (fame), "prasansa" (appreciation), and "power" as some of the rewards that MEs value.

15. He was elected as a representative to the state assembly (known as MLA in India) from the region a few times. Former rebels trusted him more than others because he and his wife were known to have been friends with Ramakrishna, a well-known rebel leader from the region.

16. After his electoral victory in 2004, Congress Chief Minister Rajasekhar Reddy (aka YSR) initiated the peace talks October 11–20, 2004. For more information see Radhakrishna (2016).

17. Based on the interviews, 75% of former rebels described their local interlocutors by identity markers like behavioral characteristics, profession, caste, age, gender rather than names.

18. Activist A29 interviewed August 2013 in Warrangal, Telangana.

19. Activist A31 interviewed August 2013 in Nalgonda, Telangana.

20. Transaction costs are the costs of collecting information, bargaining, communicating, decision-making, and enforcing contracts between individuals and the state. The perception of such costs as exogenously impeding trade or inhibiting the formation of complete contracts suggests that reducing, eliminating, or avoiding those costs is generally welfare enhancing. As the quality of institutions is thought to be a part of what explains those transaction costs, the implication is that better institutions improve economic outcomes.

21. For example, if several countries join a pact to reduce air pollution, a downwind country that has the most to gain from clean air may make a side payment to an upwind country to give it some incentive to participate in what would otherwise be a losing proposition.

Chapter 5

1. The Tritiya Prastuti Committee (TPC) was formed in 2002 when several cadres broke away from CPI(Maoist) in Jharkhand due to the perceived domination of Yadavs over

other castes, particularly the Ganjus who are lower down the caste order than Yadavs. TPC's area of influence is spread over the districts of Latehar, Palamu and Chatra, with extensions in nearby Ranchi and Hazaribagh.

2. Often the assassinations of Maoists by mafia members are reported as encounters with security personnel.

3. Laloo Prasad Yadav was the chief minister of Bihar between 1990 and 1997 (with Rabri Devi) and the railway minister between 2004 and 2009. Nitish Kumar, belonging to the Kurmi caste, was the chief minister between 2005 and 2014. Their rise opened up political space for Yadavs and Kurmis within the democracy.

4. Jharkhand has 24 districts, which are further divided into 38 subdivisions, 262 blocks, and 32,620 villages. Jharkhand has 29% forest cover, one of the highest percentages in the country. The state is primarily rural with rich mineral deposits.

5. Between the 1980s and 1990s, India saw an overall decline in the population growth rate from 23.9% to 21.3%. However, during the same time period, Bihar saw a sharp increase in the population growth rate from 23.4% to 28.4%. The 2011 census shows that the population density of Bihar is phenomenally high at 880 persons per square kilometer compared to the national average of 234.

6. In an overpopulated state like Bihar, land ceiling was hard to justify on the basis of sound economic considerations. Economists point out that it is futile to try resolving the problem of rural poverty by redistributing land, which is in short supply, because enforcing extremely low land ceilings will not yield results worth the cost of enforcing those ceilings. Supply of cheap labor always exceeded the demand, and the best cure for poverty was investing in irrigation systems and other technocratic approaches to increase agricultural productivity.

7. One of the key promises made by Nitish Kumar after becoming the chief minister of Bihar was that he would carry out land reforms. The Land Reform Commission was initially granted a period of one year, which was subsequently extended to two years and expired in June 2007. The full report of the Commission was eventually submitted to the chief minister in April 2008. The Bihar government has not taken even the first minimum step of making the report public. For more details, please see https://www.mainstreamweekly.net/article1547.html.

8. Some of the early tribal uprisings in the region were the Khewar rising among the Santhal tribe in 1871, the Birsa rising among the Munda tribe from 1895 to 1900, and the Tana Bhagat movement among the Oraons during World War I. Following the fierce agitation against these land-grabbers under the leadership of Birsa Munda in the late 1800s, the British government ordered a survey and settlement of the country and passed the 1908 Chotanagpur Tenancy Act, which legitimized the Khuntkatti system enabling the tribals of Chotanagpur to clear forest and live and cultivate there.

9. Several tribal groups that formed during the same period, like Chotanagpur Unnati Samaj (Chotanagpur Improvement and Prosperity Society) formed in 1928 and Kissan Sabha (Conference of Peasant) in 1935–1936, worked to improve the socioeconomic condition of the tribals. All of these small groups united to form the Adivasi Mahasabha in 1938 that was to serve as the single spokesperson of tribal plight. Under the leadership of Jaipal Singh, an Oxford-educated Christian convert who was elected

chairman of the Chotanagpur Adivasi Maha Sabha in 1939, the movement gathered momentum.

10. The long history of intense ideological debate within the Indian left over the nature of the state and who would lead the revolution (workers or peasants) as discussed in Chapter 2 provides the context for this divide.

11. I'm grateful to journalist Anumeha Yadav for introducing me to Ranjan Yadav.

12. I was not able to meet Paulus Surin, the JMM legislator who was brought from Simdega jail for his MLA swearing in ceremony in 2009. He, and two other former Maoists from PLFI faction, were still in jail when they ran for office on the JMM ticket. Surin was arrested in 2009 and fought for the assembly poll on the JMM ticket from Torpa assembly constituency. Surin was the only former Maoist leader who won the assembly poll. As many as six former Maoist leaders were in the fray and four were contesting as JMM candidates. For more details, please see https://www.hindustantimes.com/india/develop-villages-to-end-maoist-insurgency-says-ex-maoist/story-OuRM5FcQvjGh5VEhMLKYXK.html (accessed November 28, 2013).

13. I was able to find most of the names during my research at Taraknath Das Research Center in Kolkata, where newspaper clippings from all major newspapers are filed under various categories. I found most of the surrender news in the North in *The Telegraph* and *Hindustan Times*. Among the most notable local journalists I was able to talk to was Harivansh (J2 in interview sample), the editor of *Prabhat Khabar*, and I met Faisal Anurag (J3 in interview sample). During meetings with Dayamani Barla (A1 in interview sample) at her tea shop and Stan Swamy (A2 in interview sample) at his ashram, they shared their insights on the Maoist retirement and tribal rights in Jharkhand.

14. I do not reveal his identity by referring to his last name because Ghanju is the name of his caste, and there are many rebels from this caste group in Chatra-Latehar districts in Jharkhand.

15. Yadav came to this meeting as well. He knew the owner of the bar.

16. The intelligence officers showed me identification on request. They checked my credentials; I showed them my research proposal and letter from my adviser and assured them that I would not submit my interview with Mr. Ghanju (MN8 in interview sample) to any newspaper. They requested my interview notes, but I had not yet transcribed the interview and did not have names and dates of persons in paper. They were courteous and professional but warned me that I should not meet any more "dangerous, wanted criminals" involved in many kidnaps and extortion for my own safety. The experience was somewhat unnerving.

17. In the 1980s, following the Bhoodan movement of Binobha Bhabe and Total Revolution of Jayprakash Narayan (JP), a small group of very committed activists from Chhatra Yuva Sangharsh Vahini of the JP movement began organizing peasants in both armed and democratic struggles. He never joined PU and eventually broke from it in a public spat. There were serious disagreements on the secondary status of mass organizations in the PU hierarchy and on the annihilation of landlords by Maoist cadres, which subjected the members of their mass organizations to severe police repression.

18. There were four names in the list of surrendered rebels that the police gave me who took one or two installments of the surrender money but not all of it. They were marked deceased. When I asked, it was clarified by the police that their former comrades killed them. On cross-checking about them with local journalists, I found that some might have been killed for failing to be helpful to the local real estate mafia or the various other extortion projects underway in Jharkhand.

19. RN11 mentioned that his former comrades took out death warrants against him. I have seen handwritten death warrants on walls in villages, written in dilute red ink against anyone who collaborated with the police. They warn of death for informers and their entire families. His cousins and their families avoid all contact with him.

20. In 2015, evidence came to light that many BJP leaders, including Murli Manohar Joshi, C. P. Thakur, and former Prime Minister Chandra Shekhar were complicit in the Bihar Dalit massacres committed by the Ranvir Sena, while the backward-caste governments of Nitish Kumar, as well as his arch rivals Lalu Prasad Yadav and Rabri Devi, declined to order investigations into the massacres despite knowledge of them. In addition, the police camps established outside villages to apprehend Maoists were jointly manned by the police and upper-caste militias. Bereft of housing and sanitation facilities, the security forces were lodged in landlord's houses.

21. Levels of violent crime in Jharkhand and Bihar have been significantly higher than the national average. Murder accounts for 4.73% of total reported crime in Jharkhand compared to a national average of 1.8%.

22. Satyendra Dubey was an Indian Engineering Service officer. He was the project director in the National Highways Authority of India (NHAI). Road contract mafia allegedly killed him when he identified large financial irregularities and threatened to expose the police, bureaucrats, politicians, and the mafia. For more details, see https://www.thebetterindia.com/163087/satyendra-dubey-iit-whistleblower-vajpayee-news/.

23. There are many mafias in the North designated by the industry they are associated with. Some examples include the coal mafia, timber mafia, construction mafia, contractor mafia, real estate mafia. For example, see https://web.archive.org/web/20070822134101/http://www.indiadaily.com/editorial/3897.asp.

24. The People's Liberation Front of India (PLFI), the Tritiya Sammelan Prastuti Committee (TSPC), Pahadi Cheetah, Shanti Sena, and Jairam Sahu Giroh are among a long list of such groups in Jharkhand. Almost every district with a Maoist presence also has a powerful non-Maoist armed group. The first to emerge was the TPC following a caste dispute within the Maoists. During interviews in the police headquarters in Ranchi, police officers who wanted to remain unnamed, remained ambivalent about the collusion between the police and these breakaway Maoist factions. Instead they asked if it would be so bad if the police wanted to weaken the Maoist insurgency by engineering and perpetuating violent splinter groups.

Chapter 6

1. Known as white flag incident (2009), hundreds of surrendered Tamil militants were killed by the Sinhalese army after the demobilization of the Liberation Tigers of Tamil Elam. An analysis of the available evidence points to an organized government plan at the highest level not to accept the surrender of the top civilian, administrative, and political leadership of the Liberation Tigers of Tamil Elam—but rather to execute them.

2. Rebels in Kashmir killed their comrade "suspecting him of planning to surrender before the government forces." For further details see http://kashmirdispatch.com/2016/01/06/anti-india-rebel-killed-by-own-men-who-suspected-him-of-surrendering/4180/.

3. http://www.aljazeera.com/indepth/features/2014/06/kashmir-former-fighters-regret-homecoming-201462214440675226.html.

4. For more on the execution of surrendered rebels in Burundi see https://news.vice.com/article/at-least-47-surrendered-rebels-executed-as-burundi-makes-a-bloody-start-to-2015.

5. Surrendered fighters in Syria were attacked, See, e.g., https://www.almasdarnews.com/article/video-daraa-rebels-disturb-reconciliation-kill-surrendered-fighters/.

6. The Ministry of Home Affairs published the IAP at http://mha.nic.in/naxal_new available on June 7, 2016.

Appendix 1

1. The annual Maoist surrender events based on newspaper reports are available at SATP's website: https://www.satp.org/satporgtp/countries/india/maoist/data_sheets/maoist_datasheet.html.

2. In my conversation with Ajai Sahni who oversees data collection in SATP, he suggested that it is possible that some surrender incidents were not reported in the national media but logged in police records. MHA, based on police records, can be slightly higher than SATP.

3. The MHA does not recognize CMAS, a popular tribal organization, as Maoist. That 1,765 surrendered over a few months in a single year is political propaganda by state governments. I cross-checked with police and bureaucrats with work experience in Koraput and Malkangiri. For example, in 2013, during my meetings with R. Vineel Krishna, who was abducted by the Maoists when he was in Malkangiri in Odisha, he confided that such abruptly high surrender is highly unlikely. He doubted if there were that many Maoists in the area.

4. Naturally suspicious of All India Radio (AIR), the rebels are known to prefer BBC because BBC has done reporting from the Naxalite heartland in Chhattisgarh with a reporter stationed in Bastar. I excluded these extreme observations, which had a strong effect on the size of confidence intervals around the regression line, from further analysis.

5. For the IHDS 2 data set, some of the ME variables are positively correlated with the number of retired rebels whereas others are negatively correlated (ME2, ME3, and ME11). Thus, the effect of the organizational density within this data set might be underestimated.

6. The CapEx database contains cost and ownership information on projects at different stages—announced, under implementation, completed, abandoned, stalled—across a wide variety of industries at the district level. The amounts invested in various industries are very heterogeneous for all types of investments. The approximate time period covered by the database is from the mid-1990s to the current year. For purposes of this analysis, all projects that had a date of announcement before or during 2009 were included—projects in all stages were included in the analysis to maximize coverage. As the industrial classification of the different projects in the CapEx is at a significant disaggregated level, the particular classification from CapEx was matched against the National Industrial Classification (2008) categories (major industries, e.g., mining, and their subcategories, coal-lignite) published by the government of India.

7. The Maoists, like other insurgent groups, prefer the forested and hilly tribal areas—and not the plains—as strategic areas where Base Areas can be set up.

8. However, I noticed in preliminary analysis that there is not much variation in this crime data between the two surveys. I also found that variables LC1, LC2, LC3 are positively correlated with the preliminary explanatory variable of interest organizational density (orgdens), while LC4 is negatively correlated. That is intuitive because high perception of crime leads to voluntary neighborhood watch programs. In construction of the crime variable, I exclude LC4 to avoid confusion in interpretation of results.

9. One could also use OLS but there are many values of 1 and 2 for *RTRMT*, which might bias the estimator. Another model of count data is the Poisson regression. However, the assumption that the conditional variance is equal to the conditional mean is violated. Therefore, the more general regression model is appropriate.

Appendix 2

1. These decisions were based on my previous fieldtrips to India during the summers of 2009–2011, when I found that structured and semi-structured interviews were ineffective in breaking the ice with former rebels. I had a local institutional affiliation with the Center for Economic and Social Sciences in Hyderabad, and I lived in the CESS campus in 2013. In the North, I stayed in Ranchi and Khunti where most of the retired rebels lived. I worked with a team of research assistants who were affiliated with the Indian Institute of Management in Ranchi and had ongoing projects in the Maoist-affected Saranda and Palamu regions.

2. The primary difficulty I faced in using surveys came from the inability or unwillingness of respondents in conflict zones to disseminate discrete information on sensitive issues accurately. I have personally administered the two pilot surveys to ordinary people in the conflict zones (100 respondents each in the North and South), where

I saw how traumatic experiences of loss and violence inhibit the ability and willingness of respondents to communicate them. The survey was more easily administered in the South than in the North in general. In the North, people in villages would promptly shut their doors and ask us to leave the moment they heard "Maoists." Both in the North and in the South, the sight of printed survey material made people skeptical of leaving a "paper trail" of their responses that could potentially land them in trouble. In addition, surveys in rural India can hardly be done one on one, with neighbors, family, and passers-by coming in and freely joining the conversation, making it impossible to ensure that respondents do not pick answers that they think others want them to (social desirability bias).

3. Snowball sampling can be very useful in revealing key actors or networks unknown to a researcher, thereby expanding the sample frame.

4. Since the research question is how rebels quit and not why some rebels quit and others don't, it was not imperative for me to create a balanced sample of both current and retired rebels. Current rebels with no plans to quit are not expected to have as valuable insights about the process of retirement as rebels who have been through the process of retirement.

5. I spoke to Derek O'Brien of Trinamool Congress on the phone because he was in New York at the time. I was unable to meet Mr. P. Chidambaram, in the original sample frame, who was the home minister of India (2008–2012) known to be instrumental in shaping the counterinsurgency policy, including the surrender and rehabilitation policy of former Maoists. But his interviews on the subject, and those of the other state chief ministers and party chiefs, were publicly available. I primarily targeted MLAs in conflict zones for interviews under Category 2.

6. I prepared a database of retired rebels in the South based on media reports, and I reached out to rebels directly with the help of my local network of researchers. In the North, the police shared their database of retired rebels, and I was able to reach out to all of them. However, admittedly I was not able to interview as many current rebels as retired rebels due to obvious personal security reasons. I was however able to speak to some current rebels, both men and women, who had not yet formally disarmed but wanted to quit, more in the North than in the South.

7. A representative sample did not need to include current Maoist guerrillas, who have no intention of quitting, because I'm interested in the process of retirement and not in the reasons for retirement. Besides security and accessibility were important considerations too. Instead I interviewed some current rebels who want to quit but have not yet, particularly in Jharkhand.

8. This approach reduces the number of study cases, but the combination of careful comparisons within a shared political setting and militant group, attention to path dependence, and rich empirical details of the causal processes make my inferences more credible than those that I might have drawn from a more heterogeneous and less detailed set of cases. In addition, each of these five districts is large and varied, and should not be thought of as a single case, but rather as the locations where I engaged in in-depth research of several case studies.

9. A mandal is an administrative division in the state of Andhra Pradesh that has come to replace the system of *tehsils*. A mandal is generally smaller than a *tehsil* and is meant for facilitating local self-government in the *panchayat* system.

10. In Giridih (in the east, contiguous with West Bengal), the Palamu district (in the North, contiguous with Bihar), and the West Singhbhum district in southeast, contiguous with Orissa), movement intensity is high, and surrender is moderately high. In the Dhanbad district, movement intensity is high, but surrender is very low. Contiguous with the East Singhbhum district is the West Midnapore district (Jangalmahal) of West Bengal, where I worked mostly in Binpur I & II and in Gopiballabhpur I & II subdivisions. I had offers from two competing activist networks and from the police to visit rural areas of Jharkhand. It is impossible to work in rural Jharkhand without an adequate network of protection. I picked an activist network affiliated with the Indian Institute of Management, Ranchi. This choice was deliberate, and, in hindsight, might have restricted access to certain areas and persons. In Palamau, I had developed personal connections with retired Maoists turned politicians from the area, and the ordinary people I spoke to were most likely aware of that.

11. The release of transcripts (even to an archive) undermines any promise of anonymity or confidentiality that we make to any individual. As Boston College researchers discovered, a country with extradition treaties can request the US government to subpoena interview materials and render them to the government of the foreign state. The subpoena of interview materials (full transcripts and audio tapes) led to the arrest of at least two ex-conflict participants, neither of whom had any involvement in the interviews—or any opportunity to offer "consent" to the release of materials implicating them in murders. Northern Ireland residents will generally attest to the destabilizing impact of the Boston College fiasco on the peace process, since one of the arrestees (Gerry Adams) is himself a major figure in the peace deal of 1998. Read more at http://www.chronicle.com/interactives/belfast.

12. I felt the need to edit out parts of the quotes from former rebels and various local, as well as more well-known, activists that I included in earlier drafts of my dissertation to protect their identities and to more closely follow IRB requirements. I have been questioned by an intelligence agency about my research, and my experience in Ranchi in October 2013 convinced me that there should be nothing in my writing that outside of illustrating an understudied and underreported process of rebel retirement could become bases for any harm including arrests, career backlash, or violence.

Bibliography

Ahluwalia, Montek S. 2002. "State Level Performance under Economic Reforms in India." In *Economic Policy Reforms and the Indian Economy*, edited by Anne O. Krueger, 91–125. University of Chicago Press.

Ahluwalia, Montek Singh. 2013. "Regional Balance in Indian Planning." In *The New Bihar: Rekindling Governance and Development*, edited by N.K. Singh. HarperCollins India.

Alden, Chris. 2002. "Making Old Soldiers Fade Away: Lessons from the Reintegration of Demobilized Soldiers in Mozambique." *Security Dialogue* 33 (3): 341–56.

Appu, P.S. 1975. "Tenancy Reform in India." *Economic and Political Weekly*, 1339–75.

Arjona, Ana. 2014. "Wartime Institutions: A Research Agenda." *Journal of Conflict Resolution* 58 (8): 1360–89.

Arjona, Ana. 2016. *Rebelocracy*. Cambridge University Press.

Arjona, Ana, Nelson Kasfir, and Zachariah Mampilly. 2015. *Rebel Governance in Civil War*. Cambridge University Press.

Auerbach, Adam Michael. 2016. "Clients and Communities: The Political Economy of Party Network Organization and Development in India's Urban Slums." *World Politics* 68 (1): 111–48.

Auyero, Javier. 2001. *Poor People's Politics: Peronist Survival Networks and the Legacy of Evita*. Duke University Press.

Auyero, Javier. 2013. "Gray Zone of Politics and Social Movements." *The Wiley-Blackwell Encyclopedia of Social and Political Movements*. Wiley-Blackwell.

Baaré, Anton. 2005. "An Analysis of Transitional Economic Reintegration." Swedish Initiative for Disarmament, Demobilisation and Reintegration (*SIDDR*), Ministry of Foreign Affairs, SIDDR Working Group 3.

Bach, Daniel, C. 2011. "Patrimonialism and Neopatrimonialism: Comparative Trajectories and Readings." *Commonwealth & Comparative Politics* 49 (3): 275–94.

Balcells, L. 2012. "The Consequences of Victimization on Political Identities: Evidence from Spain." *Politics & Society* 40(3): 311–47.

Baker, Christopher. 1975. "Figures and Facts: Madras Government Statistics 1880–1940." In *South India: Political Institutions and Political Change 1880–1940*, 204–31. Palgrave Macmillan.

Bakke, Kristin M., Kathleen Gallagher Cunningham, and Lee J.M. Seymour. 2012. "A Plague of Initials: Fragmentation, Cohesion, and Infighting in Civil Wars." *Perspectives on Politics* 10 (2): 265–83.

Balagopal, K. 1981. "Revival of Encounters in Andhra." *Economic and Political Weekly* 16 (38): 1524–5.

Balagopal, K. 1990. "The End of Spring?" *Economic and Political Weekly*, 1883–88.

Balagopal, K. 2000. "A Tangled Web: Subdivision of SC Reservations in AP." *Economic and Political Weekly*, 1075–81.

Balagopal, K. 2005. "Naxalites in Andhra Pradesh: Have We Heard the Last of the Peace Talks?" *Economic and Political Weekly*, March.

Balagopal, K. 2006. "Maoist Movement in Andhra Pradesh." *Economic and Political Weekly*, 3183–87.

Balagopal, K. 2007. "Land Unrest in Andhra Pradesh-I: Ceiling Surpluses and Public Lands." *Economic and Political Weekly*, 3829–33.

Balagopal, K. 2011. *An Ear to the Ground: Writings on Caste and Class*. Navayana.

Balcells, Laia. 2017. *Rivalry and Revenge*. Cambridge University Press.

Ballabh, Vishwa, and Sushil Pandey. 1999. "Transitions in Rice Production Systems in Eastern India: Evidence from Two Villages in Uttar Pradesh." *Economic and Political Weekly*, A11–16.

Bandyopadhyay, D. 2001. "Tebhaga Movement in Bengal: A Retrospect." *Economic and Political Weekly*, 3901–7.

Bandyopadhyay, D. 2006. "A Visit to Two 'Flaming Fields' of Bihar." *Economic and Political Weekly*, 5302–4.

Bandyopadhyay, D. 2009. "Lost Opportunity in Bihar." *Economic and Political Weekly*, 12–14.

Banerjee, Abhijit. 2004. "Who Is Getting the Public Goods in India? Some Evidence and Some Speculation." In *India's Emerging Economy: Performance and Prospects in the 1990s and Beyond*, edited by K. Basu, 183–213. MIT Press.

Banerjee, Abhijit, and Esther Duflo. 2007. "The Economic Lives of the Poor." *Journal of Economic Perspectives* 21 (1): 141–67.

Banerjee, Abhijit, and Esther Duflo. 2009. "Improving Health Care Delivery in India." Paper presented at Deaton Festshrift Conference, September. Princeton, NJ. http://economics.mit.edu/files/5172.

Banerjee, Abhijit, and Lakshmi Iyer. 2005. "History, Institutions, and Economic Performance: The Legacy of Colonial Land Tenure Systems in India." *American Economic Review* 95 (4): 1190–213.

Banerjee, Aloke. 2003. *Inside MCC Country*. K DasPublishing.

Banerjee, S. 1980. *In the Wake of Naxalbari: A History of the Naxalite Movement in India*. Subarnarekha.

Banerjee, S. 1984. *India's Simmering Revolution: The Naxalite Uprising*. Zed Books.

Barakat, B., and H. Urdal. 2009. "*Breaking the Waves? Does Education Mediate the Relationship between Youth Bulges and Political Violence?*" The World Bank .

Basu, P. 2000. *Towards Naxalbari (1953-1967): An Account of Inner-Party Ideological Struggle*. Progressive.

Bates, Robert H. 2008. "State Failure." *Annual Review of Political Science* 11: 1–12.

Batson, C. Daniel, Nadia Ahmad, David A. Lishner, and J. Tsang. 2016. "Empathy and Altruism." In *Oxford Handbook of Hypo-Egoic Phenomena: Theory and Research on the Quiet Ego*, edited by Brown, Kirk Warren, and Mark R. Leary, 161–74. Oxford University Press.

Berman, Sheri. 1997. "Civil Society and the Collapse of the Weimar Republic." *World Politics* 49 (3): 401–29.

Berman, Sheri. 2009. *The Social Democratic Moment: Ideas and Politics in the Making of Interwar Europe*. Harvard University Press.

Bernstorff, Dagmar. 1973. "Eclipse of 'Reddy-Raj'? The Attempted Restructuring of the Congress Party Leadership in Andhra Pradesh." *Asian Survey* 13 (10): 959–79.

Bhaduri, Amit. 1973. "A Study in Agricultural Backwardness under Semi-Feudalism." *The Economic Journal* 83 (329): 120–37.

Bhaduri, Amit. 1977. "On the Formation of Usurious Interest Rates in Backward Agriculture." *Cambridge Journal of Economics* 1 (4): 341–52.

Bharadwaj, Krishna. 1982. "Regional Differentiation in India." *Economic and Political Weekly* 17, 605–14.

Bhatia, Bela. 2005. "The Naxalite Movement in Central Bihar." *Economic and Political Weekly*, 1536–49.

Bilgin, Pinar, and Adam David Morton. 2002. "Historicising Representations of 'Failed States': Beyond the Cold-War Annexation of the Social Sciences?" *Third World Quarterly* 23 (1): 55–80.

Bjornlund, E., G. Cowan, and W. Gallery. 2007. "Election Systems and Political Parties in Post-conflict and Fragile States." *Governance in Post-Conflict Societies: Rebuilding Fragile States*, 64–85.

Blair, Harry W. 1980. "Rising Kulaks and Backward Classes in Bihar: Social Change in the Late 1970s." *Economic and Political Weekly*, 64–74.

Blattman, C., and E. Miguel. 2009. "Civil War." NBER Working Paper No. 14801.

Bleich, Erik, and Robert Pekkanen. 2013. "How to Report Interview Data." *Interview Research in Political Science* 1: 84–105.

Bleie, T. and R. Shrestha. 2012. *DDR in Nepal: Stakeholder Politics and the Implications for Reintegration as a Process of Disengagement*. University of Tromso.

Boone, C. 2003. *Political Topographies of the African State: Territorial Authority and Institutional Choice*. Cambridge University Press.

Bouton, Marshall M. 2014. *Agrarian Radicalism in South India*. Princeton University Press.

Bradburn, Norman M., Seymour Sudman, Ed Blair, and Carol Stocking. 1978. "Question Threat and Response Bias." *Public Opinion Quarterly* 42 (2): 221–34.

Brancati, D., and J.L. Snyder. 2013. "Time to Kill: The Impact of Election Timing on Postconflict Stability." *Journal of Conflict Resolution* 57(5): 822–53.

Bühler, Georg, trans. 1964. *The Laws of Manu. Translated with Extracts from Seven Commentaries by G. Bühler*. Motilal Banarsidass.

Burns, Justine, Susan Godlonton, and Malcolm Keswell. 2010. "Social Networks, Employment and Worker Discouragement: Evidence from South Africa." *Labour Economics* 17 (2): 336–44.

Büthe, Tim, Alan M. Jacobs, Erik Bleich, Robert Pekkanen, Marc Trachtenberg, Katherine Cramer, Victor Shih, Sarah Elizabeth Parkinson, Elisabeth Jean Wood, and Timothy Pachirat. 2015. "Transparency in Qualitative and Multi-Method Research: A Symposium." *Qualitative and Multi-Method Research: Newsletter of the American Political Science Association's QMMR Section* 13 (1): 2–64.

Carothers, T. 1997. "The Rise of Election Monitoring: The Observers Observed." *Journal of Democracy* 8(3): 17–31.

Chaitanya, Krishna. 1991. "Social Justice, Bihar Style." *Economic and Political Weekly*, 2612–3.

Chakrabarty, Dipesh. 2000. "Subaltern Studies and Postcolonial Historiography." *Nepantla: Views from South* 1 (1): 9–32.

Chakravarti, Anand. 2001. "Caste and Agrarian Class: A View from Bihar." *Economic and Political Weekly*, 1449–62.

Chakravarty, Anuradha. 2015. *Investing in Authoritarian Rule: Punishment and Patronage in Rwanda's Gacaca Courts for Genocide Crimes*. Cambridge University Press.

Chandran, Suba, and Alok Kumar Gupta. 2002. "India, Caste Violence and Class in Bihar: The Ranvir Sena." In *Searching for Peace in Europe and Eurasia: An Overview of Conflict Prevention and Peacebuilding Activities*, 546–578. Lynne Rienner Publishers.

Chatterjee, Moyukh. 2017. "The Impunity Effect: Majoritarian Rule, Everyday Legality, and State Formation in India." *American Ethnologist* 44 (1): 118–30.

Chatterjee, Partha. 1991. "Whose Imagined Community?" *Millennium* 20 (3): 521–25.

Chaudhry, Praveen K. 1988. "Agrarian Unrest in Bihar: A Case Study of Patna District 1960–1984." *Economic and Political Weekly*, 51–56.

Chesterman, S. ed. 2001. *Civilians in War*. Lynne Rienner Publishers.

Christia, Fotini. 2012. *Alliance Formation in Civil Wars*. Cambridge University Press.

Coase, R.H. 1960. "The Problem of Social Cost." In *Classic Papers in Natural Resource Economics*, 87–137. Palgrave Macmillan.

Cohen, N. and T. Arieli. 2011. "Field Research in Conflict Environments: Methodological Challenges and Snowball Sampling." *Journal of Peace Research*, 48(4): 423–35.

Collier, P. 2000. "Economic Causes of Civil Conflict and Their Implications for Policy." *World Bank* 15: 20011107-4.

Collier, Paul, and Anke Hoeffler. 2004. "Greed and Grievance in Civil War." *Oxford Economic Papers* 56 (4): 563–95. https://doi.org/10.1093/oep/gpf064.

Colomer, Josep M. 2000. "Strategic Transitions: Game Theory and Democratization." Johns Hopkins University http://works.bepress.com/josep_colomer/9.

Cook, Karen S., Russell Hardin, and Margaret Levi. 2005. *Cooperation without Trust?* Russell Sage Foundation.

Corbridge, Stuart. 1987. "Industrialisation, Internal Colonialism and Ethnoregionalism: The Jharkhand, India, 1880–1980." *Journal of Historical Geography* 13 (3): 249–66.

Corbridge, Stuart, and John Harriss. 2000. *Reinventing India: Liberalization, Hindu Nationalism and Popular Democracy*. Polity Press..

Cyr, J. 2016. "The Pitfalls and Promise of Focus Groups as a Data Collection Method." *Sociological Methods & Research* 45(2): 231–59.

Daly, Sarah Zukerman. 2016. *Organized Violence after Civil War: The Geography of Recruitment in Latin America*. Cambridge University Press.

Das, Arvind, N. 1986. "Landowners' Armies Take over 'Law and Order.'" *Economic and Political Weekly*, 15–18.

Das, V., D. Poole, V. Das, and D. Poole. 2004. "Anthropology in the Margins of the State." *PoLAR: Political and Legal Anthropology Review* 30(1): 225–52.

Dasgupta, Aditya, Kishore Gawande, and Devesh Kapur. 2017. "(When) Do Anti-povertyPrograms Reduce Violence? India's Rural Employment Guarantee and Maoist Conflict." *International Organization* 71(3): 605–32..

Datt, Gaurav, and Martin Ravallion. 1998. "Why Have Some Indian States Done Better than Others at Reducing Rural Poverty?" *Economica* 65 (257): 17–38.

Dauphinée, Elizabeth. 2016. *The Ethics of Researching War: Looking for Bosnia*. Manchester University Press.

Deaton, Angus, and Jean Dreze. 2002. "Poverty and Inequality in India: A Re-Examination." *Economic and Political Weekly*, 3729–48.

Debos, Marielle. 2016. *Living by the Gun in Chad: Combatants, Impunity and State Formation*. Zed Books.

DeMaio, Theresa J. 1984. "Social Desirability and Survey." *Surveying Subjective Phenomena* 2: 257.

Dhanagare, D.N. 1976. "Peasant Protest and Politics—The Tebhaga Movement in Bengal (India), 1946–47." *The Journal of Peasant Studies* 3 (3): 360–78.

Dhar, Hiranmay. 1990. "Institutional Constraints to Land Reform in Bihar." Paper Presented for Study Group on Land Reforms as Common Property Resources, Giri Institute of Development Studies, Lucknow.

Donner, H. 2004. "The Significance of Naxalbari: Accounts of Personal Involvement and Politics in West Bengal." *Occasional Papers Series* 3 (2): 1–22.

Dyregrov, Atle, Rolf Gjestad, and Magne Raundalen. 2002. "Children Exposed to Warfare: A Longitudinal Study." *Journal of Traumatic Stress* 15 (1): 59–68. https://doi.org/10.1023/A:1014335312219.

Elman, C., D. Kapiszewski, and L. Vinuela. 2010. "Qualitative Data Archiving: Rewards and Challenges." *PS: Political Science and Politics* 43(1): 23–7.

Elliot, Carolyn. 1970. "Caste and Faction among the Dominant Castes: The Reddies and Kammas of Andhra." In *Caste in Indian Politics.* edited by Rajni Kothari, 129–69. Orient Longman.

Elliott, Carolyn, M. 1974. "Decline of a Patrimonial Regime: The Telangana Rebellion in India, 1946–51." *The Journal of Asian Studies* 34 (01): 27–47.

Evans, P.B. 1989. "Predatory, Developmental, and Other Apparatuses: A Comparative Political Economy Perspective on the Third World State." *Sociological Forum* 4: 561–87.

Evans, P.B., Rueschemeyer, D. and Skocpol, T. 1985. *Bringing the State Back In.* Cambridge University Press.

Fafchamps, M. and Lund, S., 2003. Risk-sharing networks in rural Philippines. *Journal of development Economics*, 71(2), 261–87.

Fearon, J.D. and Laitin, D.D. 2003. "Ethnicity, Insurgency, and Civil War." *American Political Science Review* 97 (1): 75–90.

Findley, Michael, and Peter Rudloff. 2012. "Combatant Fragmentation and the Dynamics of Civil Wars." *British Journal of Political Science* 42 (4): 879–901.

Fisher, M.H. 1998. *Indirect Rule in India: Residents and the Residency System, 1764-1858.* Oxford University Press, USA.

Fjelde, Hanne, and Desirée Nilsson. 2012. "Rebels against Rebels Explaining Violence between Rebel Groups." *Journal of Conflict Resolution* 56 (4): 604–28.

Forrester, Duncan B. 1970. "Subregionalism in India: The Case of Telangana." *Pacific Affairs* 43 (1): 5–21.

Fortna, V.P. 2008. *Does Peacekeeping Work?: Shaping Belligerents' Choices after Civil War.* Princeton University Press.

Frankel, Francine R. 1989. "Caste, Land and Dominance in Bihar: Breakdown of the Brahmanical Social Order." *Dominance and State Power in Modern India: Decline of a Social Order* 1: 46–132.

Fuller, C.J. and John Harriss (2000) "For an Anthropology of the Modern Indian State." In *The Everyday State in Modern India*, edited by C.J. Fuller and Veronique Benei, 1–30. Social Science Press.

Furlong, Paul. 2012. "Informal Governance in Higher Education Reform: The Bologna Process in Europe." In *International Handbook on Informal Governance*. Edward Elgar Publishing.

Gambetta, Diego. 2000. "Mafia: The Price of Distrust." *Trust: Making and Breaking Cooperative Relations* 10: 158–75.

George, A.L. and A. Bennett. 2005. *Case Studies and Theory Development in the Social Sciences*. MIT Press.

Ghatak, M. and Eynde, O.V. 2017. "Economic Determinants of the Maoist Conflict in India." *Economic & Political Weekly*, 52(39): 69.

Ghosh, S.K. 2009. *Naxalbari: Before and after: Reminiscences and Appraisal*. New Age.

Gilligan, Michael J., Eric N. Mvukiyehe, and Cyrus Samii. 2013. "Reintegrating Rebels into Civilian Life Quasi-Experimental Evidence from Burundi." *Journal of Conflict Resolution* 57 (4): 598–626.

Girod, D.M. 2008. *Foreign aid and Post-Conflict Reconstruction*. Stanford University.

Goodwin, J., and T. Skocpol. 2000. "Explaining Revolutions in the Contemporary Third World." *Revolution: Critical Concepts in Political Science* 17 (4): 178.

Gordon, Ruth. 1997. "Saving Failed States: Sometimes a Neocolonialist Notion." *Proceedings of the ASIL Annual Meeting*, 91: 420–22. Cambridge University Press.

Gough, K. 1968. "Peasant Resistance and Revolt in South India." *Pacific Affairs* 41 (4): 526–44.

Gough, Kathleen. 1974. "Indian Peasant Uprisings." *Economic and Political Weekly*, 1391–412.

Gourevitch, Alex. 2004. *The Unfailing of the State*. JSTOR.

Goyal, Yugank. 2018. "The Coal Mine Mafia of India: A Mirror of Corporate Power." *American Journal of Economics and Sociology* 77 (2): 541–74.

Granovetter, M.S. 1973. "The Strength of Weak Ties." *American Journal of Sociology*, 78(6):1360–80.

Gudavarthy, Ajay. 2005. "Dalit and Naxalite Movements in AP: Solidarity or Hegemony?" *Economic and Political Weekly*, 5410–18.

Gudavarthy, Ajay. 2013. *Politics of Post-Civil Society: Contemporary History of Political Movements in India*. SAGE India.

Gudavarthy, Ajay. 2017. *Revolutionary Violence versus Democracy: Narratives from India*. SAGE India.

Guha, R. 1999. *Elementary Aspects of Peasant Insurgency in Colonial India*. Duke University Press Books.

Guha, Ramachandra. 2007. "Adivasis, Naxalites and Indian Democracy." *Economic and Political Weekly*, 3305–12.

Guha, Ranajit. 1982. "On Some Aspects of the Historiography of Colonial India." *Subaltern Studies*, 1.

Gupta, Akhil. 1995. "Blurred Boundaries: The Discourse of Corruption, the Culture of Politics, and the Imagined State." *American Ethnologist* 22 (2): 375–402.

Gurr, T.R. 1970. *Why Men Rebel*. Princeton, NJ.

Gwande, Kishore, Devesh Kapur, and Shanker Satyanath. 2012. "Natural Resource Shocks and Conflict in India's Red Belt." Work in Progress.

Hansen, Thomas Blom, Finn Stepputat, Julia Adams, and George Steinmetz. 2001. *States of Imagination: Ethnographic Explorations of the Postcolonial State*. Duke University Press.

Hanumantha Rao, C.H. 2011. "Sri Krishna Committee Report on Telangana: Recommendations at Variance with Analysis." *Economic & Political Weekly* 46 (5): 33–36.

Haque, T., and G. Parthasarathy. 1992. "Land Reform and Rural Development: Highlights of a National Seminar." *Economic and Political Weekly*, 395–97.

Haragopal, G. and Balagopal, K. 1998. "Civil Liberties Movement and the State in India." In *People's Rights: Social Movements and the State in the Third World*, edited by M. Mohanty and Partha N. Mukherji, 353–72. Sage Publications.

Haragopal, G., and K. Balagopal. 1998. "Civil Liberties Movement and the State in India." *People's Rights: Social Movements and the State in the Third World*, 353–72.

Hardin, R. (2001). "Conceptions and Explanations of Trust." In *Russell Sage Foundation Series on Trust, Vol. 2. Trust in Society*, edited by K.S. Cook, 3–39. Russell Sage Foundation.

Harsh, Matthew. 2005. "Formal and Informal Governance of Agricultural Biotechnology in Kenya: Participation and Accountability in Controversy Surrounding the Draft Biosafety Bill." *Journal of International Development* 17 (5): 661–77.

Harstad, Bård. 2007. "Harmonization and Side Payments in Political Cooperation." *American Economic Review* 97 (3): 871–89.

Harstad, Bård. 2008. "Do Side Payments Help? Collective Decisions and Strategic Delegation." *Journal of the European Economic Association* 6 (2–3): 468–77.

Hartman, Alexandra C., and Benjamin S. Morse. 2015. "Wartime Violence, Empathy, and Intergroup Altruism: Evidence from the Ivoirian Refugee Crisis in Liberia." Working Paper. http://cega. beerkely. edu/assets/miscellaneous_file/119_-_HartmanMorseViolenceEmpathy-May_.

Heller, P. 2009. " 'Democratic Deepening in India and South Africa." *Journal of Asian and African Studies*, 44(1): 123–49.

Helmke, Gretchen, and Steven Levitsky. 2004. "Informal Institutions and Comparative Politics: A Research Agenda." *Perspectives on Politics* 2 (4): 725–40.

Henningham, Stephen. 1979. "Agrarian Relations in North Bihar: Peasant Protest and the Darbhanga Raj, 1919-20." *The Indian Economic & Social History Review* 16 (1): 53–75.

Herring, R. 1997, May. Fanaticism, jacquerie, movement, party: ratchet politics and peasant mobilization in South India, 1836–1956. In *Symposium "Power, Agrarian Structure and Peasant Mobilization in Modern India,"* University of Virginia, Charlottesville, May (Vol. 25).

Herring, Ron. 1997. "'Fanaticism,' Jacquerie, Movement, Party: Ratchet Politics and Peasant Mobililization in South India, 1836–1956." In *Symposium "Power, Agrarian Structure and Peasant Mobilization in Modern India,"* University of Virginia, Charlottesville, May (Vol. 25).

Herring, Ronald J. 1986. "Agrarian Radicalism in South India. By Marshall M. Bouton. Princeton, NJ: Princeton University Press, 1985." *The Journal of Asian Studies* 45 (05): 1093–94.

Herring, Ronald J. 1991. "From Structural Conflict to Agrarian Stalemate: Agrarian Reforms in South India." *Journal of Asian and African Studies* 26 (3–4): 169–88.

Hill, Jonathan. 2005. "Beyond the Other? A Postcolonial Critique of the Failed State Thesis." *African Identities* 3 (2): 139–54.

Hironaka, Ann. 2009. *Neverending Wars: The International Community, Weak States, and the Perpetuation of Civil War*. Harvard University Press.

Hoelscher, Kristian, Jason Miklian, and Krishna Chaitanya Vadlamannati. 2012. "Hearts and Mines: A District-Level Analysis of the Maoist Conflict in India." *International Area Studies Review* 15 (2): 141–60.

Hooker, John. 2009. "Corruption from a Cross-Cultural Perspective." *Cross Cultural Management: An International Journal* 16 (3): 251–67.

Horgan, John, and Kurt Braddock. 2010. "Rehabilitating the Terrorists?: Challenges in Assessing the Effectiveness of De-Radicalization Programs." *Terrorism and Political Violence* 22 (2): 267–91. https://doi.org/10.1080/09546551003594748.

Humphreys, Macartan, and Jeremy Weinstein. 2005. "Disentangling the Determinants of Successful Disarmament, Demobilization, and Reintegration." Paper presented at 101st Meeting of the American Political Science Association. September. Washington, DC.

Husain, Syed Arshad, Jyotsna Nair, William Holcomb, John C. Reid, Victor Vargas, and Satish S. Nair. 1998. "Stress Reactions of Children and Adolescents in War and Siege Conditions." *American Journal of Psychiatry* 155 (12): 1718–19.

Hwang, Julie Chernov. 2018. *Why Terrorists Quit: The Disengagement of Indonesian Jihadists.* Cornell University Press.

International Peace Academy. 2002. *A Framework for Lasting Disarmament, Demobilization and Reintegration of Former Combatants in Crisis Situations.* International Peace Academy.

Irschick, Eugene F. 1969. *Politics and Social Conflict in South India: The Non-Brahman Movement and Tamil Separatism, 1916–1929.* University of California Press.

Iyengar, S. Kesava. 1951. *Rural Economic Enquiries in the Hyderabad State, 1949–51.* Government Press.

Jaffrelot, Christophe. 2003. *India's Silent Revolution: The Rise of the Lower Castes in North India.* Orient Blackswan.

Jaffrelot, Christophe, and Sanjay Kumar. 2012. *Rise of the Plebeians?: The Changing Face of the Indian Legislative Assemblies.* Vol. 2. Routledge.

Jaffrelot, India's Silent Revolution. 2002. "The Rise of Low Castes in North Indian Politics." *Delhi, Permanent Black,* 227.

Jaoul, Nicolas. 2011. "Manju Devi's Martyrdom Marxist-Leninist Politics and the Rural Poor in Bihar." *Contributions to Indian Sociology* 45 (3): 347–71.

Jenkins, J. Craig. 1983. "Resource Mobilization Theory and the Study of Social Movements." *Annual Review of Sociology* 9 (1): 527–53. https://doi.org/10.1146/annurev.so.09.080183.002523.

Kalyvas, S.N. 2006. *The Logic of Violence in Civil War.* Cambridge University Press.

Kalyvas, Stathis N. 2008. "Ethnic Defection in Civil War." *Comparative Political Studies* 41 (8): 1043–68.

Kamra, L. and Chandra, U. 2017. "Maoism and the Masses: Critical Reflections on Revolutionary Praxis and Subaltern Agency." In *Revolutionary Violence Versus Democracy: Narratives from India,* edited by A. Gudavarthy, 191–221. Sage Publication.

Kannabiran, Kalpana. 2013. *Tools of Justice: Non-Discrimination and the Indian Constitution.* Routledge India.

Kannabiran, Kalpana, Sagari R. Ramdas, N. Madhusudhan, S. Ashalatha, and M. Pavan Kumar. 2010. "On the Telangana Trail." *Economic and Political Weekly,* 69–82.

Kapiszewski, D., L.M.MacLean, and B.L. Read. 2015. *Field Research in Political Science: Practices and Principles.* Cambridge University Press.

Kaplan, Oliver, and Enzo Nussio. 2018. "Explaining Recidivism of Ex-Combatants in Colombia." *Journal of Conflict Resolution* 62 (1): 64–93.

Kapur, Devesh, Kishore Gawande, and Shanker Satyanath. 2012. "Renewable Resource Shocks and Conflict in India's Maoist Belt." Mimeo.

Kasara, K. 2009. *Electoral Geography and Conflict in Kenya: Examining the Local Level Causes of Violence in Rift Valley Province after the 2007 Election.* Working Paper.

Katznelson, Ira. 1982. *City Trenches: Urban Politics and the Patterning of Class in the United States.* University of Chicago Press.

Kaviraj, Sudipta. 2010. *The Imaginary Institution of India: Politics and Ideas.* Columbia University Press.

Kelley, J. 2008. "Assessing the Complex Evolution of Norms: The Rise of international election Monitoring. *International Organization*, 221–55.

Kennedy, Jonathan, and Sunil Purushotham. 2012. "Beyond Naxalbari: A Comparative Analysis of Maoist Insurgency and Counterinsurgency in Independent India." *Comparative Studies in Society and History* 54 (4): 832–62.

Khanna, Gaurav, and Laura Zimmermann. 2014. "Fighting Maoist Violence with Promises: Evidence from India's Employment Guarantee Scheme." *The Economics of Peace and Security Journal* 9 (1): 30–6.

Khusro, Ali Mohammed. 1958. *Economic and Social Effects of Jagirdari Abolition and Land Reforms in Hyderabad.* Osmania University Press

Kishore, Avinash. 2004. "Understanding Agrarian Impasse in Bihar." *Economic and Political Weekly*, 3484–91.

Kocher, Matthew Adam. 2010. "State Capacity as a Conceptual Variable." *Yale Journal of International Affairs* 5: 137.

Kohli, Atul. 1988. "The NTR Phenomenon in Andhra Pradesh: Political Change in a South Indian State." *Asian Survey* 28 (10): 991–1017.

Kohli, Atul. 1997. "Can Democracies Accommodate Ethnic Nationalism? Rise and Decline of Self-Determination Movements in India." *The Journal of Asian Studies* 56 (2): 325–44.

Kohli, Atul. 2002. "State, Society, and Development." *Political Science: The State of the Discipline*, 84–117.

Kolenda, Pauline Mahar. 1964. "Religious Anxiety and Hindu Fate." *The Journal of Asian Studies* 23 (S1): 71–81.

Krishna, A. 2002. *Active Social Capital: Tracing the Roots of Development and Democracy.* Columbia University Press.

Krishna, Anirudh. 2006. "Pathways out of and into Poverty in 36 Villages of Andhra Pradesh, India." *World Development* 34 (2): 271–88.

Krishna, Anirudh, Mahesh Kapila, Sharad Pathak, Mahendra Porwal, Kiranpal Singh, and Virpal Singh. 2004. "Falling into Poverty in Villages of Andhra Pradesh: Why Poverty Avoidance Policies Are Needed." *Economic and Political Weekly*, 3249–56.

Kumar, Anand. 2010. "Understanding Lohia's Political Sociology: Intersectionality of Caste, Class, Gender and Language." *Economic and Political Weekly*, 64–70.

Kumar, Ashutosh. 2013. "Development Focus and Electoral Success at State Level: Nitish Kumar as Bihar's Leader." *South Asia Research* 33 (2): 101–21.

Kumar, Ashwani. 2008. *Community Warriors: State, Peasants and Caste Armies in Bihar.* Anthem Press.

Kunnath, G.J. 2006. "Becoming a Naxalite in Rural Bihar: Class Struggle and Its Contradictions." *Journal of Peasant Studies* 33 (1): 89–123.

Kurtenbach, Sabine, and Herbert Wulf. 2012. "Violence and Security Concerns in Post-Conflict Situations." Research and Advisory Project, Instruments and Procedures of German Development Cooperation in Post-Conflict Situations—Project Working Paper No. 3.

Lalwani, Sameer. 2014. "Understanding India's Counterinsurgency Strategy against the Naxal Threat." Centre for the Advanced Study of India, India in Transition.

Lange, M. 2009. *Lineages of Despotism and Development: British Colonialism and State Power.* University of Chicago Press.

Larsson, Marie. 2006. "'When Women Unite!': The Making of the Anti-Liquor Movement in Andhra Pradesh, India." Department of Social Anthropology, Stockholm University.

Lauth, Hans-Joachim. 2000. "Informal Institutions and Democracy." *Democratization* 7 (4): 21–50.

Ledeneva, Alena V. 2006. *How Russia Really Works: The Informal Practices That Shaped Post-Soviet Politics and Business.* Cornell University Press.

Lehmann, E.L. and J.P. Romano. 2006. *Testing Statistical hypotheses.* Springer Science & Business Media.

Leonard, John G. 1967. "Politics and Social Change in South India: A Study of the Andhra Movement." *Journal of Commonwealth & Comparative Politics* 5 (1): 60–77.

Leonard, Karen. 1978. "The Mulki-Non Mulki Conflict." In *People, Princes and Paramount Power: Society and Politics in the Indian Princely States,* edited by R. Jeffrey, 91–92. Delhi and New York, Oxford University Press.

Leonard, Karen, and Susan Weller. 1980. "Declining Subcaste Endogamy In India: The Hyderabad Kayasths, 1900–75." *American Ethnologist* 7 (3): 504–17.

Levitsky, Steven. 2003. *Transforming Labor-Based Parties in Latin America: Argentine Peronism in Comparative Perspective.* Cambridge University Press.

Lichbach, M.I. 1987. "Deterrence or Escalation? The Puzzle of Aggregate Studies of Repression and Dissent." *Journal of Conflict Resolution,* 266–97.

Lichbach, Mark I. 1994. "What Makes Rational Peasants Revolutionary? Dilemma, Paradox, and Irony in Peasant Collective Action." *World Politics* 46 (3): 383–418. https://doi.org/10.2307/2950687.

Louis, Prakash. 2000a. "Class War Spreads to New Areas." *Economic and Political Weekly,* 2206–11.

Louis, Prakash. 2000b. "Shankarbigha Revisited." *Economic and Political Weekly,* 507–9.

Lupia, A. and C. Elman. 2014. "Openness in Political Science: Data Access and Research Transparency. *PS, Political Science & Politics* 47(1): 19.

Mahadevan, Prem. 2012. "The Maoist Insurgency in India: Between Crime and Revolution." *Small Wars & Insurgencies* 23 (2): 203–20.

Mahoney, J. 2000. "Path Dependence in Historical Sociology." *Theory and Society* 29(4): 507–48.

Mahoney, J. 2010. *Colonialism and Postcolonial Development: Spanish America in Comparative Perspective.* Cambridge University Press.

Mahoney, J. and D. Schensul. 2006. "Historical Context and Path Dependence. In *The Oxford Handbook of Contextual Political Analysis.* Oxford University Press.

Mamdani, M. 1996. "Indirect Rule, Civil Society, and Ethnicity: The African dilemma. *Social Justice* 23(1/2) (63-64): 145–50.

Mampilly, Z.C. 2012. *Rebel Rulers: Insurgent Governance and Civilian Life during War.* Cornell University Press.

Mander, Harsh. 2004. "Towards Peace, Democracy and Justice: Committee of Concerned Citizens." *Economic and Political Weekly* 39 (12): 1206–8.

Manning, C. 2008. *The Making of democrats: Elections and Party Development in Postwar Bosnia, El Salvador, and Mozambique.* Springer.

Manning, Carrie, and Ian Smith. 2016. "Political Party Formation by Former Armed Opposition Groups after Civil War." *Democratization* 23 (6): 972–89.

Mao, Zedong. 1967. *On Protracted War.* Foreign Languages Press.

Matanock, Aila M. 2017. *Electing Peace: From Civil Conflict to Political Participation.* Cambridge University Press.

Matanock, Aila M., and Paul Staniland. 2018. "How and Why Armed Groups Participate in Elections." *Perspectives on Politics* 16 (3): 710–27.

Mazumdar, Charu. 1967. "It Is Time to Build Up a Revolutionary Party." *Liberation* 1 (1): 62–79.

Mazumdar, Charu. 2001. *Charu Mazumdar Rachana Sangraha*. New Horizon Book Trust.

Mazurana, Dyan E., Susan A. McKay, Khristopher C. Carlson, and Janel C. Kasper. 2002. "Girls in Fighting Forces and Groups: Their Recruitment, Participation, Demobilization, and Reintegration." *Peace and Conflict: Journal of Peace Psychology* 8 (2): 97–123. https://doi.org/10.1207/S15327949PAC0802_01.

McLauchlin, Theodore D. 2011 "Can You Home Again? Desertion and Control ofHometowns in Civil Wars." IBEI Working Papers 34, McGill University, Montreal, Quebec, Canada.

Mearns, Robin, and Saurabh Sinha. 1999. *Social Exclusion and Land Administration in Orissa, India*. World Bank.

Merkel, Wolfgang, and Aurel Croissant. 2000. "Formale Und Informale Institutionen in Defekten Demokratien." *Politische Vierteljahresschrift* 41 (1): 3–30.

Merkel, Wolfgang, and Aurel Croissant. 2004. "Conclusion: Good and Defective Democracies." *Democratization* 11 (5): 199–213.

Migdal, Joel. 1988. *Strong Societies and Weak States: State-Society Relations and State Capabilities in the Third World*. Princeton University Press.

Migdal, J.S. 2001. *State in Society: Studying How States and Societies Transform and Constitute One Another*. Cambridge University Press.

Migdal, Joel S. 2018. "The State in Society." In *New Directions in Comparative Politics*, edited by H. Wiarda, 63–79. Routledge.

Miklian, Jason, and Scott Carney. 2010. "Fire in the Hole: How India's Economic Rise Turned an Obscure Communist Revolt into a Raging Resource War." *Foreign Policy* 6 (181): 104–5.

Misra, Vinod. 1987. *The Flaming Fields of Bihar: A CPI (ML) Document*. Prabodh Bhattacharya.

Mohan, R. 1971. *Maoism in India*. Vikas.

Mohanty, M. 1977. *Revolutionary Violence: A Study of the Maoist Movement in India*. Sterling.

Moravcsik, A. 2010. "Active Citation: A Precondition for Replicable Qualitative Research." *PS: Political Science & Politics* 43(1): 29–35.

Mosley, L. ed. 2013. *Interview Research in Political Science*. Cornell University Press.

Mukherjee, Shivaji. 2013. "Colonial Origins of Maoist Insurgency in India: Historical Legacies of British Indirect Rule." In *APSA 2013 Annual Meeting Paper*.

Munda, Ram Dayal, and S. Bosu Mullick. 2003. *The Jharkhand Movement: Indigenous Peoples' Struggle for Autonomy in India*. IWGIA.

Munshi, K., and M. Rosenzweig. 2006. "Traditional Institutions Meet the Modern World: Caste, Gender, and Schooling Choice in a Globalizing Economy." *American Economic Review*, 96 (4): 1225–52.

Nadeau, Richard, Richard G. Niemi, and Timothy Amato. 1995. "Emotions, Issue Importance, and Political Learning." *American Journal of Political Science*, 558–74.

Nardin, Luis G., Giulia Andrighetto, Rosaria Conte, Áron Székely, David Anzola, Corinna Elsenbroich, Ulf Lotzmann, Martin Neumann, Valentina Punzo, and Klaus G. Troitzsch. 2016. "Simulating Protection Rackets: A Case Study of the Sicilian Mafia." *Autonomous Agents and Multi-Agent Systems* 30 (6): 1117–47.

Nordstrom, Carolyn, and Antonius C.G.M Robben. 1995. *Fieldwork under Fire: Contemporary Studies of Violence and Culture*. University of California Press.

North, D.C. 1993. "Institutions and Credible Commitment." *Journal of Institutional and Theoretical Economics* 149: 11–13.

North, Douglass C. 1990. "A Transaction Cost Theory of Politics." *Journal of Theoretical Politics* 2 (4): 355–67.

Nussio, Enzo. 2011. "How Ex-Combatants Talk about Personal Security. Narratives of Former Paramilitaries in Colombia." *Conflict, Security & Development* 11 (5): 579–606.

O'Donnell, G., Schmitter, P.C. and Whitehead, L. 1986. Woodrow Wilson International Center for Scholars Latin American Program, Woodrow Wilson Rehabilitation Center, and P. P. S. P. C. Schmitter. *Transitions from Authoritarian Rule: Tentative Conclusions about Uncertain Democracies.* Johns Hopkins University Press. https://books.google.com/books?id=CHKGBjFbI-MC.

Ojha, Gyaneshwar. 1976. *Land Problems and Land Reforms (a Study with Reference to Bihar.* S Chand and Sons.

Oppenheim, Ben, Abbey Steele, Juan F. Vargas, and Michael Weintraub. 2015. "True Believers, Deserters, and Traitors: Who Leaves Insurgent Groups and Why." *Journal of Conflict Resolution* 59 (5): 794–823.

Ostrom, E. 2000. "Collective Action and the Evolution of Social Norms." *Journal of Economic Perspectives* 14 (3): 137–58.

Otto, Sabine. 2018. "The Grass Is Always Greener? Armed Group Side Switching in Civil Wars." *Journal of Conflict Resolution* 62 (7): 1459–88.

Pachirat, Timothy. 2011. *Every Twelve Seconds: Industrialized Slaughter and the Politics of Sight.* Yale University Press.

Paes, Wolf-Christian. 2005. "The Challenges of Disarmament, Demobilization and Reintegration in Liberia." *International Peacekeeping* 12 (2): 253–61.

Paige, J.M. 1975. *Agrarian Revolution.* Free Press.

Pande, Rekha. 2000. "From Anti-Arrack to Total Prohibition: The Women's Movement in Andhra Pradesh, India." *Gender, Technology and Development* 4 (1): 131–44.

Panikkar, Kandiyur N. 1989. *Against Lord and State: Religion and Peasant Uprisings in Malabar, 1836–1921.* Oxford University Press.

Panjabi, Kavita. 2010. "'Otiter Jed' or Times of Revolution: Ila Mitra, the Santals and Tebhaga Movement." *Economic and Political Weekly*, 53–59.

Parkinson, S.E. and Wood, E.J. 2015. Transparency in Intensive Research on Violence: Ethical Dilemmas and Unforeseen Consequences. *Qualitative & Multi-Method Research* 13(1): 22–7.

Parulekar, Godavari. 1975. *Adivasis Revolt: The Story of Warli Peasants in Struggle.* National Book Agency.

Patnaik, Prabhat. 2000. "Economic Policy and the Political Management in the Current Conjuncture." In *Transforming India: Social and Political Dynamics of Democracy*, edited by Francine R Frankel, Zoya Hasan, Rajeev Bhargav and Balveer Arora, 230–53. Oxford University Press.

Patnaik, U. 1987. *Peasant Class Differentiation.* Oxford University Press.

Pavier, Barry. 1974. "The Telengana Armed Struggle." *Economic and Political Weekly*, 1413–20.

Planning Commission. 2008. "Development Challenges in Extremist Affected Areas." Government of India, New Delhi.

Pradhan, Prasad, 1994, "Poor Peasant Movement in Central Bihar." In *Peasant Struggles in Bihar, 1831–1992: Spontaneity to Organization*, edited by Kaushal Kishore Sharma. Janaki Prakashan.

Prasad, N. Purendra. 2015. "Agrarian Class and Caste Relations in 'United' Andhra Pradesh, 1956–2014." *Economic and Political Weekly* 50 (16): 77.

Przeworski, Adam. 1991. *Democracy and the Market: Political and Economic Reforms in Eastern Europe and Latin America.* Cambridge University Press.

Puetter, Uwe. 2004. "Governing Informally: The Role of the Eurogroup in EMU and the Stability and Growth Pact." *Journal of European Public Policy* 11 (5): 854–70.

Putnam, Robert D. 1995. "Bowling Alone: America's Declining Social Capital." *Journal of Democracy* 6 (1): 65–78.

Putnam, Robert D., Robert Leonardi, and Raffaella Y. Nanetti. 1994. *Making Democracy Work: Civic Traditions in Modern Italy.* Princeton University Press.

Radhakrishna, G.S. 2016. "Malkangiri Encounter: Ill-Fated Peace Talks in 2004 with Andhra Govt Reason Behind Recent Bloodbath." *Firstpost*, November 7. https://www.firstpost.com/india/malkangiri-encounter-ill-fated-peace-talks-in-2004-with-andhra-govt-reason-behind-recent-bloodbath-3091790.html.

Ramakrishna, V. 1993. "A Background Study to the Emergence of Caste Consciousness in Coastal Andhra Pradesh." In *Caste and Communal Politics in South Asia*, edited by S. Bandopadhyay and S. Das, 99–118. KP Bagchi.

Ramana, P.V. 2006. "The Maoist Movement in India." *Defense & Security Analysis* 22 (4): 435–49.

Ramana, P.V. 2009. "A Critical Evaluation of the Union Government's Response to the Maoist Challenge." *Strategic Analysis* 33 (5): 745–59.

Ramaswamy, Uma. 1978. "The Belief System of the Non-Brahmin Movement in India: The Andhra Case." *Asian Survey* 18 (3): 290–300.

Rao, C.H. Hanumantha. 2014. "The New Telangana State." *Economic & Political Weekly* 49 (9): 11.

Rao, K.N. 1972. *Telangana: A Study in the Regional Committees in India.* Minerva Associates.

Rao, K. Ranga. 1979. "Peasant Movements in Telangana." In *Social Movements in India*, edited by M.S.A. Rao, Vol. I, 152. Manohar Publications.

Rao, K. Ranga. 1979. "Peasant Movement in Telangana." *Social Movements in India* 1.

Rasul, M. Abdul-lah. 1969. *The History of Kishan Sabha.* Calcutta Publishers.

Ravallion, Martin, and Gaurav Datt. 2002. "Why Has Economic Growth Been More Pro-Poor in Some States of India than Others?" *Journal of Development Economics* 68 (2): 381–400.

Reddy, D. Narasimha, and Arun Patnaik. 1993. "Anti-Arrack Agitation of Women in Andhra Pradesh." *Economic and Political Weekly*, 1059–66.

Regani, S. 1972. *Highlights of the Freedom Movement in Andhra Pradesh.* Ministry of Cultural Affairs, Government of Andhra Pradesh.

Reno, William. 2000. "Shadow States and the Political Economy of Civil Wars." In *Greed and Grievance: Economic Agendas in Civil Wars*, edited by M. Berdal and D. Malone, 43–68.

Ribetti, M.M. 2002. *Some Conflicts may not End: The Stability of Protracted Violence in Colombia* (Doctoral dissertation), University of Texas at Austin.

Ribetti, Marcella. 2009. "Disengagement and Beyond: A Case Study of Demobilization inColombia." " In *Leaving Terrorism Behind: Individual and Collective Disengagement*, edited by ToreBjørgo and John Horgan, 152–69. Routledge, .

Richards, John F., James R. Hagen, and Edward S. Haynes. 1985. "Changing Land Use in Bihar, Punjab and Haryana, 1850–1970." *Modern Asian Studies* 19 (3): 699–732.

Richards, Paul, Steve Archibald, Bah Khadija, and James Vincent. 2003. "Where Have All the Young People Gone? Transitioning Ex-Combatants Towards Community Reconstruction After the War in Sierra Leon." Unpublished Report. Submitted to the National Commission for Disarmament, Demobilization and Reintegration, Government of Sierra Leone.

Robin, Cyril. 2004. "Bihar Elections: Laloo against Who?" *Economic and Political Weekly*, 5361–62.

Robins, S., R.K. Bhandari, and Ex-PLA Research Group, 2016. *Poverty, Stigma and Alienation: Reintegration Challenges of Ex-Maoist Combatants in Nepal.* Berghof Foundation.

Rogaly, Ben, Barbara Harriss-White, and Sugata Bose. 1999. *Sonar Bangla?: Agricultural Growth and Agrarian Change in West Bengal and Bangladesh.* Sage.

Rosenzweig, M.R., 1988. Risk, implicit contracts and the family in rural areas of low-income countries. *The Economic Journal*, 98(393), 1148–70.

Rosenzweig, M.R. and Stark, O., 1989. Consumption smoothing, migration, and marriage: Evidence from rural India. *Journal of political Economy*, 97(4), 905–26.

Rothermund, Dietmar, Erhard Werner Kropp, and Gunther Dienemann. 1980. *Urban Growth and Rural Stagnation: Studies in the Economy of an Indian Coalfield and Its Rural Hinterland.* Vol. 2. Manohar.

Rothermund, Dietmar, and Wadhwa, D.C. 1978. *Zamindars, Mines and Peasants: Studies in the History of an Indian Coalfield.* Manohar Book Service.

Roy, A.K. 2000a. "Fighting the Dhanbad Mafia: Life and Death of Gurudas Chatterjee." *Economic and Political Weekly*, 1701–3.

Roy, A.K. 2000b. "Jharkhand: From Separation to Liberation." *Economic and Political Weekly*, 3631–33.

Ruis, Arjan, and Aart de Zeeuw. 2010. "International Cooperation to Combat Climate Change." *Public Finance & Management* 10 (2): 379–404.

Saab, B.Y. and A.W. Taylor. 2009. "Criminality and Armed Groups: A Comparative Study of FARC and Paramilitary Groups in Colombia." *Studies in Conflict & Terrorism* 32(6): 455–75.

Sachs, J., A. Varshney, and N. Bajpai. 2000. *India in the Era of Economic Reforms.* Oxford University Press.

Sahay, Gaurang R. 2008. "Naxalism, Caste-Based Militias and Human Security: Lessons from Bihar." Centre for Development Studies. Tata Institute of Social Sciences., Mumbai.

Sanchez, Andrew. 2010. "Capitalism, Violence and the State: Crime, Corruption and Entrepreneurship in an Indian Company Town." *Journal of Legal Anthropology* 2 (1): 165–88.

Sankaran, S.R. 2002. *Committee of Concerned Citizens, Third Report, 1997–2002.* Committee of Concerned Citizens, Hyderabad.

Sanyal, Kanu. 1968. "Report on the Peasant Movement in the Terai Region." *Liberation* 2 (1): 28–53.

Sarma, Eas. 2010. "SR Sankaran: In Memoriam." *Economic and Political Weekly*, 25–27.

Scott, James C. 1977. *The Moral Economy of the Peasant: Rebellion and Subsistence in Southeast Asia.* Yale University Press.

Scott, James C. 1987. *Weapons of the Weak: Everyday Forms of Peasant Resistance.* Yale University Press.

Sen, Rumela, and Emmanuel Teitelbaum. 2010. *Mass Mobilization and the Success of India's Maoists*. Ralphe Bunche Institute for International Studies.

Sen, Sunil Kumar. 1972. *Agrarian Struggle in Bengal, 1946–47*. Peoples' Publishing House.

Sengupta, Nirmal. 1980. "Class and Tribe in Jharkhand." *Economic and Political Weekly*, 664–71.

Seymour, Lee J.M. 2014. "Why Factions Switch Sides in Civil Wars: Rivalry, Patronage, and Realignment in Sudan." *International Security* 39 (2): 92–131.

Shah, A. 2006. "Markets of Protection." *Critique of Anthropology* 26 (3): 297.

Shah, Alpa. 2009. "Morality, Corruption and the State: Insights from Jharkhand, Eastern India." *The Journal of Development Studies* 45 (3): 295–313.

Shah, Alpa. 2013. "The Tensions over Liberal Citizenship in a Marxist Revolutionary Situation: The Maoists in India." *Critique of Anthropology* 33 (1): 91–109.

Shapiro, Jacob N., Oliver Vanden Eynde, Katherine Ingram, and Emefa Addo Agawu. 2017. Indian State Counterinsurgency Policies: Brief Historical Summaries, ESOC. https://scholar.princeton.edu/sites/default/files/jns/files/svia_2017_india_state_coin_histories.pdf.

Sharma, Alakh N. 2005. "Agrarian Relations and Socio-Economic Change in Bihar." *Economic and Political Weekly*, 960–72.

Sharma, H.R. 1994. "Distribution of Landholdings in Rural India, 1953–54 to 1981–82: Implications for Land Reforms." *Economic and Political Weekly*, A12–25.

Sharma, Kaushal Kishore, Prabhakar Prasad Singh, and Ranjan Kumar. 1994. *Peasant Struggles in Bihar, 1831–1992: Spontaneity to Organisation*. Centre for Peasant Studies in association with Janaki Prakashan.

Shugart, Matthew Soberg. 1992. "Guerrillas and Elections: An Institutionalist Perspective on the Costs of Conflict and Competition." *International Studies Quarterly* 36 (2): 121–52.

Simhadri, Somanaboina, and P.L. Vishweshwer Rao. 1997. *Telangana: Dimensions of Underdevelopment*. Centre for Telangana Studies.

Singhal, Saurabh, and Rahul Nilakantan. 2012. "Naxalite Insurgency and the Economic Benefits of a Unique Robust Security Response." HiSN Working Paper 127, University of Sussex.

Sinha, A. 1978. "Class War in Bhojpur: II." *Economic and Political Weekly* 13 (3): 90–92.

Sinha, Arvind, and Indu Sinha. 2001. "Ranveer Sena and 'Massacre Widows.'" *Economic and Political Weekly*, 4095–99.

Skocpol, T. 1979. *States and Social Revolutions: A Comparative Analysis of France, Russia, and China*. Cambridge University Press.

Söderberg-Kovacs, M. 2007. "From Rebellion to Politics." In *The Transformation of Rebel Groups to Political Parties in Civil War Peace Processes*. Uppsala University.

Söderberg Kovacs, Mimmi, and Sophia Hatz. 2016. "Rebel-to-Party Transformations in Civil War Peace Processes 1975–2011." *Democratization* 23 (6): 990–1008.

Srinivasulu, K. 2014. "Telangana Peasant Movement and Change in the Agrarian Structure: A Case Study of Nalgonda District." Unpublished PhD thesis. Jawahar Lal Nehru University, New Delhi.

Srinivasulu, Karli, and Prakash Sarangi. 1999. "Political Realignments in Post-NTR Andhra Pradesh." *Economic and Political Weekly*, 2449–58.

Staniland, Paul. 2012a. "Between a Rock and a Hard Place: Insurgent Fratricide, Ethnic Defection, and the Rise of pro-State Paramilitaries." *Journal of Conflict Resolution* 56 (1): 16–40.

Staniland, Paul. 2012b. "Organizing Insurgency: Networks, Resources, and Rebellion in South Asia." *International Security* 37 (1): 142–77.

Staniland, Paul. 2014. *Networks of Rebellion: Explaining Insurgent Cohesion and Collapse.* Cornell University Press.

Stevenson, Jonathan. 2017. "General McMaster's Sandwich." *Survival* 59 (2): 211–20.

Stiglitz, Joseph E. 2000. "Formal and Informal Institutions." In *Social Capital: A Multifaceted Perspective*, edited by P. Dasgupta and I. Serageldin, 59–68. World Bank.

Subedi, D.B. 2014. "Conflict, Combatants, and Cash: Economic Reintegration and Livelihoods of Ex-Combatants in Nepal." *World Development* 59: 238–50.

Sundar, Nandini. 2013. "Insurgency, Counter-insurgency, and Democracy in Central India." In *More than Maoism: Politics and Policies of Insurgency in South Asia*, edited by Robin Jeffrey,Ronojoy Sen, and Pratima Sen, 149–68. Manohar.

Sundarayya, P. 1972. *Telengana People's Struggle and Its Lessons.* Calcutta: Communist Party of India (Marxist).

Sundarayya, P. 2006. *Telengana People's Struggle and Its Lessons.* Foundation Books.

Suri, K. C. 1996. "Caste Politics and Power Structure in India: The Case of Andhra Pradesh." In *Political Science Annual,* edited by S. Mukherjee and S. Ramaswamy. Deep and Deep.

Tanner, Victor, Jérôme Tubiana, and Michael Griffin. 2007. *Divided They Fall: The Fragmentation of Darfur's Rebel Groups.* Small Arms Survey, Geneva, Switzerland.

Tansey, O. 2007. "Process Tracing and Elite Interviewing: A Case for Non-probability Sampling." *PS: Political Science and Politics* 40(4): 765–72.

Tedeschi, Richard G., and Lawrence G. Calhoun. 2004. "Posttraumatic Growth: Conceptual Foundations and Empirical Evidence." *Psychological Inquiry* 15 (1): 1–18.

Thakur, R. N. 2002. "For the Future of Prosperous Bihar." Economic Association of Bihar Conference, Samastipur College, Samastipur.

Thirumali, Inukonda. 1992. "Dora and Gadi: Manifestation of Landlord Domination in Telengana." *Economic and Political Weekly,* 477–82.

Thirumali, Inukonda. 2003. *Against Dora and Nizam: People's Movement in Telangana, 1939–1948.* Kanishka.

Thorner, Alice. 1982. "Semi-Feudalism or Capitalism? Contemporary Debate on Classes and Modes of Production in India." *Economic and Political Weekly,* 1961–68.

Tilly, Charles. 1985. "War Making and State Making as Organized Crime." *Violence: A Reader,* 35–60.

Tilly, Charles. 2003. *The Politics of Collective Violence.* Cambridge University Press.

Tourangeau, Roger, and Ting Yan. 2007. "Sensitive Questions in Surveys." *Psychological Bulletin* 133 (5): 859.

Tsai, Kellee S. 2006. "Adaptive Informal Institutions and Endogenous Institutional Change in China." *World Politics* 59 (1): 116–41.

Tsai, Lily L. 2007. "Solidary Groups, Informal Accountability, and Local Public Goods Provision in Rural China." *American Political Science Review* 101 (2): 355–72.

Tullock, Gordon. 1971. "The Paradox of Revolution." *Public Choice* 11 (1): 89–99.

Urdal, H. 2008. "Population, Resources, and Political Violence: A Subnational Study of India, 1956–2002." *Journal of Conflict Resolution* 52(4): 590–617.

Vaishnav, Milan. 2017. *When Crime Pays: Money and Muscle in Indian Politics.* Yale University Press.

Varese, Federico. 2001. *The Russian Mafia: Private Protection in a New Market Economy.* Oxford University Press.

Varshney, A. 2003. *Ethnic Conflict and Civic Life: Hindus and Muslims in India.* Yale University Press.

Varshney, A. 2000. "Is India Becoming More Democratic?" *The Journal of Asian Studies* 59 (1): 3–25.

Varshney, A. 2001. "Ethnic Conflict and Civil Society: India and Beyond." *World Politics* 53 (3): 362–98.

Vaugier-Chatterjee, A. 2009. "Two Dominant Castes: The Socio-Political System in Andhra Pradesh. In *Rise of the Plebeians?*, edited by C. Jaffrelot and S. Kumar, 277–312. Routledge.

Venkatarangaiah, M. 1965. *The Freedom Movement in Andhra Pradesh.* Vols., Hyderabad, Government of Andhra Pradesh.

Venugopal, N. 2007. "Fake Encounters: Story from Andhra Pradesh." *Economic and Political Weekly*, 4106–11.

Verghese, Ajay. 2016. *The Colonial Origins of Ethnic Violence in India.* Stanford University Press.

Volkov, V. 2002. "Patrimonialism versus Rational Bureaucracy: On the Historical Realities of Cor-ruption," In *Bribery and Blat in Russia*, edited by S. Lovell et al., 35–47. Macmillan.

Waldman, Matt. 2010. *Golden Surrender: The Risks, Challenges, and Implications of Reintegration in Afghanistan.* Afghanistan Analysts Network.

Weingast, Barry R. 1997. "The Political Foundations of Democracy and the Rule of Law." *The American Political Science Review* 91 (2): 245. https://doi.org/10.2307/2952354.

Weinstein, J.M. 2006. *Inside Rebellion: The Politics of Insurgent Violence.* Cambridge University Press.

Wendt, Alexander. 2001. "Driving with the Rearview Mirror: On the Rational Science of Institutional Design." *International Organization* 55 (4): 1019–49.

Williamson, Claudia R. 2009. "Informal Institutions Rule: Institutional Arrangements and Economic Performance." *Public Choice* 139 (3–4): 371–87.

Wilson, Kalpana. 1999. "Patterns of Accumulation and Struggles of Rural Labour: Some Aspects of Agrarian Change in Central Bihar." *The Journal of Peasant Studies* 26 (2–3): 316–54.

Witsoe, Jeffrey. 2011. "Corruption as Power: Caste and the Political Imagination of the Postcolonial State." *American Ethnologist* 38 (1): 73–85.

Witsoe, Jeffrey. 2012. "Everyday Corruption and the Political Mediation of the Indian State." *Economic & Political Weekly* 47 (6): 47.

Wolf, Eric R. 1969. *Peasant Wars of the Twentieth Century.* University of Oklahoma Press.

Wood, Elisabeth Jean. 2003. *Insurgent Collective Action and Civil War in El Salvador.* Cambridge University Press.

Wood, Elisabeth Jean. 2006. "The Ethical Challenges of Field Research in Conflict Zones." *Qualitative Sociology* 29 (3): 373–86.

Yadav, Y. 1999. "Electoral Politics in the Time of Change: India's Third Electoral System, 1989–99." *Economic and Political Weekly* 34 (34): 2393–99.

Yadav, Yogendra. 2010. "On Remembering Lohia." *Economic and Political Weekly*, 46–50.

Index